DREAM
BEYOND
SHADOWS

DREAM BEYOND SHADOWS

BY

KARTIKEYA LADHA

White Falcon Publishing

www.whitefalconpublishing.com

Dream Beyond Shadows
Kartikeya Ladha

www.whitefalconpublishing.com

ISBN - 978-93-88459-17-4

DEDICATION

This book is dedicated to my mother and all the mothers of this world, who exhale every breath with a selfless desire to protect, love and support their children.

The Earth is our mother, so it blesses all mothers who reside on its lands with enduring limitless strength, to persist with the most powerful role a being can carry out, with the ultimate responsibility of guiding their children through times of suffering onto a path of kindness that leads to the transformation of an animate being into a pure soul.

INTRODUCTION

S EATED ON A CHAIR with a pair of eyes fixed at an illusory point on a plain white wall, a mind loses its sense of time and morphs past the wall to enter another dimension of mirage, aided by a lifetime of unforeseen events that happened in the Amazon Jungle.

That dimension is far removed from the uproar of traffic and excessive turmoil of our prevailing civilization, and allows the mind to only perceive hooting birds, racketing insects and echoing animals. It is filled with crisp air making it easier for human nostrils to breathe and nurse the mind so that it feels more connected with nature. The trees residing in that jungle transmit messages with other species by establishing uninterrupted channels of communication among all the living beings of the region. They foster awareness in the mind and extend to it the chance to be fully synchronized with Mother Earth.

℘ ℭ

Being in such a peaceful environment can certainly make us question why we are building our civilizations at the expense of destroying nature. Are we really developing our nations or are just demolishing our world by the imprudent construction of "cosmopolitan cities", marking the importance of human achievement?

We think we know it all and let our ego, fear, pride and anger guide us into manifesting a mindset that is doomed by greed. Our longing for power and superior status has led us to forget our real purpose in life. We have become ignorant and are free-falling inside a bottomless hole, we have dug for ourselves in this illusionary world.

We rely on our material possessions and the dimensions of our houses to impress others. They aid construction of our image of being superior to others. We believe that we're the most intelligent beings in this world and think that we know everything about what's happening in it, because of how well-versed we are in the current political scenario and all the other frivolous news relating to the contemporary global situation. We like to argue to prove others wrong, so that we can feel better about ourselves. Society has trained our minds to deem that knowing more than others is what maintains our supremacy in this world. The pity in our souls evoked by seeing the helpless around us, assures us that we need to predominate in the world. We tell ourselves that we have achieved an imperishable milestone because of the quantum of capital we have stacked in our bank accounts. This frame of mind characterizes our existence in the world we have fabricated for ourselves.

It is painful for us to consider that we could ever be wrong, because of how gravely immersed we are in our own vanity.

Our fabrications have led us to forget the true purpose of human existence.

We lack devotion to grow in love and compassion, to acknowledge the importance of family, to assimilate our duty to be kind and forgiving toward our fellow brothers and sisters.

Living in peace and harmony with others taxes our heart, as it has stopped beating for anyone but our venal self.

We are not able to recognize the sublimity of Mother Nature and the ingenious ecosystems sheltered by her.

In pursuit of this truth, the writer renounced his American dream of building a life in New York, to embark upon a journey to Peru, South America. During his odyssey, he followed his calling to the depths of the Amazon Jungle and there he visited a shaman, and experienced the mystical healing powers of Ayahuasca, which launched him on a quest to uncover the deep-rooted purpose of his life, and inspired him to tell this story and serve his duty as a Messenger of the Jungle.

This story has not been derived from the writer's imagination but from the writer's actual experience, which has given him the opportunity to breathe freely for every second of his life, regardless of how deplorable a situation is.

Tasting real freedom, even for a second, makes life worth living.

This story is not an attempt to craft intellectual discussion, or to prove a point, nor to show others what inspired the writer to narrate the story.

It is solely written for the seekers of this world, who need an affirmation that it is possible to discover their true path in life and then create their own reality based on their truth – as distinct from being controlled by a never-ending circle of desires.

The writer realized that the only way for him to find his true purpose in life was to completely surrender himself to this world and begin the process of cleansing the accumulated rubbish from his being. Only when he'd freed himself from this world's conditioning and futile societal beliefs, could he begin to relearn the realities of life and remove himself from the delusions we have all been socialized to be a part of, delusions that force us to deny the possibility that something mightier and more vigorous than us could exist in this world. Delusions that stop us from composing a life beyond the measures of normalcy and keep us oblivious of the possibility that other realities could exist in this abstruse totality.

TABLE OF CONTENTS

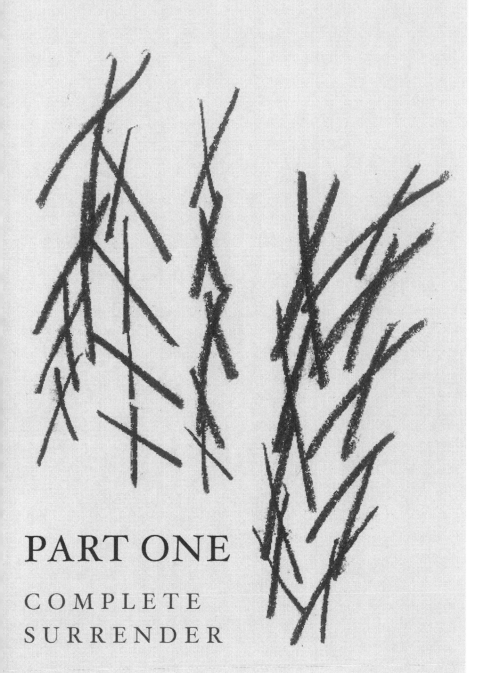

PART ONE

COMPLETE
SURRENDER

I. THE HIGH RISERS

I BECAME AN ANOMALY TO myself in the absence of light and when shades of darkness surrendered. My mind was then tempted to question what lay behind that selfless "I".

Who is this "I"?

What is this "I"?

And… why is this "I"?

The story to be told here begins with the emergence of this egoless "I".

෯ ෬

The story of this "I", begins in a city where the American dream shimmers among its towering estates – New York City, branded as the greatest city on this planet. A city that never sleeps. A city that welcomes people from all around the world. A city where hard work and ambition make it possible for people to live the American dream and create a better life for themselves and their families. A city where the statement, *If you work hard, your dreams will come true and the world will be at your feet,* drives people to wake up every morning with determination, and walk the never-ending crowded streets in the pursuit of their dreams. A city where individuals breathe for themselves and are always running away from something and toward something else. Where everybody is trying their best to win and become the best at what they do. Where your work defines you, not your fundamental values in life. Where your status is based upon the neighborhood you live in, rather than how big your heart is.

A society where I experienced becoming the best at what I did, only to realize that I have so much more to offer to this world than to blindly follow the herd.

We have sealed our minds, therefore, we do not see that we are all living bubbles, which only continue to expand with time. Not until my time in New York City, did I see that even though it seemed like we were growing and achieving something significant, it only truly pertained to our own bubbles, and was a delusion created by our own minds to satisfy ourselves. That same delusion stops us from seeing things as they really are, and to endlessly add expendable layers onto our little bubbles. It is only when the mind bursts out of its bubble that it can experience the actuality of life and witness the real splendor our world contains.

ℬ ℭ

It was December of 2016 and I was working as a door-to-door salesman for a solar energy startup based in Brooklyn, New York. It was my first job out of college, and it couldn't have been a more exciting opportunity for an ambitious college graduate. My office was based above a car wash at the edge of Sunset Park, an increasingly popular neighborhood in Brooklyn. It was a classic startup, and I loved everything about it.

When I first visited the office, I was very much taken aback by its whole arrangement, which was nothing like any I'd seen before. It contained only two desks, as it was primarily a training facility for all its salespeople. The idea was to have an open environment for everyone to interact and be enculturated by the sales training. It was an in-the-field job, so no one spent much time in the office anyways. It didn't make any business sense for the company to spend money on useless office items. There were folding chairs for us to sit on when the occasion demanded, and charts for us to write the sales targets for various teams. The office was made up of enthusiastic and dynamic professionals; there was really nothing more to the office than its people.

After starting my job, I found a room at an affordable rent in an apartment located in Park Slope, a cheerful and welcoming neighborhood and only a short commute of two train stops from the office. That was a major advantage in New York; so many individuals spent hours of their invaluable time commuting every day.

The apartment was on the fourth floor of an old red-brick building at the intersection of 7th Avenue and 7th Street, beside Brooklyn's Methodist Hospital. My job demanded I spend hours in the field, going door-to-door in various Brooklyn neighborhoods and influencing homeowners to go solar. Many of my friends and family members were confused about why I'd taken the door-to-door-salesman job after graduating from one of the top-ranked business programs in the U.S. But it was because of the limitless learning potential it offered.

I was entirely responsible for my own growth, and my finances were totally in my control. I understood how sales was about freedom: financial and personal. My sales numbers and attitude spoke for me and I was the master of my own destiny every single hour at the job. That job taught me that we have the ability to motivate and influence others. If you train your mind to create a desirable future for yourself, you understand human behavior on an entirely different level. A friend and co-worker, Kenneth used to describe door-to-door sales quite explicitly, "One month of door-to-door sales teaches four years' worth of communication at prominent business schools".

The common beliefs that "college is what defines your future", and "a degree is what makes you knowledgeable and educated", are not particularly accurate. Yes, there are many benefits of going to college, but the real thing is out in the world, which abounds with limitless possibilities. What years of college experience didn't teach me, being a door-to-door salesperson taught me in just a few months. It taught me even about the littlest of human personality twists, through multiple live-screenings of distinct personalities every single day. My job required me to interact with hundreds of individuals on a weekly basis and spawned multiple scenarios so my mind was constantly processing immense amount of information. My mind grew exponentially every day, and the learnings from the daily exchanges with numerous customers, who'd migrated to New York from all over the world, were endless.

Brooklyn is one of the most diverse places on the planet, so my customers varied by ethnicity, race, culture, religion, and any other characteristic that could possibly be distinguished. I went from knocking doors at the richest neighborhoods to the most dangerous in Brooklyn. I witnessed the divide that existed in the mindsets of American people, based on their political beliefs and wealth. Every individual looked at the world differently and thought his or her way was the correct way of doing things. From Trump supporters to Obama applauders, I met with all kind of individuals. It was an epic job that allowed me to gain real hands-on-knowledge of bona fide American culture.

Before taking up that job, I'd never been involved in sales but my preceding traveling and constant self-learning came in handy, as they'd trained me superbly to build relationships with strangers. During my time at the solar company, I became one of the best salespersons in the organization with the finest numbers anyone in my role could have. It resulted in early promotion, which persuaded me to take responsibility of managing a team. That new role helped me develop myself into a leader: my mission then became to teach others the skills I'd repeatedly applied at my sales job, so they'd gain positive results for the team. Fortunately, I was able to use that opportunity to build a strong team and train individuals to master "the art of selling". I gained more than I'd ever imagined possible very early in my career and was so grateful for the openings that kept pushing me to climb the ladder of success.

It was an ideal life for someone in my shoes. I was living in the most exciting city on the planet, working in a job I relished. My leisure time was spent at the city's prime locations meeting fascinating new people and partying with wonderful friends. I thought I had it all figured out.

I had work-life balance. I had other job opportunities to look at. And basically, everything I'd worked for till then had come to fruition. I was on the path of success in terms of how society defined success – but I myself was living in the delusion that I was happy with everything.

℘ ℭ

A Broken Ladder

Moving incessantly up the ladder,
with steps shrinking in size and water streaming from the clouds,
my heart was stranded in a spineless dream.

The more I climbed up, the further I drowned beneath a hollow tree.

There I was, but no one was there…

Only a wire torn away from the source,
with a surge-less covering.

The ladder seemed broken,
its top getting smudgy among the ghostly figures.

My body was in shock from following its usual mechanical movement,
When suddenly a release flickered and
swayed the frozen corpse away from the seamless clouds,
into a novice world.

A. Something Was Missing, But I Didn't Know What It Was

One night as I lay down on my bed, after observing the Grey Avenue with its dissonant traffic and spectral shadows hurrying past one another through the small window of my cozy room, I heard something…

It was a voice from deep inside my core: *the reason you feel something is missing in your life is because you have no idea what the world can truly offer. All you have to do is surrender yourself to the world.*

I ignored the voice at first, but somehow, I couldn't let it go. It'd really got to me. At the same time, what it said made no sense, as I believed, I was already applying that voice in my life. In theory, I wanted to follow the voice and simply take the first step toward the unknown, but in reality it was the most demanding voice to follow. My in-built fear prevented me from streaming against the norm. I was scared by the notion that I'd lose everything I'd worked for. Theory is always so much easier than practicality! I'd have to muster immeasurable courage to be able to take that "leap of faith", and seek a voice, which would take me onto an obscure path requiring me to risk everything I'd worked for.

There was a point, when I realized that I was living in an illusion fabricated by my own mind.

Illusion governs our lives and instills society's superficial beliefs within us, that what we have (intellect, fame, a good job, money, house, car, etc.) is the greatest gift life can offer. The shattering of that illusion does not ring a bell in your mind. Instead, it foments an upheaval of unmitigated emptiness at the core of your vitality. You recognize that everything you've learned and lived for is nothing but sheer falsehood. You admit to yourself that everything you've ever believed to be true, is nothing but a fallacy created by us over the past centuries that takes us far away from the truth.

When you feel absolutely lost, you question yourself, what type of life is worth living for? And it's not just for the lack of an intellectual quest! You ask yourself...

How do I find meaning in life?

What does it even mean to be happy in life?

What is my actual path in life?

What is my true purpose?

AND

Who am I?

And you ask these questions not out of confusion, but suspicion that your existence seems worthless.

Could there be a world that doesn't exist in front of our eyes, but exists beyond our imagination? Could there be a world that is as real as anything can get, while what we are living in right now is just the default? How do we break away from this default mode of living to look for something that cannot be imagined, but only experienced?

The emergence of these questions is an inevitable invitation for fear to take over our minds. We feel defenseless and the fear further paralyzes us from even exploring the possibilities. Our civilization has advanced to a stage where most people are accustomed to living with regrets. That's a bold statement, but it's the truth.

We live our lives encompassed by fear of the unknown, enslaved to a life where our decisions are governed by fear. We are the first to blame or judge others for their actions but are not willing to improve upon our own actions. The fear that burdens our soul, forces us to do what others want us to do and spurs us to blame others for our blunders. We are not afraid of dying, we are terrified of living.

In that frame of mind, I knew everything that I'd achieved meant nothing. I had to get all my innate fears out of my being and break out of the illusion that had taken over my life, to discover the truth behind my existence.

B. Decision

I knew nothing could be the same after that night, and I gave myself the target of December 31 2016 to make a decision for myself. I had to make a life-choice and bring peace to my mind, which was in a delirious state. I couldn't talk about it at the office or with my parents because I didn't want the decision to be affected by biased opinions or have a rumor emerge in the office, when I couldn't be assertive about the decision myself. The only person I spoke to about it was my flat mate.

I lived with a young married couple, Brian and Monica. Since the day I'd moved into their apartment, Brian and I had become wonderful friends. I used to call him Sensei Brian because of his innate ability to bestow meaningful advice. Brian was a lawyer in his early thirties, with an oval-shaped face, a bald head, and an Irish-blooded beard that distinguished him as a certified ginger man. He was wise and genuine with his every statement. He was a keen meditator, who was always a good person to talk to about life.

On the up-coming weekend, I intended to shut myself off from the external world in my room, solely to meditate and get in touch with that deep voice again, which had left me stranded on a deserted island. Before commencing the task, I told Brian about what had happened on an evening walk in Prospect Park in Brooklyn, just a block away from our apartment building.

He asked, "Are you going to quit your job?" I replied, "I have given myself a deadline of 31 December to make the decision... and

I am locking myself in my room for the coming days to submerse myself with this question." He smiled and said, "Let me know, what you decide."

The next day, I disconnected myself from all means of communication and sealed my room's door to begin my soul-searching session, hoping for deeper insight and a broader perspective on the matter. I played a music album of nature recordings of rain, ocean waves, birds and animals to connect my mind to nature instead of being slowly absorbed into the spectral shadows on the streets, which vanish into thin air of New York City after a while.

I shut my eyes with the absolute determination to get past the stage where I was about to fall inside a black hole with no clear vision for myself about which path to choose. It was extremely challenging to meditate, as I felt so agitated. But I vowed to myself that even if I might die, I wouldn't leave my room until I'd made a decision. It was so hard staying in the room to meditate, but I knew if I could continue despite the deep emotions coming to the surface, I would be able to focus deep within and hear my inner voice.

That inner voice is an inherent human capacity. It has different names depending on your culture and personal beliefs: gut feeling, intuition or xyz… and so on. But it doesn't matter what you call it; what does matter is that it is real, and it's your true guide. Over time, as we humans have evolved we've lost the ability to hear it. We block it out, as our current system only accepts rational and logical thinking. So we reject intuitive, feeling or emotion-based decisions and, instead, we blindly follow a methodical structure formulated by society to restrict the limitless potential of our minds. We are easily manipulated and have been trained to think and act in a certain way and live an enchained life without even realizing it.

We are actually in a system, which deludes us into thinking that what we experience is freedom! But that's a fraudulent idea we've been beguiled into believing. I was trusting my inner voice to get me out of that trap by helping me make a decision to move my life forward. I didn't move for even a second, because I knew that time was crucial. I had to re-connect with that voice, as it would lead me on the right path.

Going deep into my mind in an intense meditational experience was not the normal thing for a casual weekend afternoon in New York City! Despite struggling to come to a decision, I tried my very best to stay true to the whole experience and have no expectations about what was to come from it. On such occasions, it's better to surrender yourself and be completely present with every moment of your breath.

We really are our worst enemies: instead of focusing on what's happening inside our minds, we invest so much energy on the pointless distractions surrounding us. They come in all forms and we've been overtaken by them: media, politicians, preventable unrest, wars, conflicts, arguments over needless topics and so on. We spend so much energy talking about such things, which in the long run don't matter, and in the whole charade we are consumed by ignorance, self-centeredness, ego, and greed. What are we trying to achieve by destroying our world? Every possible external stimulus, which is not inspired by progressive and noble ideals, is nothing but a distraction from the truth.

Increasing self-awareness helps us acknowledge the war concealed within and spurs us to question the common route we've been told to follow since childhood—about how to live and what to believe. It's an institutionalized and fear-breeding system that only takes us away from our purpose in life and fetters us to every possible form of distraction.

When you realize that everything you've been told and made to believe is nothing but a lie, you don't only feel lost but downright shattered – and directionless. The goals or dreams you've had till then seem inconsequential and somehow false.

You have to begin a new life with a breath of fresh air and start the process of unlearning everything you've digested till then. You have to let go of it all and get past every single impediment leading you away from the truth and away from the journey of finding your true purpose in life.

ઠા ભ

The world was being born again for me.

I lost track of time and my room was hidden in the obscurity of the night. It ended with my eyes unfolding. I unlocked the door of my room and made my way through the narrow walkway that led to the old kitchen with a window at its end equipped with fire-escape stairs. I stepped out into the limited space to breathe in some juicy air and look at the hazy sky.

With my first breath out in the open, I knew I had made a decision.

೮೦ ෆ

I was having breakfast early next morning at the dining table, when Brian walked in with some groceries. "So, what did you decide?" he asked. With a sigh of relief, I replied that I'd decided to quit my job, leave the U.S., and go travel to Peru. Not unsettled by my response, he asked when was I thinking about going. I smiled and told him that I wasn't entirely sure. "First I have to quit my job, and then tell my family. But I am thinking in January." Brian was a well-traveled individual, and had been to Peru in the past. He was extremely supportive of my decision and thought it would all work out for good.

Now that I knew what I had to do, my next move was to take prompt but thoughtful action. I broke it down into orderly steps: first, quit my job, second, leave the U.S., and third, go to Peru. They were big steps for setting out on my path to discover my true purpose. I couldn't figure out the logical reasons behind it all, but I was certain that the decision was guided by my inner voice, which was good enough for me. There was no way to analyze it, because there was no rational thinking behind it, but I was convinced from the core of my vitality that that was what I had to do.

I was mentally prepared to face every obstacle that would come in the way of my decision. I knew people around me were going to be bewildered by my actions, but none of it would matter. My heart was in the right place, and my actions were governed by something much more tenacious than me, which gave me the strength to act upon my life-choice, despite it being looked down upon by society as unreasonable, as running away, or as a rebellious act. But it was so much more than that. It was about how our lives are to be lived, to experience living in congruence with breathing, and to feel every moment for what it really is.

It was time to get into action mode and bring the words into reality. There is no point in going through such an introspective time, if you are not able to take action to back your decisions. Our actions are what define us: if we are persistent and consistent with our actions, they will drive results. The key is to take actions that derive from positive intentions for yourself and others, as they generate more meaning.

We shouldn't consider taking action as inconsequential because affirmative actions are what spur the growth of humanity. Not being able to follow up on our words and finish what we originally wanted to do, is simply an act of disrespect to ourselves and our own words. It's better to be quiet than utter words lacking conviction. It only creates a scenario, where people don't take our words seriously, and by doing so we fill our lives with regret and disappointment.

I have been guilty of the same in the past, but a life of regrets and disappointments is not a life worth living. Being able to live up to your word, turns you into an individual who whole-heartedly respects others for taking risks and following their zeal to build the life of their dreams.

However, it's not easy to take that momentous step and break away from the usually defined path.

II. LESS INACTION

THE MOMENT HAD ARRIVED; it was time for me to act. I knew what steps I had to take and even though I wasn't entirely sure why they were the steps, I was absolutely certain that they were what my heart truly wanted.

I told myself, if I don't build up the strength to leave everything behind now, I wouldn't be able to take that step in the future, and would live a regretful and purposeless life. Yes, people were going to be surprised, curious, judgmental, worried and a substantial number of questions were going to come my way. But I would respond to every criticism with a smile, and not let a single external voice affect my decision, which was inspirited by that deep-seated voice.

It's only when you decide to do something that's not considered "normal" and challenge everything that you usually live for is when you are actually onto something. You recognize that it's something much bigger than yourself, and it's not solely about you. There's a powerful force, which I don't have a name for that works with you in every step of the way to take you on an incredible path where amazing things happen to you, and your whole world changes.

I reassured myself that if a young boy born in a small town in India can end up in New York City living the American dream, anything is possible in this world. The opportunities that you can create for yourself are endless: all you have to do is listen to your heart and act upon your words.

The heart guided by your inner voice will merge with the universal energy that will strengthen you on every step of your true journey, where obstacles are to be cherished and life becomes meaningful.

A. Path to Freedom

Several days had passed since I made the decision to begin my journey by not pursuing somebody else's path but discovering my own. I felt at peace and was relieved at my core to have reached my verdict well before December 31. I still hadn't spoken about it with anyone but Brian, as I didn't want a buzz around the whole thing until I'd acted upon my decision. The Annual Office Christmas Party was held on December 17 on Long Island and I went along with all my Brooklyn colleagues and friends. The morning after that amazing night, I decided to send my resignation email to my boss. That way, I could end my time at the company with the wonderful memories from the previous night.

After taking that first step, I could then focus on the next steps.

I was on a car ride with my colleagues back from Long Island, when I wrote my resignation email, without them knowing what I was writing. It was a cold morning in New York, and I pressed the send button on my phone as we arrived in Brooklyn.

It's funny how in life everything can change in a matter of a few seconds. After I pressed the send button, a notification popped up on the screen stating that it had been sent, and with that a chapter had ended. I felt a little nervous, but more so, ecstatically relieved from having taken that first step.

With deep exhilaration and a steady tone of voice I announced, "I quit my job." Kenneth, the guy who'd been driving the car had just parked, and stared at me with his big green eyes not saying a word. We walked to his apartment, and everyone was very quiet after hearing me, probably stunned for words. Kenneth, a lean man with a neat hairstyle and elegant manners was one of the best salesmen I'd come across in my life. He was always high in spirits and enthusiastic about life. He asked if he could read the email, so I handed over my phone to him.

Hey Keith,

Hope everything's well!

This email is in regard to a decision I have made about my life so that I can continue the journey toward my goals and dreams. I have decided to start traveling again. Even though my time at Level Solar has been amazing and beautiful, I have to keep moving forward on my life-path.

This was a very hard decision to make as I have never been in an office with people of such quality. Every single person there has touched my heart with their spirit and life goals, and that's why it's been challenging to do this.

I don't want to say more in the email, as I would like to come and speak with you in person when we all get back in January. If it's OK with you, I would like to come in to see everyone as a Level Solar employee one last time to share my experience with them and thank them for everything they have done for me.

It's been a pleasure working under you Keith. Having you as my mentor has been a privilege. I promise you, wherever I go, I'll speak and think very highly of you.

Best wishes,

Kart

P.S. Thank you so much for your present. It touched my heart :)

Kenneth finished reading the email and passed it on to my co-workers, who were so much more to me than mere professional acquaintances. We'd become really good friends and had basically spent all our hours together on and off the field. After reading the email, they were dumbstruck. Apparently, all of them had the same thought in their minds - this is for real, he's seriously leaving.

The next step was to tell my family about my decision and then figure out the logistical details for traveling to Peru. In four days, I was leaving for Miami to spend Christmas and New Year on a trip planned in October, which had not been the slightest bit influenced by my sudden life-changing decision. Christmas and New Year in Miami would now become a celebration of my wonderful years in the U.S. and a goodbye to my original life-plan.

When I told my family about my decision, they couldn't understand it at first. They thought it was because I wanted to move in with them and start working in India. When I told them, I would be traveling to Peru and living there for several months, my mother asked me where Peru was, as she'd not even heard of it. My parents were obviously bewildered by my decision, though since childhood, I'd managed to surprise them with every life-choice I'd ever made. My curiosity and desire to question everything as a child had at times been overwhelming for them. Still, my parents, unlike the majority of parents and contrary to the traditional beliefs of Indian society, had always supported my decisions.

But this time they were more astonished than ever before and all I could say to them was that there was only one thing I was completely sure about: I had to do this. Yes, it was confusing and difficult for them to understand, rightly so because they cared about me and wanted me to succeed in life. I couldn't tell them what was going to happen in the coming months, but I knew in my heart that if I didn't do this now, I would never be able to live for a purpose bigger than myself. As their son, I was asking for their blessings and the rest would take care of itself. Solemnly looking through the screen of their phone, my parents told me that they were always with me, no matter what, and that was the only statement I needed to hear, before commencing upon my unknown journey.

After ending the call with my parents, the first thing I did was to find a cheap flight to India as I really wanted to see my family before leaving for Peru. I booked one from New York to New Delhi for January 15, which allowed me around twelve days after my return from Miami to get rid of every unnecessary object I owned. That was plenty of time to say goodbye to all my friends, and soak in the energy of New York City till my departure. It would be my time to transition into leaving. There was no need to rush through that transition and generate discomfort in my mind. Instead, it was to be treasured before my eternal surrender to the world.

B. The Glowing Sky

On the midnight of December 31 2016, the New Year began with a blast of blazing fireworks above the ocean at Miami. My feet were lodged in sand, as I looked up at the sky mesmerized by the colorful illuminations celebrating another year nearer to our deaths.

That is when I commemorated the teachings America had given me, and let go of all the emotional constraints that had piled on me over the years I'd spent there. There were no hard feelings in my heart against America. Gazing at the dazzling fireworks, I confirmed that a huge part of who I was that day had come from my time living there. Every person I'd met during that time had aided in my growth and self-discovery. It had made me into a self-confident person who was always willing to give his best and be the best at what he did. If not for America, I wouldn't have reached the stage where I could coin the bravery to leave it all and start again from rock-bottom.

I didn't feel nervous anymore. The material pleasures were withering away, and my unwarranted cultural guards were collapsing. I left New York for New Delhi exactly a month after I'd decided to leave the U.S. and travel to Peru. That period seemed to have flown by in a matter of seconds. It was time to move on from my old life and start the new one.

My friend, Kenneth drove me to the airport, a kind gesture of our friendship. He asked me during the ride, how I was feeling. I told him that those final weeks of my time in the U.S. had been sentimental and memorable, and that I would never forget the countless hugs, virtuous tears, sincere smiles, and simple good-byes in them. As I walked away from him to board my flight, I told him to take care of himself, and that in the long run, it was all going to be worth it.

☙ ☘

Dreamers

In the darkness of night, under the radiating sun was when I became free.
The shadows had evaporated into the clouded sea.
Leaving the high risers, unfilled with soulless sprees.
I flew over the sky, away from an illusory world,
Not knowing what I'd see.
But willing to die for the unforeseeable dreams.

ഇ൫

The flight to New Delhi set off a numbing sensation in my body, as that was the first time I'd flown to India feeling lost and not entirely sure about how I was going to deal with the numerous queries from all my family members, friends and acquaintances. What are your plans for the future? What's your goal? What now? How was New York? Are you going to start your own solar company now? Have you thought about working with your father? Are you moving back to India? Why did you leave New York? What job are you going to do? Et cetera … et cetera … et cetera.

It wasn't that I lacked confidence in my decision, but it would plainly be difficult for people to understand an impractical choice. I mentally groomed myself to stay mute through the infinite questions that were going to be fired my way. I told myself that ultimately what really mattered was that I knew my parents' hearts were with me, and that was enough for me to stay quiet through the irrelevant questions and suggestions. My decision wasn't to be debated or discussed, but just acted upon.

When I made the decision to leave New York, I was willing to face every objection and hurdle that would appear on the way. I knew it wasn't going to be an effortless path, but that would make the whole journey even more extraordinary. That decision became such a crucial part of my life, even beyond what I'd envisioned it to be.

Whenever an individual decides to do something in his or her life, it's intriguing how others are more interested in that person's life-plans, than in reflecting on their own plans. I think there's some kind of human pleasure attached to getting someone else listen to what we think is the best thing for them to do with their life. We do that, rather than craft an environment where we can listen to our own voice and connect deeply within ourselves to figure out how to move forward in the direction suited for our genuine endeavors.

In my situation, people seemed to think it was an opportunity for them to persuade me to do what they thought I should do. It all seemed to revolve around money – money as the end-goal.

And the arguments in India were to be, as they always are, that you can learn to love finance/technology/business and it will provide you with money in life and we all know money is the most important thing. It's not the people in your life or doing something that you love that matters the most; the amount of money you have in your bank balance reflects your true identity. Money lives forever; it's not just a piece of paper with some intangible value based on the economy of the country, but a collector's piece that can only be earned by ignoring your soul and killing your dreams. Right?

Seated on a plane, far away from anyone's reach, I was flying away from that notorious concept of money being the end-goal. It wasn't a condemnation of money or individuals who seek nothing but money in their lives per se. I accepted the realism that money is an essential part of surviving in our world, but it's no more than a mere tool. Money was not designed to be our end-goal. People who do that forget what a gift human life is. Human life is so precious; it's a blessing to be alive as a species, which has an unbounded capacity to transcend its physical form. If we spend our blessed life as a human, not creating, learning, discovering, growing, exploring, giving, helping, and providing value to others, what are we doing then? Poor or rich, everyone can play their part in doing the best they can.

It's so crucial to see money and life as different entities because everything tangible is perishable. It's only the intangible that really matters. Yes, money allows us to have many luxuries in life that can provide us with intangible pleasures, and there is nothing wrong with that. But it's quintessential to understand that money is not going to be with us forever. It's a reward for our actions, and it's up to us how we use it for a concrete meaningful purpose beyond ourselves. If we devote our lives to becoming greedy and selfish by simply making money for ourselves, we are laying the foundation for a miserable life. Instead of focusing our attention on just earning money, dedicating our time to creating something of value to others is much more satisfying to the soul.

Our values should be erected upon the indestructible bridges of selfless love, gratitude and kindness toward others. Where we don't just live with the end-goal of comparing bank balances with our peers, but create an ecosystem instead, where others can feel inspired by our actions, and are compelled to learn from them to do what motivates them. That is what being human is all about.

Flying over the Atlantic Ocean, miles above our civilization, I promised myself that until my heart ceased beating, I was not going to spend my precious time, this gift of life, burning my soul to produce cinders of agony, regret and fear.

C. Indian Curry

"Indira Gandhi Antarashtriya airport mein aapka swagat hai."

My eyes unsealed as my ears registered that announcement from the pilot. I looked out of the plane's window and acknowledged the smoggy atmospheric conditions of New Delhi. It had been approximately one and a half years since my last visit and even though my life had substantially changed during that period, I was to find out that the majority of people in my pre-existing groups could not understand that, as they were living more or less the same lives.

Experiences drive change, and accepting change is what determines an individual's growth. Contrary to the common belief, age is not the most prominent factor in defining a person's maturity, expertise, wisdom, knowledge and so on. No doubt, it's a crucial part of it, but it's truly relative to the individual's personal capacity for accepting change. Not everyone welcomes change for what it is. Some accept it, but do not make a determined effort to change more than what's needed for survival. The ones who embrace change and develop the ability to constantly evolve through hard-earned experiences, are the ones who move past their past to transform themselves.

When we interact with new people from different backgrounds than our own, and experience the variety of what the world has to offer by traveling to different cultures, our subconscious mind functions at an unprecedented rate from processing all the new information it receives. That processing causes brain cells to multiply and new neural pathways to form. These major transformative changes can't be quantified, but they can be felt by the release of suppressed emotional layers in our mind. The change in the subconscious mind is so dramatic that it awakens new thoughts, fosters creative ideas, important realizations, and enlivens the body with a spirited energy.

After going through such internal dramatic changes, your external physical structure looks more or less the same to the human eye, but your mental and emotional states acquire different contours. It can be difficult to convey the change in words to other people, who have never experienced a similar process in their lives. In fact, it's even difficult for them to relate to the idea of it, as it's an alien concept.

Our first instinct as humans is to not accept something we are not familiar with, because we don't know what it entails, and fear of the unknown always prevails. As a result, you have to find a way to explain to your loved ones what you have been through, and in a manner so that they can understand its importance.

As humans, we are always expected to act perfectly, which results in us pretending, and critically leading lives that are built on numerous lies. In a social setting especially, we want to portray our best and be branded by others as someone who has figured it all out. Thus, all of us live in a world, where everyone acts the roles they have embodied to their minds. The only difference is that some are good at it and some are bad. Subconsciously immersed in representing these diverse characters, we can't even differentiate between the characters we play and our true identity, and forget to ask ourselves who we are.

Our mind conceives what it sees, and we believe what others see.

Going to India is always accompanied with an overflow from a bag filled with emotions. It's such a fascinating country, which stimulates the mind beyond its capabilities. It's a country of paradoxes where there is peace amongst chaos and chaos amongst peace. And everything else falls in between.

It's an exciting, colorful, extremely diverse, multi-cultured, and multi-faceted country, which offers everything from the imaginable to the inconceivable. As soon as I walked out of the Indira Gandhi International Airport, memories of the past surfaced onto the unguarded layers of my recent self.

India is not a very formal country. It's like a big family, where strangers can ask personal questions without hesitation and guests are hailed as gods, so I was prepared for the hundreds of opinions that were going to be pitched my way as soon as I stepped my foot out of the airport's entrance.

Instead of being demeaned by that, I had started to cherish it dearly as an Indian cultural norm. My decision was firm and that's what mattered. Dealing with people on a personal level on a regular basis is an essential part of living in Indian society, which I was aware of and more importantly accepted. My job in New York had polished my diplomatic skills and negotiation tactics, which were going to aid me in dealing with the people of my community.

I had prepared myself with a strategy. Apply your learning. Listen to everyone, but only respond when it's essential. Filter out the received information, and only retain what you think might be important for your path. Say the minimal amount and be sincere with your actions. Don't indulge in arguments, and don't hurt anyone's feelings. There is no need to explain yourself. Let your actions speak for you.

And most important of all: be patient with yourself and others, because in the long run it will be worth it.

Instead of being concerned about all of that, I diverted all my energy into assembling what I needed to get me to Peru.

In the week after my return from Miami, I'd asked Brian about Peru one day and whether he had done Ayahuasca when he was there. "That's why I went there," he replied. I gently nodded my head and told him that at first, I hadn't been sure why my intuition had directed me toward Peru, but during my introspective time, I'd had a lengthy vision of me standing in the midst of a jungle. At first, I couldn't understand why I'd had that vision, but was later convinced that Ayahuasca was the prime reason for my inner voice pointing me toward Peru. Brian simply stared at me and asked, "You're going to go to the Amazon Jungle?" I said, "If it is truly in my path, which I think it is, the Amazon will call me."

I didn't tell anyone, but Brian and few other friends knew about my intention of going to the Amazon Jungle and doing Ayahuasca, which is a brew prepared from vines grown in the Amazon Jungle. It is used as a traditional spiritual medicine by the indigenous communities there. I could have researched more about it on the internet, but didn't. I wanted to get to Peru first, and then figure out for myself what it was. I didn't want any negative remarks on the internet about it to skew or formulate my opinion on it. I preferred, instead, to accumulate information directly about it from individuals who'd done it in the past. I sincerely believe that people's words are much more credible when they are an expression of their own experience, rather than a quotation of what they've read from an unreliable source on the internet.

I purposely didn't mention Ayahuasca to my family or friends in India, because I didn't know what it really was and didn't want to talk about it, without having experienced it. I truly believe that you need to experience something first, before talking about it. Only then, can words be discharged from your heart.

During my last days in New York, I'd also looked at various volunteer work opportunities in Peru, some place where I could help a local community to achieve its mission. After browsing through a bunch of websites for few hours, I came across an organization that was working with a local community in one of the districts of Lima called Villa El Salvador.

The organization provided free integrated educational workshops for the children of its community. They focused on practical learning and enhancing the educational system. They designed study environments where the children learned by doing activities rather than sitting on chairs and staring at someone talk at them. I liked what they were doing and got in touch with the organization's founder, Emily, who lived in the U.S. She'd founded the organization several years previously, when she'd visited Peru. It was built on a sound foundation, which let it grow organically over time.

Emily and I started exchanging emails and after learning about our priorities, we set up a call for us to discuss the possibility of my helping the organization to achieve one of its goals. The call with Emily was brief and to the point. Both of us were very happy to hear what the other had to say. The result was that Emily invited me to go stay in Peru with a local family, who would host me at their house in a district in Lima called Villa El Salvador while I worked for the organization to create a social entrepreneurship course in their youth leadership program.

Staying with a local family was a great opportunity to experience the culture of Peru. It would give me meaningful insights into the daily lives of Peruvian people, and when Emily had asked me on our call, if I would like to go work with them, I had immediately said yes. So, when people asked me in India, what I would be doing in Peru, I simply answered, "I will be crafting a social entrepreneurship program for a non-profit organization."

Far from what I could envision, Peru was going to be much more than crafting a program. It was going to be an exhilarating, invaluable, unpredictable, and animated journey. I booked my flight from New Delhi to Peru for February 15, 2017, which was exactly a month from when I'd left New York. The Peruvian visa allowed Indians to stay in Peru for 90 days, which meant I had to leave Peru in exactly three months from that date in May.

After spending an essential month of re-connecting with my family in India, it was time for me to finally begin the journey. Since being a kid, I had been used to leaving home and saying goodbye to my parents, but this time there was an odd feeling attached to it, because I wasn't sure what I was getting myself into. My parents were standing at the door of their apartment when I hugged them goodbye. My mother with moisture in her eyes and my father with a solemn smile replied, "Bye, take care of yourself and remember to regularly keep in touch."

I strapped my backpack on my shoulders and commenced my Peruvian journey. I didn't know anybody in Peru and wasn't sure what was going to happen, but I indisputably believed in the voice that had got me to that point. Beginning my walk on an unknown path, stimulated fear in my nerves, but to fight through it, I opened my arms to the sky to free my body. A storm was headed my way, but I was equipped with courage in my heart to stand firm through it, and let it pass through me.

Eternal Surrender

It was time to surrender.
Surrender myself to the world.
World beyond realms of despair.
Despair to be broken.
With hope.
Hope to love.
Love to see.
See the world.
The world that exists inside and outside.

III. HOLA PERU

I F YOU GLANCE AT the globe, it's quite evident that Peru is situated around the world from India, which makes it an extensive trip all the way from India. There was no direct flight, so I had to book a connecting flight via Western Europe. Originally, I'd decided to fly to Peru directly from New York, which would have shortened my travel time, but that would also have cut out my family visit to India.

Something told me that I had to see my family, before leaving for Peru. I knew it didn't make sense logistically but when I left New York, I'd left my logical thinking behind. The way I looked at it was that I needed to complete the circle of my whole U.S. journey by ending it where it had begun – at my home in India. And I wanted to begin my new chapter only after receiving blessings from my parents, and elders at home in person.

It was a traditional approach, certainly, but I felt immense gratification toward my parents and family elders, who had worked so hard throughout their lives to provide me with the opportunities that allowed me to take such a path. Not until later, was I to discover how going to India and seeing my family would become a crucial aspect of getting me past my evils in the Amazon.

As I embarked upon my flight from India to Peru, ruminations about the closure of my American dream and my recent transition time in India played through my head, together with the echo of the airplane's turbines. New York was my last chapter in America, the end of a story that had developed my character as a boy, who knew it all, into a man who knew nothing. It led me to open a new chapter, which was to start upon my leaving America. India was essential for my acceptance of the upheaval that was to change my life and help bring closure to the American story with a sense of comfort.

Closure is a key ingredient in every story. It appears after the end of a story and needs to be dealt with delicately, because it is vital for the new story to begin without any backwash from the previous one. Closure is what helps us move on from the past, without letting the past take over the present. It's critical for us to accept the past for what it was and not let it become our new present.

My visit to India had increased the magnitude of vulnerability in my soul, because there were so many people I'd met there, who simply couldn't understand why I was going to Peru. Every single one, without exception, wanted me to do something that resonated with the sound of money. I was happier not to know what I wanted to do and discover it for myself than give in to someone else's idea of what I should become.

It is a common struggle for our generation, when we find ourselves not sure of what we want to do in life and somebody else walks in telling us what we need to do – which only further confuses us. Really, the most important thing for us to do at that stage is to accept our defenseless state, then use it to spur deep introspection so that we can detect what truly lies in our heart. And finally, to shore up all the courage we can to follow our heart with everything we have.

Hours on the plane on my way to Peru gave me plenty of time to calm myself and get acquainted with the fact that Peru was happening. When you are a dreamer and live your life creating new visions for yourself, nothing seems more unreal than when that vision is in the process of coming to life, even if it's been proposed by an intangible voice inaudible to human ears.

It feels surreal when you actually find yourself breathing in a moment, which was featured in your dreams. It spawns a sedative-like sensation of absolute nothingness in your brain and then synchronizes your being with everything that surrounds you. It's like being in a dream within a dream, which befuddles your mind so it can't differentiate between what's real and what's unreal. You feel awakened in a manner you haven't experienced before, which allows your soul to enter an ephemeral dimensional space, where time magically stops without your conscious awareness of it.

Revelation of this new space occurred on the flight to Peru. It was an indication that I'd surrendered myself to receive the ceaseless teachings of the world.

Pilot

Fly in. Fly out.
Stay in. Stay out.
Breathe in. Breathe out.
Peru in. India out.
Peace in. Peace out.

ॐ ॐ

"We will be shortly landing in Lima," announced the pilot, inspiring a sense of relief among the passengers. Being on a plane for a very long time is claustrophobic, so everyone was thrilled to be getting out of the closed space and getting their blood flowing again.

My landing in the unexplored territory of Peru, inflamed me with excitement and curiosity. For some people, being in a completely new environment can be scary, but for me it was the opposite. I was jubilant and energized to have arrived there. No jet lag or any sort of tiredness in my body undermined me. I was alive, and ready to explore what Peru had to offer.

"Welcome to Jorge Chavez International Airport," the pilot said. When I heard that, my heart started beating strongly and I could feel the adrenaline-rush in my veins. I didn't want to control that, instead experience what it was like for a few words to have such a biological impact on my body. My brain demanded blood, which made my legs move rapidly through the airport out into the openness of Lima, so that I could taste Lima's energy and conclude that I had arrived in Peru.

Emily had arranged a pick-up for me at the airport. Eve, the Program Director of the organization, was coming, as she was the only person who could speak English in the community where I was going to live. I'd got to Peru with zero proficiency in Spanish, which made everything even more exciting because the challenge of communicating elementary ideas with people was going to be a hefty task. My brain wasn't even grooved with basics of that language! I'd have to use my body language and get creative with my hand gestures, to convey a simple message. In such circumstances, the brain develops visceral skills to decode the words/sentences it receives so that it can make sense of what the person might be saying.

It's fascinating how much you can communicate with other humans, regardless of your ability to speak their native language. I am not saying that language is not necessary for communication – of course, it's a quintessential part of any culture, but not being able to speak someone's native language doesn't restrict you from connecting with them. It demonstrates the potential of the unspoken word. It forces you to explore how to communicate and bond with others through pure emotion. It fosters growth of new ways of expressing yourself to individuals, who can't interpret your language.

The key is to not expect the locals of the country you are in to speak your language, but to respect theirs. Your genuine efforts to communicate without being able to speak the native language, generates sympathy among the locals, who then tune in to your efforts out of respect and try to assist you in solving your dilemma. It's also one of the best ways to learn a language. You have no choice, but to speak the native tongue, which forces your brain to grasp its semantics very quickly, compared to being in a comfortable setup where people around you can speak your language.

As a solo traveler in a foreign land with no friends, family or the native language to support you, the only thing you can depend on is the nobility and goodwill of strangers. It can be very frustrating at times to not be able to communicate the gist of what you are trying to say, but it's humbling how people from completely different backgrounds to yours, can be so cooperative and kind.

When we are on our couches at home, watching the TV news or streaming something on the internet, we are constantly taking in negative information about a country and its people. Our brain then generalizes people and countries based on those few incidents, thus giving birth to stereotypes and incomplete hypotheses. We lose hope in people, and let fear take over our judgments by believing that humanity is distressing. We give in very easily to the world's controllers, who then mold our thinking into the restrictive frameworks they find so useful.

When you are at your most vulnerable in an absolutely new environment, feeling nothing but downright lost, it's those same people who were negatively stereotyped that come to your rescue and prove the world's naysayers wrong. So, why let a few negative incidents be decisive factors in our assessment of a country? For as long as humanity persists, there will always be good in the world to keep us moving forward as a species.

The baggage took longer than usual to arrive, and I had a powerful urge to step outside the airport for a moment to expand my chest, stretch the arms, close my eyes and breathe in Lima's air in commemoration of my arrival in Peru, but the carousel started turning slowly, and my backpack was third in the line. Its sight brought immense relief to my eyes. I grabbed it, hoping to sight Eve as soon as possible.

I got into the airport arrival hall only to witness the ritual common at every airport around the world; loads of people holding name cards for the arriving strangers they were to pick up. The carrier is a central component of your journey at the moment of your arrival; they embody your excitement and also convey your first impression of the country you've just landed in. They are like silent guardians, who take you to an unfamiliar place, where everything is new and puzzling.

That unknown place is where the new chapter of your life begins, a place, where nobody knows you and you know nobody; an extraterrestrial land you invade as an alien, where you walk amongst the crowd searching for your identity in the world. The carrier is a Messenger of the Gods, who transports you to where you belong.

Marching past the many carriers, I saw a hand waving at me from the distance. It had to be Eve... an Indian man with a backpack on his shoulders kind of stands out in the crowd. "*Hola* Eve! Nice to meet you! How are you?" I said to her, as the gap between us shortened. She greeted me the Peruvian way with a kiss on the cheek and replied with, "Nice to meet you, I'm good. Hope the flight wasn't too long." "It was long, but I enjoyed it. I am excited to be finally here," I replied. She smiled and said, "Great! Let's go to the parking lot, where a taxi is waiting for us."

Eve was originally from California, and had been working in Peru under a fellowship program after finishing her Bachelor degree from Brown University. She had a slender body, with brownish skin framing her brown eyes for viewers to treasure. She had curly hair that went well with her casual dressing style and easy-going attitude. Her Spanish was fluent and she could have easily passed as a Peruvian by how well she'd acclimatized to the local setting. I followed her outside and soon, we were in the taxi on our way to Villa El Salvador, a district in Lima for middle-lower class families.

It took us an hour to reach our destination. The great thing about the taxi ride was that I was so easily able to converse with Eve, who was very friendly and provided me with most of the necessary survival information about Lima and Villa El Salvador that I needed to know. She told me that I'd be staying at Nancy's house, my host mother. Her younger sister, Ana Maria worked with us and was the one who'd show me how to get to our Community Center. I asked if any of them spoke English, to which she responded with a mischievous smile, "Not at all."

It was late at night, when we entered Villa El Salvador. The roads were dusty and most of the houses were incomplete brick constructions. It was evidently not the most affluent part of the city. There were no impressive buildings or expensive cars, but I was very enthusiastic about meeting my host family. The area was a contrast to where I'd lived in New York, and was stimulating in a manner that it was going to test my adaptive skills.

"Here we are," said Eve, and with that statement, the taxi stopped at the corner of a block in front of a white house. The front gate was open, an obvious hint that the residents were expecting a guest.

Eve told me, she was going to her family's house as it was late, and that Ana Maria would take care of me now. "Great, thanks Eve! See you tomorrow and good night," I replied as I walked in through the front gate, where Ana Maria was waiting for me. She greeted me with a kiss on the cheeks, and sincerely said, "*Hola, como estas? Mi nombre es Ana Maria.*" I somehow understood what she said and replied with my almost zero Spanish in a terrible accent, "*Hola Ana Maria, mucho gusto! Mi... nombre... es... Kart...*" Ana Maria replied in her thick Peruvian accent, "*Mucho gusto Kaaartt.*"

She was so lively and extremely thrilled to receive me; her eyes were beaming in the dark and her candid smile radiated joy. We took a sharp right from the front gate to climb up a narrow spiral staircase to the floor above, where a woman was standing outside a wooden door to welcome me. Ana Maria said looking at me, while pointing her finger at the woman, "*Esta Nancy.*"

Nancy was even livelier than Ana Maria, and the resemblance between their faces was plainly visible. Anyone could guess they were sisters. Nancy greeted me with a kiss on the cheeks as well, and as I walked in through the door, the entire family was there to welcome me. It was a small rectangular living room with couches at both sides and a round dining table at the end. Nancy's husband, Herald and her son Andres shook my hand. Her youngest sister, Anita, kissed my cheeks. Every single one of them was so cheerful about having me in their house. It was the first time they'd met someone from India, and they were ecstatic. A few hours into the country, and I'd found a family, a family consisting of a Peruvian mother, father, brother and two lovely sisters!

None of them spoke any English, except my Peruvian brother, Andres who spoke a few words. He was in his teens and very mellow for his age. I spoke zero Spanish, so it was hysterical. All of them were speaking words at me, and I couldn't understand anything, but it was still great. Their hospitality was phenomenal. All our conversations happened via hand gestures and physical movements. It was a hilarious sight! I was already getting hands-on experience into the Peruvian householder's lifestyle.

I truly believe that an essential part of experiencing a country is to live in neighborhoods where many families are troubled by various problems and are exploited by the corrupt and powerful of their country.

I continued my interaction with the family. We somehow managed to communicate with one another, without understanding a single word each one of us was saying. They served me *Pollo a la braza* for dinner, a classic Peruvian dish similar to Rotisserie chicken. After spending more than twenty hours in flight, I was famished. They were quick to grasp that and the dinner was a reward for concluding the long journey.

Even the slightest bits of my tiredness dissipated, because of the energy in the living room. They'd never met anyone from India and their glittery eyes were filled with astonishment and curiosity. They were asking loads of questions in Spanish, which I responded to by trying to speak Spanish. I absolutely failed, of course, but they adored the fact that I was trying.

After I'd finished eating the delicious food, they took me on a tour of the floor upstairs, which was where I was going to stay. The narrow stairway leading up was just next to the dining table. It was a huge space, built for hosting volunteers from abroad, who came to help the organization. Ana Maria was the link between the family and the organization. The space was built on a concrete floor and was partially covered over by a roof. It had a kitchen, dining table and four rooms. They asked me to choose one of the rooms, and I picked the one with an open window and a view of the main street.

It was easy to see that the floor was built without any sort of planning. The roof gaped in many spots, and defective shed pieces had been used to cover parts of it. The rooms were separated by inexpertly fixed thin wooden walls. The incompleteness of the roof allowed the clamor of traffic to sneak in through the gaps, leaving the space exposed to the outside noise. It wasn't the most ideal of places to stay but somehow, I loved it! I got some kind of adrenaline rush out of the space and promptly accepted it as my temporary home. The family's warm spirit also made me feel very comfortable in an environment that was very distinctive and so different from my usual residences.

After I picked my room, the family let me rest for the night as I had to go to the Community Center the next morning with Ana Maria. She tried to convey the time we had to leave in the morning as she was walking down the stairs. She held her palms in front of my eyes, with eight fingers pointing up, to express the time we had to depart, followed by repeatedly wobbling her right palm, with her index finger pointing downwards. I deciphered her act right away; we would leave from downstairs at 8 am.

The family went downstairs cheerfully saying, "*Buenas noches*", which, by then, I knew meant good night. I gladly replied with "*Buenas noches!*"

As the family left, I was struck with a jolt. It took a second for me to accept the reality of that moment. How had I got there! I'd arrived in another world, which had not been part of any life-plan. The plan had been to keep working in Brooklyn and climb the success ladder. Living in a Peruvian household had never been a component of my life scheme! And being in an unfamiliar environment was unanticipated to the extent that entombed emotions were arising out of my old rotten core.

I threw my backpack down on the floor of my tiny room, which had a small bed, a dresser and a window with the view of the main street. The set-up was fine to fulfill all my basic needs; it had everything I needed to keep me going. It was in accord with the idea that the less stuff we own, the more satisfied we feel.

When I was leaving New York, I'd even disposed of any extra pieces of clothing that were no longer required. I didn't just want to live for these months in Peru with minimal stuff. I intended to build a lifestyle around minimalist living. Owning fewer materials doesn't just make us feel less burdened, it cultivates seeds for more productivity, creativity and efficiency. We become more aware of our surroundings, and the space we're in suddenly becomes crucial for our mental expansion. Most of our possessions are nothing but distractions that cripple our ability to achieve our full potential.

We create an illusory web of belongings for ourselves and then feel stuck because of the obsession we develop over time with them. There is nothing wrong with owning material things, but it's crucial to not be bound by them. The mind feels at ease once it's free from impermanent materialist belongings, which only provide us with temporary happiness.

I'm not denouncing the habit of buying luxury items. In the past, I have been guilty of owning certain things that I could have comfortably lived without. However, it's imperative to not undermine ourselves and be consumed by consumerism culture, which curtails our capacity to differentiate between our needs and our wants. We don't need to buy millions of products or services to keep ourselves busy. The best way to understand this in a modern setting is to think of ourselves as a startup. If a business starts allocating its funds to unnecessary expenses, it will ignore its staple needs. It won't work efficiently because it's been diverted away from what it really needs to achieve for its vision.

Humans are the same: each of us is our own "business entity". We shouldn't spend our time and money on things that don't deserve our attention. If we don't need something for a specific purpose, why enchain our minds in the vicious and endless cycle of owning it?

It's amazing how much we can achieve by practicing minimalist living and getting rid of unnecessary stuff. When I first grasped that in New York, I thought I barely owned anything anyway. Then I began the exercise of getting rid of needless junk, and to my surprise, I had so much disposable material! That's when I chose to restrict my belongings to just two backpacks, and to move forward without buying anything unnecessary. Focusing our attention on things that truly matter is what makes life worth living. If we can build a healthy lifestyle doing what we love, we don't need more than the basics, and it's much simpler for our minds to center attention on what we are trying to achieve.

The only things that I owned were a few clothes, shoes, laptop and a phone. That's it. Nothing more, and that's more than enough to sustain myself happily anywhere on the planet for however long. If it were not for the modern society we live in, I wouldn't even keep the phone and laptop with me, but with the world evolving at a fast pace, technology has become a crucial part of today's world, so a phone and a laptop are considered basic needs. I need them for work and traveling purposes, but at no point do I feel attached to them – and that is the most crucial aspect of minimalist living. If we want to make changes for the better, we have to work from within and accept the modifications that come along with evolving times.

I lay down on the bed exhausted, as the travel hours had kicked in. That household was going to be my home for a little while. My brain was a little overwhelmed by the fact that I was lying down on a bed in an unknown residence in Peru, and at that point, I had to convince myself that everything around me was real and not some kind of a dream. With that thought, I entered the dream state of sleep and finished my arrival in Peru.

IV. DUSTY STREETS OF VILLA EL SALVADOR

MY FIRST DAY IN Peru began with a dusty wind flowing through my window and hitting my nostrils in harmony with a wave of traffic noise blowing in my ears. It wasn't a view of a beach, mountains or a skyline but a busy street with various vehicles like old public buses, rusty cars and merchandise-carrying trucks. A tiny park in between the two streams of traffic functioned as a traffic divider.

It was a newly-built park, with hardly any grass in it. They were constructing a pathway for bicycles at its edges, and had recently planted many trees in it as well. It wasn't the view a traveler comes to a new country for, but I already knew I wasn't in the most affluent district of Lima. I was there to work for an organization, and that's what really mattered. It wasn't a district that had been built to attract tourists, but one where many locals struggled to make ends meet. They faced plenty of challenges in their daily lives, and I was pleased to begin my Peruvian journey from such a district, where I wasn't going to be drawn into some tourist attraction, but would gain real insights into the actual conditions of the working-class people of the country.

I was very enthusiastic about living and working in Peru. Even though the conditions were beyond my imagination, it was an invigorating change that was to bring out an uncharted side of me.

I was downstairs at the front gate by 8 am, as per Ana Maria's instructions. She greeted me with a kiss on the cheek and a merry, "*Hola Kaartt!*" I responded with a "*Hola!*" as well, and then we left for a school, that had recently collaborated with the NGO (Non-governmental Organization) I was going to be working for to run a few workshops a week. As it was my first day in the district, Ana Maria took me to the school by taxi.

In the taxi, I completely involved myself in observing my surroundings to get a sense of the area I was in. The district was still developing, built by people who'd migrated to Lima from villages and small towns in search of jobs. It reminded me of other developing countries and India, where it's common to see the poor inhabitants from the countryside migrating to the land around big cities for their survival. It's a stab at survival by needy people whose village or town area has been demolished. They're forced to live in brick houses and poor living conditions just to survive by working in jobs that would be classified as "blue collar" in America.

Because of the way our capitalism-driven civilizations are based on tyrannical core values around the world, individuals at the bottom of the food-chain always suffer. Under the flag of profit and development, they face the machinations of big corporations and those in power who are corrupt. Instead of empowering and educating the poor, our greed-enslaved society tears their bodies apart and sucks out every drop of their blood and sweat, leaving them masked in hatred for the powerful. It's a cruel reality in every country of the world, the proportion of maltreatment varying in different countries but existing everywhere. Until a significant change takes place at a fundamental level around the globe, our civilizations will continue like this on a macro-scale for a long time.

The taxi stopped in front of a white building, when Ana Maria said something in Spanish to the taxi driver. *Escuela* was written outside the building, which I knew meant school in Spanish. We'd arrived at our destination! It was situated in a neighborhood called Oasis, which wasn't the most secure part of that district, as I found out later from local neighborhood volunteers who'd been robbed there at gun-point several times.

I followed Ana Maria through a black steel gate only to be captivated by the vast open space the school had to offer for the children of the community. The classrooms were designed in a square, leaving the middle of the facility exposed and available for use. It wasn't solely used for school purposes but was also rented out to community members for cultural functions. Ana Maria took me to a classroom, where Eve and some other young locals were seated.

Eve said to me, as we walked inside the classroom, "*Hola* Kart, how are you?" She then introduced me to all the individuals in the room. She told me that they heavily depended on local volunteers to keep running. It was magnificent to see young people taking such positive actions for their community. I told Eve that I thought it was amazing and asked her, if any of the local volunteers spoke English. She smiled with a definite "No," so I knew I would really be picking up Spanish quickly.

Class time went by with I trying to communicate with the local volunteers and simply observing children's educational activities. The local volunteers were extremely welcoming, and even though we didn't have a common language, we somehow managed to get along and learn about one another. I said to all of them in my broken Spanish, "*Tu professor mi espanol, mi professor tu ingles.*" It was grammatically wrong, but they understood what I meant! The idea was to generate dialogue, so they'd teach me Spanish and I'd teach them English.

When the workshop ended, Eve said that she'd take me to the La Encantada neighborhood, where our Community Center was located, and where I'd be working every day, and then to other places I needed to know about. Visiting our Community Center for the first time was fascinating. It was located on top of a hill in an even poorer part than the other parts of Villa El Salvador I knew. The streets were dusty and not paved; the houses were damaged with street dogs roaming around everywhere. The Community Center was at ground-level, and that's where the organization held all its educational workshops for the community. It comprised of a hall, a study, a small kitchen, and a tiny office. The walls were colorful, packed with charts and paintings. It was a very vibrant and nurturing place, where children could feel comfortable and freely express themselves.

A. I Adored It!

Next, we went to the Municipality around ten minutes away from La Encantada by a tuk-tuk (a three-wheeled vehicle, Peruvians called a "*mototaxi*", and commonly referred to as an "auto rickshaw" in India). Tuk-tuks were the easiest way of getting around in Villa El Salvador. The main market was where the only secure ATM for the entire district could be found, installed inside a bank. It was also the busiest area of the district. After seeing its location, we continued to our next stop, the radio station, only another block further on.

At the radio station, I met Jesus, our organization's local partner. He was a short Peruvian man, with a glistening face and sharp features. He radiated a sense of calmness and gentility and shook my hands with placidity in his veins. Jesus was simply a remarkable man, who also adored taking pictures with his phone. He gave Eve and me a quick tour of the radio station and introduced us to several of his colleagues. We then took a tuk-tuk back to La Encantada, and lunched at Jesus's house. He lived on the floor above the Community Center with his wife Martha and their children. It was a very basic setting, with limited space and no luxury products in it. The children shared one room, and they'd given one room to Eve, who conveniently worked only a staircase away from where she lived.

Jesus and Martha were not wealthy, but were graced with kindness. Instead of using the floor beneath them for themselves, they'd willingly offered it for the children of their community. Martha was a very welcoming woman, who loved to cook. She'd prepared a delicious fish delicacy for us. As Lima is a coastal city, fish features in most Peruvian dishes. Martha served the pan-seared fish with a vast chunk of rice and beans. It was a large portion, but a typical meal size in Peru, Eve said, as they always had a huge serving of carbohydrates. I knew, it was going to take me weeks to get accustomed to the meal size. No wonder, siesta was part of the Peruvian culture. During my stay in the community, Martha's house was my primary go-to place for lunch.

The day then followed its course. Eve went back to the Community Center to run the post-lunch workshops. Jesus took me on a walking tour of La Encantada. We made our way up the neighborhood hill, with Jesus introducing me to some locals on the way. It was a very community-motivated setting, where all the households were adjoined. We soon arrived at the plateau on the top, which contained the last few houses in that neighborhood, and also presented us with a hypnotizing panorama of Villa El Salvador, which was unparalleled to anything I had ever seen before. Jesus took me till the end of the plateau where a crumbling brick wall announced the end of the neighborhood. Beyond the wall was a descending sandy slope leading our eyes onto the enthralling sight of the ocean.

Throughout our walk, many domesticated dogs had tried to attack us, as we rambled past their territory, but Jesus would just say, "*Tranquilo… tranquilo,*" to me whenever the dogs approached us. If we'd reacted to their barking, they would have attacked us. The strategy was to stay as still as possible and slowly walk past them and simply neglect their presence by not looking into their eyes. Even though I was fearful because of how aggressive and robust they were, not letting them sense any fear was vital for getting away unharmed. The abundance of untied dogs was certainly a reason for me to be constantly aware of my surroundings, because they were a real physical threat and I didn't want to get bitten in Peru.

The first day in that district was like being in another world. It was such an overwhelming change of environment that my mind was drained from processing everything. I told myself, as we were walking back to the Community Center, that was what I was there for. I was back at level zero and it was refreshing to start from the bottom. By the time we got back to the Community Center, it was around 5 pm, which was the hour for me to go back to the house with Ana Maria. As we were leaving, Eve told me not to walk around in the district alone when it was dark, because it was not safe.

Ana Maria took me back via public transport, which comprised a van-ride, followed by a quick bus ride to drop us outside Nancy's house. We took the van-ride from La Encantada to the main crossing called *Ovalo Mariategui* on *Avenida Jose Carlos Mariategui*; the house was located further down that avenue. The local *mercado* (market), was also situated at the crossing. Before getting on our bus, Ana Maria showed me around the market, which was very active and multicolored, and packed with local merchants selling all kinds of wares. I bought some groceries from the local vendors. The market was mid-way to Nancy's house from the Community Center, which was very convenient for me as I could simply pick up fresh ingredients for cooking on my way back to the house every evening.

On our arrival back at the house, I said, "*Ciao*" to Ana Maria, who gleefully replied "*Ciao*" with a kiss on my cheeks. She walked in through the door on the ground floor, and I went up to my floor to end that overwhelming and compelling first day in an alien land. Traveling and working in different communities can really open your eyes because of the distinctive cultural norms, you come across. It provides you with a fresh perspective and challenges you beyond anything your mind has conceived before.

I had arrived in Peru during February, the second last month of the southern hemisphere summer season. The NGO was to end its summer semester in two weeks, at the end of February. A course schedule was already in place for those two weeks. During those weeks, I assisted the local volunteers in any way I could and managed the NGO's social media platforms. The NGO was not to function the following week, which was reserved to plan for the next semester. The planning week was when Emily asked me to design a six-week social entrepreneurship course for their youth leadership program and to assist Eve in going door-to-door around La Encantada to meet with the families and enroll their children for the coming semester.

The two weeks until the planning week went by in no time. I was fully engaged in absorbing the community's local culture and visited the other districts of Lima on the weekends to get an overall idea of the city. I couldn't do much around Villa El Salvador other than the community work itself, but that was extremely rewarding as it led to the development of sincere relationships with the local volunteers and children of the community. The nights were spent mostly at the house, as it wasn't safe for me to walk around Villa at night by myself. I would hang out with the family sometimes, or practice Spanish on my computer.

The NGO was the least commercial organization I had ever worked for, and I was the first international volunteer Eve had received during her entire time working there. It was completely dependent on the sincere efforts of local volunteers to successfully run their workshops. Most of the local volunteers were in their late teens, or early twenties, a mix of both sexes, who had been associated with the NGO for several years by then. Many of them were enrolled at University, and some of them were very bright students. One of the girls, Claudia was studying medicine and another girl, Indira was studying business. A guy named Jean Paul was a gifted artist and another fellow, Brian was a talented musician. These were few of the many volunteers who made me feel very welcome and were thrilled to have an international person in their community.

My having come to Peru from India added to the enthusiasm of the local volunteers and crammed them with extra curiosity. I was the first person from India every single person in my community had ever met, and that was sensational for them. It was staggering, how much all of them wanted to learn about Indian culture. They were familiar with American culture, so they didn't ask much about America, but India was always at the top of their list of questions. It was difficult for me to sometimes explain in Spanish the specific rituals or practices in Indian culture they would ask about, but somehow it always worked out, and the end result was that we had a laugh together. Language was never a barrier; rather it functioned as a tool for me to try and communicate more with the local volunteers. They encouraged me to always speak in Spanish, which improved my Spanish skills very quickly. I didn't have much choice, anyway, but to use my voice in a language they could understand.

It didn't take much time for me to become familiar with the already formulated curriculum at the NGO. The local volunteers made it easy for me to be of help, and the children were delighted to have a new face come in to their lives. Ana Maria, Nancy and the rest of the family accepted me as one of their own and couldn't have been any nicer or more helpful. I didn't feel like a volunteer anymore, but a representative for the billions of people who identify themselves as Indian. Traveling to another land is about learning a new culture, but I realized how I was the source for the natives to learn about Indian culture. It was an exchange of cultures, and my actions were significant for the perceptions they were to develop about Indians. Because I was the first tangible representative from India, they'd had the chance to interact and communicate with in-person that in itself instilled in me a sense of responsibility to act in a manner a billion people from my home country could feel proud of.

Based on my experiences, the two weeks prior to the planning week were divided in two parts: weekdays and weekends. My working days with the NGO were from Tuesday to Saturday, so those days were my weekdays; Sunday and Monday were regarded as my weekend.

During the weekdays, I got accustomed to the rudiments of residing in Villa, which required constant effort and awareness on my part to get along in uncertain and sometimes risky situations. I regularly reminded myself to act like the locals and be confident in my approach to every circumstance. Being a foreigner, I stood out in the crowd and not being able to speak the language, amplified my intuitive skills for subconsciously analyzing every situation I was in. Not being in the company of Eve, Ana Maria or any of the local volunteers, which was many a time, further expanded my sensibility to deal with the locals and be fearless in my attitude. Every day assured me of an augmented mental state, because of how my mind was being trained not to react to any excruciating external stimuli. I used every external stimulus to develop more mettle to breach the slabs of fear that had held me down.

Weekdays of volunteering with the NGO was a novel and priceless experience. The NGO was unlike any other organization I had ever worked for, because its efforts were majorly driven by the locals of the community. There was a sense of compassion in all the local volunteers for their community. They wanted to give their best to motivate the unprivileged children of the community to learn, so that they could have an opportunity to advance and build a better life for themselves in the future. The springs of generosity were visible in every local volunteer's efforts, and they were so grateful to receive an individual from the outside world who had come to assist the NGO on his first visit to Peru.

The weekends, on the other hand, were primarily based around getting familiarized with other districts of Lima and meeting new people. I spent most of these hours on the first two weekends at Barranco District, where Eve took me at the end of my first week of being in Peru.

Our first Saturday workshop had just concluded, when I asked Eve if she had any plans for the night. When she responded with a "No," I asked her if she wanted to go somewhere. She said, "Yes," and suggested we go to Barranco, as it was a cool neighborhood. I didn't know anything about Barranco then, but I liked the surprise element of not knowing, so I agreed.

We left for Barranco later in the evening by *Metropolitano* (the Lima bus transit system). As we got on the bus, Eve told me it would take approximately forty minutes to reach Barranco from Villa El Salvador on a bus, if there was no traffic, and as it was late evening on a Saturday, the chances of us hitting the Lima traffic were minimal.

The bus ride didn't seem that long and soon we had arrived in Barranco, but the transition from Villa El Salvador to Barranco was equivalent to entering another country: it was worlds apart...

There was no comparison and I couldn't believe how different the districts were. Barranco is known as the bohemian district of Lima. It is vibrant, colorful, energetic, and a lively neighborhood. A home to artists, musicians and creative geniuses. It was built in European-styled architecture conferring a unique identity on Barranco, and the air around it flourished with a cultural heritage of its very own. The buildings were jazzy and vivid, luring the eyes of every individual walking upon the streets of the neighborhood.

It was jam-packed with people when we got there, and I thought we had walked into a music festival, but Eve told me it was just another Saturday night in Barranco. That was my first time outside Villa El Salvador, and I was shell-struck by the difference between the two districts. We walked past *Plaza de Armas* (the main square in Barranco), which was surrounded by antique colossal structures, including a famous yellow-colored church called *Parroquia La Santísima* Cruz. For my first night outside Villa, it was a marvelous change of atmosphere.

Eve showed me around Barranco, and then took me to a fusion-based gastronomy restaurant called *Hosso Casual Nikkei.* Their food combinations were focused on combining Japanese and Peruvian cuisines, with the tastes of their exclusive dishes being exceptionally delectable. The restaurant offered a pulsating sensation, which when combined with its rich setting created a wide spectrum that reminded me of Peru's diversity and multi-ethnic society.

Throughout the history of Peru, individuals from Europe, Africa, Japan, China, and all the Americas had set their feet on that magical land. During earlier centuries, when migrants of other ethnicities came to Peru, they also mixed with the indigenous population, giving birth to blended identities. In that mixing process, it wasn't just the skin colors that blended together; there was a gradual amalgamation of distinct cultures, traditions, values and belief systems. Constant immersion over time formed a single identity that formed modern diversified Peruvian society, aka, the Republic of Peru.

The dinner at that flawless, aesthetically-ornamented restaurant was followed by our group growing in numbers. Some of Eve's friends joined us, and we ended up at a stygian bar located on *Calle Berlin* in Miraflores district, an upscale affluent neighborhood of Lima. Barranco and Miraflores were the two most popular Lima neighborhoods for travelers. Barranco attracted more of the local younger artistic crowd, and Miraflores was the prime hub where the city's rich were to be found. Miraflores was architecturally designed in an elegant and contemporary manner, and it was at least three times larger than Barranco, which was a tiny district. It was my first night outside Villa El Salvador, so Eve and I didn't stay out for too long and grabbed an Uber back to Villa from Miraflores. There was no *Metropolitano* after 11 pm, and I was surprised to discover that Uber went to Villa at night. Eve told me that Uber was the safest option for getting back to Villa at night, as the taxis were not very safe in Lima.

We drove back to Villa, and I thanked Eve for showing me around on our ride back home. I also told her that I had so much respect for her, because of what she was doing in conditions that were not very work-friendly, especially for women. She replied, "Thanks Kart. It's been challenging, but I've gotten used to it now."

The reason I said that to Eve was because after the first week of volunteering, I saw how difficult it must have been for her, coming from western society and working under such brutal conditions, where security was a huge concern for anyone, and only more awful for a woman, as the worst-case scenario for women was unfortunately way crueler than it was for men.

We want an equal society in our world, but honestly no society in any part of the world is equal. Sexism is everywhere: it's just a matter of what specific kind in each society. We consider the world to be equal for both sexes, but that is far from the reality. The sad truth is that in most places, women are not considered even near to being equal to men, because of the deep ingraining that women are beneath men. I saw Eve combat some sort of sexism every day in Peru, just because she was a woman. It wasn't that the men were being sexist on purpose; they weren't even aware how their subconscious subtle gestures, facial expressions and actions correlated with their not taking a woman in a leadership position seriously. If a man had been in charge, their reactions would have been totally different.

In every society, I have seen the privilege men have, just because they are men. Being in Peru, working under Eve was another such instance where I observed with my own eyes the kind of justifications Eve had to give others and the hardships she had to combat, just because she was a woman. It was a reminder for me to not let any preconceived notions govern my judgments and actions regarding women. Instead of just talking about equality, I had to relentlessly practice equality. It was essential to start with a mindset that was respectful and empathetic toward every human being regardless of their gender. During my stay at Villa, I was able to develop a concrete professional relationship with Eve because I deeply appreciated the work she was doing and admired her courageous spirit.

My first outing in Lima was simply an introduction to the contrasting world outside the periphery of Villa El Salvador. There were plenty more items in store for the remainder of the weekend!

V. REAL LIFE CHARACTERS

THE NEXT TWO DAYS were my first weekend in Lima. I didn't know it then, but it was going to be crucial for developing the rest of my Peruvian journey, because of four individuals who were going to play pivotal roles in guiding future events during my time in Peru. Two were travelers I'd met in the past, and the other two were new characters.

The next morning, I went back to Barranco by *Metropolitano*, as I was supposed to meet-up with a friend of mine in the afternoon, Lili – one of the four critical individuals. I knew Lilli from before - we'd first met in Paraty, a small Brazilian coastal town, situated between Rio De Janeiro and Sao Paulo. It was in the summer of 2014, and I was backpacking through southern Brazil when I stopped at a town, which used to be the Portuguese colonial center, and stayed in a beachfront hostel. Brazil was the host country of the 2014 FIFA world cup, and they'd won a game the night Lili and I met. Football is nothing less than a dominant religion in Brazil, so with Brazil having won a game in their home country, astounding celebrations were going on everywhere.

Lili had just arrived at the beachfront, where I along with many Brazilians was celebrating the country's win, when I invited her to join us. We instantly became friends and stayed in touch till I saw her again at Portland, Oregon in 2016, where she lived and ran her own nutrition company. She was originally from Lima but had moved to the U.S. at an early age. Her father still lived in Lima, so she visited Lima at least once every year. When I messaged her that

I was going to Lima in February, she'd responded with a jubilant reply, saying she was going to be in Lima in February as well.

That was it… We were to re-unite again and the story of our friendship would continue. Every traveler travels for those days: there is nothing like seeing a special someone again that you met while traveling. When we first met in Paraty, we were both leaving for another city the next morning, and there was no assurance that we'd ever get to see each other again, but we did because our lives brought us together. The connections you have with people you meet while traveling, that you share such an exclusive flicker with, can be very powerful even if it's only for a few minutes or hours. At the point of separation with such special individuals, your heart is filled with hope, which encourages you to declare with faith, "We will see each other again."

It was late morning in Barranco, when I arrived there to wander around for a while. Lili wasn't going to arrive till early evening, so I figured it would give me couple of hours to explore the neighborhood a little bit. There were very few people in Barranco during the day time, compared to the previous night when it had been bursting with people. I was back at *Plaza de Armas*, which was still a remarkable sight in the light of day. I strolled through it, with the yellow church on my right and a Starbucks across on my left to a stone-engraved space with public outdoor seating. Street artists were performing around the open area, and as I walked further along I passed striking restaurants on both sides. There were stairs at the end leading downhill onto a narrow brick pathway that headed straight toward the coast of Lima. The walls were filled with illustrative artworks, arresting my eyes.

I followed the alleyway toward the beach, only to find myself standing mid-way and staring at a wooden board with the name *Kaminu* carved on it. I asked myself if it was a hostel, but wasn't entirely sure, so I decided to find out. In modern times, hostels are the most inexpensive way for travelers from around the world to move around countries and stay in environments that are friendly and community-based. They are also great places to meet other travelers and connect with individuals who are on similar journey to yours. I walked in through the sleek green-colored wooden door, which led straight to their reception. A tall, dark man with a slender body, sharp features and fiery skin was seated at the reception – the second critical individual.

He asked me in his theatrical voice, as I entered, "Hola, como estas amigo?" I replied back in my much-improved Spanish accent, "Hola amigo, muy bien, tu hablas ingles?" To which, he replied in his American accent, "Yes. How can I help you?"

"You're American?" I asked, which he confirmed and then said, "I'm from Arkansas, but was born in Brooklyn, and now I live in Lima." When I heard the term Brooklyn, I got very excited and told him that I used to work in Brooklyn. Our common love for Brooklyn was what connected us instantly.

His name was Kofi, similar to coffee. Kofi was an amiable and helpful fellow, who'd been living in Peru for quite a while. He sustained himself by working at *Kaminu*, which was a traveler's hostel, and teaching English. It was difficult to walk past him without noticing his presence, because of his tall athletic physique, which also contributed to his doing modeling on the side. He was a very well-linked individual with numerous contacts in Lima that were to be of much help to me in the future. As we were getting to know each other better, he said, "Let me introduce you to my best friend Jack, who is a journalist and is currently seated at the bar area of the hostel. He's the guy for you." I gladly agreed.

I followed his tall figure past a stripped door next to the reception, to climb a tiny wooden stair, which escorted us out into an open-air seating area with a marvelous view of the grey cliff that Barranco was established on. I was stunned for a second, because of the view the roof offered and how humongous the roof was. There were two levels, one that was entirely uncovered and the other that was a little elevated from the uncovered area, and was sheltered to protect it from the sun. It had a kitchen along with a bar and a comfortable sitting area.

Jack was settled at one of the tables in the elevated section. His eyes captivated by the blue sky, while the tips of his right-hand fingers held a half-burnt cigarette, but as Kofi called out his name, his hazel-tinted eyes moved toward Kofi, who then announced, "This is Kart. He arrived in Lima a week ago from India and is currently volunteering with an NGO at Villa." Kofi straight away returned to his shift at the reception, while I made my way toward Jack to introduce myself. He said to me in his bulky British accent, "Nice to meet you mate. Have a seat." And that's how Jack (the third critical individual) and I met. A rare friendship ensued, which was to play a pivotal role in my journey forward.

He was a fairly tall man, with flaxen misty hair reaching down to his neck. His mouth was always pouring out stories that he had been covering around Peru. He was a journalist for a Peruvian newspaper, a writer who'd been living in South America for several years already. He was originally from London, but had left London after getting his first book, *On Cowley Road* published. Hours went by like seconds in getting to know each other. What really hit a chord with us was our shared passion for India. Jack had been to India before, and he couldn't stop talking about how much he'd loved it.

He was one of the smartest and most knowledgeable individuals I had ever met, who was a workaholic and exceptional at what he did. The entire afternoon went by as he animatedly recited the story about his visit to India. We both knew we were going to see each other again after that first sensational encounter: there was more in common between us than not and he was going to be a mentor for me in the future.

My decision to come early to Barranco was more rewarding than I could have fancied; I'd met two incredible individuals, who happened to be waiting for me just to show up.

A. So, I Did...

Everything in the world is about your network - there are no coincidences, and there is a reason you meet everyone. Sometimes meeting an individual can change your life forever, but you might not know at the moment of meeting how that will happen. The way life works is that it always leads you to an opportunity for you to pursue what's in front of you... or simply do nothing. When you break out of the pattern of doing nothing that is when unbelievable events take place, and you come across people who influence your life positively – way more than anyone else you have ever known.

I had to break up the on-going conversation with Jack when it was almost evening, to meet up with Lili, who was soon to arrive in Barranco. I had last seen her in the summer of 2016, when I was backpacking across the US and passed through Portland on my way to Seattle. Lili was an entrepreneur and a lifestyle coach, who'd built her own vegan-based nutrition company from scratch. Her story as a woman entrepreneur was phenomenal, and I saluted her ceaseless efforts to educate people about healthy living and clean eating.

I made my way back through the same pathway that had guided me to Jack and Kofi. Lili and I were to meet in the open space next to Starbucks, where the street artists were still performing. Lili was an amazing soul to be around, a little yogini with vitality unlike any other human being, who always took encouraging actions in life. Her animated velvety hair, arresting eyes and genial display combined with a heart-melting smile were enough for any human to be hypnotized by her.

I was waiting for her on one of the public benches observing the crowd around me, when I first caught sight of her. She was gracefully moving her body while listening to some music through ear-phones plugged in her ears. Lili hadn't noticed me but when she did, time stopped and the bodies around us paused. She dashed toward me roaring my name and plugged an ear-phone into one of my ears and breathlessly said, "Kart!! Listen to this music. I am obsessed with it." It was none other than *Despacito*, the most popular tune in Peru that season.

It had been a remarkable day until then, and Lili only made it better. We drifted through Barranco, to a small park skirting Barranco's cliff. It was a public park, which was to become one of my most beloved sites in Lima, where I would go countless times in the future simply to envelop myself in the ocean's spirit. The park was beside *Malecon Paul Harris* and had a remarkable view of Lima's flawless coastline. The ocean presented a heart-stirring spectacle, which when synchronized with sundown was nothing less than a marvelous affair between lovers. I was seeing a sunset for the first time in Lima, and I was glad to be sharing it with a wonderful person like Lili.

With the eclipsing of the sun, my first day out in Lima ended itself with three individuals, Jack, Kofi and Lili becoming part of my Peruvian journey. They were to appear again in my story at appropriate times as individuals, who were to somehow play roles in the significant changes that were to take place in the forthcoming days.

The next day, I was to meet up again with another traveler, Katherine (the fourth critical individual), I'd met in the past in a land far away from Lima. It was the New Year's Eve of 2015, when I was in Las Vegas to celebrate the night. Katherine was in Vegas with her cousins from the U.S. when I met them at a bar in one of the hotels at the strip. I'd ended up celebrating New Year's Eve with all of them. I barely spoke with Katherine that night because she couldn't converse much in English, but thanks to social media she'd become one of my connections. I'd never imagined our paths crossing again; I didn't even know she lived in Lima.

On my arrival in Lima, I'd posted a picture on social media, which had the destination tagged as Lima. She saw the location and messaged me asking, "Are you going to my country?" When I read the message, it took me a second to recollect the memories from Vegas and remember my interactions with Katherine. We hadn't stayed in touch or anything, but I was glad to receive a message from her. I told her I was already in Lima, to which she asked how many days I would be there, and then we made plans for lunch.

Not only did Katherine graciously offer to show me around Lima, she was the one, who was going to be the mediator connecting me with a legit Ayahuasca source in the Amazon Jungle. Her linking role was critical in my journey. If we hadn't connected as individuals even briefly in Vegas, she wouldn't have messaged me on seeing my social media post. She'd messaged me with kindness and I gladly received her hospitable gesture to meet.

She showed me *Centro Historico*, the historical district of Peru, known as the City of Kings until the middle of the 18th century. It was the capital during the era of Spanish rule, and the ancient buildings in the district had a distinct Spanish colonial-era architectural style. *Centro Historico* was much farther away from Villa than Barranco. Katherine was waiting for me at one of the *Metropolitano* stations near Barranco, where we got on a bus for *Centro Historico*. When I first saw her, she was holding a crutch under her shoulders for support. As we kissed on the cheeks, I asked her what had happened, to which she replied in her harmonious tone that she'd had an accident several months ago, but she could still get around. It was just slow.

Katherine was a valiant and caring woman, who treated me with humility and tremendous hospitality. I figured it was a Peruvian thing to be so welcoming of foreigners... it kind of reminded me of India. She was an elegant woman who had lengthy dark hair and pearl-like eyes with a serene face transmitting composure. We spent the day promenading like royalty around the enormous ancient structures built by the Spanish, while conversing in a concoction of Spanish and English. She was a talented woman, an engineer who was building her own company.

During our interaction, I told her about my willingness to do Ayahuasca. To which, she said, "I am very spiritually inclined and want to do Ayahuasca myself." In the coming week, she contacted someone in Iquitos (a city in the northern Amazon, considered the gateway to the Amazon Jungle). On my arrival in Iquitos in April that person would take me deeper into the Amazon Jungle to a small village where Ayahuasca ceremonies were guided by a powerful shaman, a spiritual leader, who had the ability to access and influence the world of spirits. Shamans are also known as medicine men or women, and use their shamanic abilities to heal individuals. A shaman receives his or her knowledge from the ancient spiritual practices of his/her indigenous culture, and is the only one who can adequately guide an individual during an Ayahuasca ceremony.

Katherine's linking me with that individual was the greatest thing she could have done for me, as my time in the Amazon Jungle would change my life forever and put me in her debt for eternity. Who would have thought that a person whom I had met briefly in Las Vegas, would enter my life again at my most vulnerable stage and make such a whopping impact on my Peruvian journey!

There are no co-incidences in life: everyone enters in your life for a reason. You might not always be able to discover the reason but if you open yourself to the world, a brief second with an individual you met at some random place can have a radical impact on your future in an unforeseeable circumstance.

It was an all-embracing day with Katherine, which, combined with my entire first weekend and weekdays in Villa, amounted to an overwhelming range of graciousness, warmth, and kindness bestowed upon a wandering soul by unknown people. The power of humanity showed its true potential. Every single person I met, was willing to help regardless of their socio-economic status, beliefs or whatever other divisive factors there are that disintegrate humanity. I realized that the way we perceive a country or its people, is so distant from what actually transpires within the country.

Living and working at projects with local volunteers at the Community Center in Villa on the weekdays, while exploring other districts on the weekends and meeting all kinds of individuals, travelers, locals and foreigners who were living in Peru, were to provide me with a broad understanding of the various aspects of the culture Lima had to offer by the end of my time there.

The week following my first weekend out in Lima was to be the culmination week of the summer semester at the NGO. All the ongoing projects were to finish by end of that week, and a celebratory picnic day was scheduled for the Saturday when the summer semester would officially conclude. The picnic was to be held at a public park in Villa El Salvador with all the children, local volunteers and the NGO staff. It would bring everyone involved with the NGO together to celebrate the achievements of the summer semester and bring it to a rewarding close.

The conclusion of the summer semester was followed up with an extravaganza in Barranco, with Eve and some other fellas including her friend, Allie, a woman from the U.S., who'd volunteered with the NGO in the past and used to live in Villa at Nancy's house. She was now working for the Peruvian Government and dwelt in an apartment at Barranco. Her boyfriend, Imanol, who was Peruvian, was also with her. He'd brought along a co-employee too, a woman named Nina from Finland who'd recently moved to Peru for a year to take up an entrepreneurship project. There was a carnival going on in Barranco that weekend, so it was even busier than on the previous weekend. It was such a lively night to be in Barranco, with musicians and dancers performing all around the area. The music from the beating drums resonated with a verve that enchanted the crowd. The atmosphere was wild and the breeze played with profusion of colors and converted the night into a spectacle.

The hours flew by as I moved around Barranco grooving with the carnival. It was around 3 am, when all of us walked to Allie's apartment in Barranco, a cozy spot not far from *Plaza de Armas*. Eve had decided to leave for Villa from there and everyone else was also done for the night by then, but I went back to *Plaza de Armas* to soak in the last bits of what was left of the carnival. It was at its ending stage by then, so I decided to call an Uber but unfortunately, couldn't find one at 4 am that would take me to Villa and a regular taxi was not an option.

My only option was to spend the night in Barranco. So, I walked around in Barranco looking for hostels, savior of travelers, to find a bed for the night. Everywhere was booked, until I came across a little sketchy looking one on *Avenida Francisco Bolognesi* that had a gigantic black steel gate at the front with a door bell next to it. It didn't seem like the most ideal place to spend a night, but I couldn't find a bed in any other hostel, so I had to try it. When I rang the bell, a guy who looked like a Peruvian wolverine opened the door for me.

He was staying at the hostel and guided me toward the reception, past the expanded empty space at the front of the building. He was also a drug-dealer and tried to sell me cocaine while accompanying me till the reception. He was harmless but annoying, but he wouldn't take a "No." So, I completely ignored him and made my way toward the reception.

A half-asleep, half-drunk man was at the reception. He was the owner of the hostel but didn't speak a word of English so I tried to ask him in my limited Spanish for a bed to crash for the night. He couldn't really process anything, because he was so drunk and the Peruvian wolverine was still trying to sell me drugs.

Luckily, a nice Argentinian man who was volunteering at the hostel was still awake and came to my rescue. A skinny man, with long curly hair and a big smile, he asked me in broken English, "What's happened?" I explained my situation to him, so he talked to the owner, whose body was swaying and eyes were rolling, and somehow managed to get me a bed for the night. He also asked the Peruvian wolverine to leave me alone. I was very thankful to him.

It was a classic South American experience. Even though I'd got a bed, I was still very skeptical about the place. I lay down on the bed with both my hands in my jeans pockets, to make sure no one would steal my phone or wallet. I woke up around 10 in the morning, glad that nothing had happened to me. All I wanted was to quickly get out of the place, but there was a problem: my phone was dead… and I needed to contact a few people. So, I went downstairs to the dining room hoping someone would have a charger for my phone.

There was a girl sitting at the dining table writing something in her diary when I interrupted her to ask if she had a charger for an iPhone, which she did. And that's how I met Ana.

Ana had fair skin with smooth coffee-shaded hair that gently brushed her delicate neck. Her body was covered with tattoos, that contrasted with her crimson lips and her eyes were concealed behind thick-framed glasses. I sat across from her at the table, putting my phone into her hands. Next thing you know – we talked for an hour. I told her the entire story of how I'd ended up at the hostel, which she found amusing and couldn't stop giggling while I was narrating it.

Ana was a musician from Argentina, who was traveling alone around South America performing everywhere she could. She would sing in restaurants, bars, on the streets and even go around on public buses to entertain the local crowd. She had the voice of an angel, which combined with her heroism and passion for music, just made her a superstar in my eyes.

Ana was to become one of my closest friends throughout my stay in Lima. I treated her as a little sister, and she would tell me about her boyfriend problems, which I would give her a hard time about. She was a genuine, kind-hearted and loving person, who always reminded me of my real sister and younger female cousins in India. Somehow, winding up in that outlandish hostel didn't seem so bad after that, because it had led me to Ana. It was one of those moments, that had me understand that you can meet someone special when you least expect it and in a place that is not ideal.

My phone was charged by the time we'd got to know each other better, and there was a message from Lili saying she'd be in Barranco soon. That reminded me that I'd had plans to see Lili that day, so instead of returning to Villa, I decided to simply continue my day from the hostel itself and even asked Ana to join me. She willingly agreed and we set off toward *Plaza de Armas*. On the way we stopped at a *Chifa* restaurant, which are very popular in Lima. *Chifa* restaurants are basically a combination of Peruvian and Chinese cuisine, with mouthwatering delicacies. It was another of Peru's exclusive and culturally-integrated cuisines.

Lili joined forces with us there, and my entire day went by in no time with Ana, Lili and JP, a friend of Lili's who lived in Barranco. I returned to Villa after witnessing the sunset from the same spot in Barranco Lili had previously taken me to. On my ride back to Villa, I felt extremely grateful to have met so many wonderful people in just two weeks of being in Peru. Working at the Community Center had been a fruitful experience and meeting individuals from different walks of life on the weekends was emancipating me from the mental constraints and thought processes that came from sheltering in bubbles all my previous life.

What's truly essential in life is to develop our own thinking based on a wholesome perspective about what's in the world. If our mindset and thinking are limited to what's in our little bubbles, and we just quote what we've read on social media or the internet, we are far removed from the actuality of what matters and what really defines us. We undermine ourselves by not realizing the potential we have and by not taking the opportunities we can create for ourselves and others, if we were only willing to take that one step toward the unknown.

VI. A MAJOR CHANGE

AFTER THE END OF the second weekend, the planning week for the next semester began. The Community Center was to be closed for that week and only Ana Maria, Eve and I were to be going there. Without the kids and local volunteers, the Community Center had lost its appeal but the quiet helped in getting the assigned tasks done quickly.

My major task was to develop a six-week Social Entrepreneurship course for the NGO's Youth Leadership Program that would be held every Saturday for a total of six weeks. The course was to focus on the practical aspects of Social Entrepreneurship, not on theory. The students were to be introduced to the concept of social entrepreneurship by using actual examples of social entrepreneurs, who'd built successful businesses in Peru by having entrepreneurs come in and explain to them the practicalities of starting a venture. We wanted to introduce them to brainstorming techniques, assign case studies pertaining to social enterprises and foster team-building exercises in every workshop.

The goal was to help them develop a mindset where they could start concentrating on problems, that they felt deeply passionate about and then, as a team, come up with a solution to a chosen problem, while keeping the business aspect in mind so that the solution incorporated a self-sustainable economic model. The Social Entrepreneurship concept was being introduced to them so that they could understand a win-win scenario for all the stakeholders involved, and then use it to empower people in the local community to make a positive change and be financially independent.

It didn't take me a long time to develop the course as the intention was to keep it simple for the students to grasp the material. When I was not working on writing the Social Entrepreneurship course, I assisted Eve with knocking doors around *La Encantada* for families to get their kids enrolled in the upcoming semester. That was equivalent to strategizing in a battlefield, as we had to beware of the dogs that could certainly attack us. It reminded me of my door-knocking days in New York, where I used to go the most dangerous neighborhoods and stand outside a door not knowing what was going to come from the other side.

There is something about being in the field that is thrilling and invigorating. You are out in the world in action-mode. You gain first-hand insights about what you're working on, and you learn about what's happening in the world ground-up. What we read and hear, is not even close to what we see and experience for ourselves. You will change substantially more than others, if your learning comes from real experience, as that is what grows your wisdom and expands your mental capacity to conquer fear.

I finished writing the Social Entrepreneurship course in three days and as my major tasks were completed and the Community Center was to be closed till the next week, I thought about going to a town near Lima for the long weekend.

It was a Wednesday night, when I was cooking boiled chicken, steamed vegetables and rice for dinner after returning home with Ana Maria, and hanging out with my host mom Nancy, who was the perkiest individual I'd ever met. I understood her Spanish the best of all the family members because her sentences would primarily consist of one word, "*Excelente.*" Whenever I conversed with her in my broken Spanish, her first reply would always be, "*Excelente* Kart," uttered in harmonic tones while delivering the biggest smile in the whole world, which always made me so happy. I loved spending time with Nancy, because of her uplifting spirit.

While I was contemplating going somewhere for the weekend, a new thought occurred to me - I wondered if I should go out that night and explore Lima by myself. I just felt like drifting through the city by myself, but something was stopping me from doing so - fear of the unknown. There would be no surety of what would happen after leaving Villa El Salvador.

Fear has to be conquered. It overpowers your subconscious mind. It gives birth to excuses, inaction, hate, anger, anxiety, laziness, etc. The fear of defeat, the fear of the unknown, the fear of xyz – whatever it is that you fear, that is the principal deterrent stopping you from walking on your real path and discovering what it is that makes your heart skip a beat.

At that moment, I was struck by fear of the unknown, which had my mind following the usual framework of excuses: it's too far; I'm already comfortable; it's too much effort to leave; what will I do by myself? It's late… etc. The list went on and I was giving in to it – unless I made a choice to break out of this usual thought-pattern and overcome my fear. Taking one step against fear makes all the difference. Not giving in to fear is the first step toward defeating it. Incredible things happen to you only when you let them happen.

It was around 9 pm when I finished eating my dinner and unleashed my strike against fear, by rushing out of the house and getting on a bus to Barranco. There was a surge of energy in my body the entire time I was on the bus, waiting to be released out into the openness of Lima. I didn't contact anyone or inform my host family before leaving for Barranco, but just left with a mission to conquest my fear.

When I placed my feet on the ground, they enchantingly led me through the streets of Barranco freeing my mind from the fear that was obstructing neurons in my brain from being electrified. At one point, I was back on the same narrow pathway that headed to the beach, when my eyes spotted a familiar name *Kaminu*, and without thinking much I walked past the same green wooden door, which had previously led me to Kofi.

Kofi was not at the reception; the seat was empty. Not giving much thought to it, I went straight up to the rooftop to admire the scenic view that had seduced my senses the first time I'd discovered that enormous open space.

The rooftop wasn't very busy, just a group of travelers sitting together on combined tables under the sky. There was no hesitation in my mind about going to their table and asking them if I could join them. In a matter of few minutes, I was part of the group and seated at one end of the table directly opposite was a man with a polished bald head. He screamed at me from the far end, "Where are you from?" I replied saying, "India, how about you?" "I'm from Germany, and was in India last year," he responded.

I sensed a connection with that man instantaneously and knew right away we were going to be friends. There was no rocket science involved in knowing that, but somehow, I just knew that was the case.

There is a powerful energy that governs many events in the life of a lone traveler, and you are bound to meet some people on your path, who end up having a substantial effect on your life. It's not something that you can plan or control, because it's beyond your domain but what makes a difference is your willingness to surrender to the world and have outright faith in that robust force. You can name it whatever you want, but if your actions and thoughts are pure, that powerful energy will support you throughout your journey and bring individuals into your life as guides for your moment of truth.

I moved my chair from my end of the table to the other end next to the man. There was a woman seated next to him, who was now facing me. I felt a similar connection with her as well. It was dreamlike, more so, outrageous. I wasn't sure if it was just my mind playing games with me, or if it was something real. I introduced myself to both of them, and they were so receptive of my presence that I knew, there was something going on.

A. And I Had to Discover it

The German man's name was Esat and he'd been on the road for almost three years, working and traveling around the globe. He wore thick glasses and had a tanned skin. He had a stubble, and a simple smile to go along with his casual attire, which included many *malas* (a string with beads) wrapped around his neck, that were a sure sign that he'd been to India.

The woman's name was Mahaut (pronounced as Mau). She was from France and had an amazing aura about her that could bewitch any life on the planet. Her blossoming smile, firm-seated posture, dusky long hair falling over a single shoulder, and transparent azure eyes consolidated with a golden heart formed a magnetic force.

The three of us became friends in a matter of a few seconds and it seemed like we knew one another from before. It was interesting to have that kind of connection with strangers I had just met. We were on the same frequency, though I didn't know it then. Meeting them was going to change my coming to Barranco from an attempt to combat fear into discovering more about the unknown path I was on. All three of us were traveling solo and it became evident that we were on similar journeys, which led to our connection only growing stronger.

It's not every day that you come across individuals you bond with in a matter of seconds and beyond logical understanding. And when you are out in the world by yourself mourning your past suffering, having your path overlap with such individuals is a significant reminder of the human connections that can exist in the world beyond plausible cognition.

In the coming hours, the three of us along with a few other travelers left the hostel to walk around Barranco and ended up at a spot, where a band of talented local musicians was performing a variety of their own creations. Their music was very rhythmic and in sync with the mental state of the entire audience, which was enraptured by their compositions. I hadn't thought I would be out for more than a couple of hours from Villa, but that's not what life had in store for me. I'd met two incredible people, who just wouldn't let me go.

When I was thinking of heading back to Villa at around midnight, Esat said, "Just stay at the hostel tonight, and you can leave tomorrow after having lunch with us. I'm cooking Indian curry for everyone at the hostel." I gladly agreed with them and enjoyed their company even more as the night progressed. I had no idea what was going to happen, but instead of thinking too much about it, I simply accepted my heart's desire to stay with them and discover why I'd met them.

Esat had begun his journey from India, where he'd spent time in ashrams and moved around religious towns to embrace India's spiritual aspect. He'd acquired knowledge about Ayurveda, holistic healing, and learnt to cook Indian food using spices and herbs, that could also be used for treating bodily ailments. He'd done several meditation courses as well, including Vipassana, which means to see things as they really are. Vipassana is one of the oldest meditation techniques in India, and was re-discovered by the Buddha himself. I had previously done a Vipassana meditation course in the U.S. and appreciated its meditation technique for its authenticity and concrete benefits.

On top of all that, Esat had recently gotten back from the Amazon Jungle after attending several Ayahuasca ceremonies, which was one of the elements that awakened my ears every time I heard the echo of the sound of its letters. Esat's desire for traveling, seeking knowledge and his efforts to understand life beyond its material aspects through the spiritual world inclined me to spend more time with him, as I really wanted to assimilate the learnings he'd gained over the years of living in different parts of the globe. The next day I'd get to spend plenty of time with him and hear about his Ayahuasca ceremonies, which would provide me with immense confidence and make my belief about my journey even fiercer.

We headed back for the hostel after the end of the band's performance, when Mahaut sighted a small burger joint and said, "Let's get some food!" It was a rare spot, which crafted its own Peruvian-styled burgers, with all kinds of ingredients. It was managed by a polite woman, who was very warm and welcoming. She stood behind the counter and greeted us with a genuine smile, delivered through her beguiling green eyes. Her soothing voice grabbed my attention. She was passionately interested in food, and the burger we had was delicious. It was unlike any other burger I'd had before and was the only burger I'd eat during my entire time in Peru.

I was trying to practice my Spanish with the woman. She was from Argentina and had been working in Lima's food industry for several months. In my broken Spanish, I was trying to tell her how

I'd met Esat and Mahaut, who were standing next to me eating their burgers and laughing at my Spanish skills. The lovely woman seemed to be enjoying the conversation as well.

I told her in my grammatically and every way possible wrong Spanish sentences, "*Mi amigo Esat (pointing at him) es preparado almuerzo manana en Kaminu hostal,*" and asked her, "*Quieres venir?*" I wasn't sure if I conveyed the proper sentence for what I was trying to say, which was that my friend Esat is preparing lunch tomorrow at Kaminu Hostel and would she like to come. She looked at me with a blank face for a whole second, and then nodded her head in agreement "*Si,*" without any hesitation, and I playfully added some Peruvian slang I had learnt from the locals in Lima, "*Buenaso!*"

Esat said to me as we were walking back to the hostel, "I am surprised she said yes," and I replied, "Me too. We'll see tomorrow if she actually comes."

On our return to the hostel, we stayed up till late talking about life on the rooftop while admiring the moonlight in the sunless vault above us.

I had no extra clothes or mental preparation for that sudden change of plan, but life doesn't work the way you plan it. Instead, it throws something completely unexpected at you with a choice: you can either stick to your original plan, or take the unexpected choice and explore how it could affect you. I'd chosen the latter and broken through my pre-conceived notions about what is what and had ended up slumbering on an empty hostel bed, without telling any of the staff members. As I dozed off, I planned to tell Kofi the next day and pay him in the morning.

The next morning, Kofi was amused by the story and told me to let him know in advance next time if I planned to stay for the night! It was around that time when I received a call from my host mother, Nancy, who was worried about where I'd been the whole night. There was no way I could explain the situation to her in Spanish, but thankfully Kofi took charge and told her not to worry, that I was fine, that everything was OK, and that I'd come back in the afternoon.

Esat was about to leave the hostel to go ingredient shopping for the feast he was going to prepare for everyone. He asked if I wanted to join him, and of course, I said, "Why not!" Then the hours of learning about Esat's Ayahuasca experience and life-quests began. We had to go to the local *Mercado* in Miraflores, as that was where the only ingredient shop in Lima that sold *garam masala* and other Indian condiments could be found. He'd figured that out by going to the Indian restaurant in Miraflores, and they'd told him about it!

So, began our day of ingredient hunting – and conversing. The sun was shining at its peak, when we got on the bus from Barranco to Miraflores, whose local *Mercado* was much bigger and cleaner than the one in Villa, which was the one I was accustomed to. The Miraflores *Mercado* was beautiful with a variety of Peru's home-grown nourishing vegetables and juicy fruits. There were many vendors there, selling everything they possibly could, but, Esat with German efficiency, bought all the ingredients in quick succession only stopping at the stores he needed to. I purchased a packet of *garam masala* too to take back with me to Villa, as Nancy had asked me to prepare an Indian dish for the family one day.

During that time, Esat spoke about his travels, Ayahuasca experiences and possible future plans. One of his realizations from Ayahuasca was that Germany was not the place where he wanted to build his life. Instead, he was planning to buy some land somewhere, possibly in Colombia and develop an Ecovillage. He went on to describe his vision for that project, and explained to me that an Ecovillage (*Ecoaldea* in Spanish) is built on bringing together members of the international community to share and live in a place, that is socially, economically and ecologically sustainable. He spoke about the project with intensity in his eyes, and a burning desire in his heart to live a healthy balanced life in sync with nature. His dedication to his mission was commendable.

It was a great outing with Esat and learning about his experiences, ideas and plans for the future was inspiring. One of the great things about traveling is meeting such distinctive individuals, who are out in the world driving the change our planet desperately needs.

We have had enough centuries of our civilization being ruled by the greedy and corrupt. It's time we recognize that our world doesn't deserve more wars. Instead of spending trillions of dollars on assembling nuclear weapons, we need to come together as a species to eradicate poverty, hunger, diseases, and illiteracy around the world. Our prime investments should be in our younger generations, who will take humanity forward and save our planet from being consumed by our own selfish desires. There are many major concerns for our world today like climate change, water crises, cyber security, etc. The list goes on. This century will define our planet's future. As humans, the most conscious of all beings, we have a huge responsibility to act as we speak, and truly come together as children of one mother: our Mother Earth.

Mother Earth is the sole mother, who sustains the balance of our world through the five elements of Earth, Water, Air, Fire and Space. These five elements are mentioned in the Vedas (Ancient Indian scriptures) and constitute every living entity on our planet. Sadly, we have altered the state of balance of our beloved earth, which thus necessitates us to protect our only planet from being annihilated and build a better world based on core values that breathes sustainably along with every animal that resides on it.

Those core values will spring from the seeds of compassion, kindness, love, care, happiness, selflessness, creativity, humility, positivity, determination, acceptance, imagination, respect, unity, wisdom, freedom, knowledge-seeking, responsibility and from the ability for human transformation. When enshrined in every beating heart, they will create a society in which we don't bring others down, but embrace all individuals so that they flourish and transcend themselves for the better.

శో ❁

In a matter of a few hours, we returned to the hostel with all the ingredients, and Esat quickly began preparing the curry, using an innovative blend of the acquired spices and herbs in a large cooking pot full of sweet potatoes and lentils. The end-result was an aromatic ethereal curry served alongside steamy white rice. The taste of the meal transported us to the streets of India and reminded me of my beloved home country. The most ludicrous part of the afternoon was that I was the one from India, but a German man was preparing Indian food in South America – and I was learning from him: it's truly a global world we live in.

The feast brought together members from four continents of the world to a single table, who shared their cultures in the name of the human spirit and produced splendid memories. The company at the table consisted of Mahaut, Kofi, a couple from Venezuela, Xoana, the Argentinian woman we'd met the night before at the burger joint, who'd also brought along her roommate, Verna, a woman from Germany who'd been living in Peru for several months while working in the food industry.

Most of us didn't speak the native languages of the others, but that didn't get in the way of us sharing a moment of naive comradeship. It reminded me of my own reasons for traveling, and that if I'd never left Villa in an effort to conquer my fear, I wouldn't have met all these wonderful people. That one decision, like all the other life-decisions I'd been taking against the grain of the mind's usual thinking patterns, had caused a chain reaction, which had directly affected all these unforeseen events.

The feast was a delight for the taste buds and an offering to the stomach, which was full beyond measure by the time we gave up trying to finish the whole pot of curry. It had to be preserved for later meals. Post-lunch, all of us went to Barranco's sunset spot and relished Lima's sunny afternoon. The thought of returning to Villa didn't even cross my mind as I was so engrossed in the present with incredible company all around me. I told myself I'd leave by the evening, but that didn't happen either.

As the day went on, our group got larger and I ended up spending my entire night and the next morning with them. None of us slept that night. More individuals from different parts of the world joined us, which only brought more solidarity and excitement into the whole equation. We went to a Latin color-throwing festival (kind of like Holi, the color festival in India) during the night, followed by a jam-packed taxi ride at dawn that took us on a tour of the whole city, and finally ended at the sunset spot at Barranco, where we began our day watching the bright sun's rays encountering every ocean wave that touched the land.

Not until mid-day, (when I went back to Villa for a few hours to let my family know I was OK) would Mahaut, Esat and I leave each other's company. It was bizarre – and wonderful!

From the time I left Villa in order to conquer my fear to when I returned, two nights passed and I had hardly slept. It was an unexpected adventure, which wouldn't end till Sunday because for some reason every single person from our group (except Esat) happened to be leaving on Sunday to continue their solo journeys. After seeing my family, I decided to return to Barranco and stay till Sunday with the rest of the group. That time I was mentally prepared with clothes and an intention to stay a few nights.

As I was packing my backpack before leaving for Barranco, I remembered that the previous week I'd accepted Lili's offer to go on a one-day sailing trip with some of her friends the next Friday. That Friday was the very next day! I decided that I'd spend the night with the group and then go sailing with Lili in the morning. Before leaving the house, I made sure I informed Nancy that I wouldn't be back till Sunday so she wouldn't worry again.

The night continued with the group in Barranco at The Point Hostel near the Barranco sunset spot. Some of us, including me, were staying there, as Kaminu was booked out for the night. Its setting was not as spectacular as Kaminu's, but it was a lively and comfy hostel with a great atmosphere. As everyone was still charged by the energy created by our union, none of us slept even during the day!

The night took off from where we'd earlier left off. It was around midnight when we headed out to wander around the streets of Barranco. We were standing outside The Point Hostel on *Jr. Batalla De Junin* and that was when Esat detached from us, as he had to leave early in the morning. It was a touching moment as in just two days he'd given me more than he was aware of. I hadn't even completed a month in Peru, and it was overwhelming to have had such a solid connection bless me at the beginning of my journey. I thanked him and told him that I'd go visit his *Ecoaldea* in Columbia for sure.

I spent the rest of the night with the group, as my mind didn't want to sleep: it so wanted to be awake and conscious of everything that was happening. I couldn't differentiate between dreaming and reality anymore. It felt like I was living in a movie, where the scenes were aligned perfectly with the script and the director was elevating the scenes from the big screen into reality.

It had been more than 48 hours since I'd last slept. All my human filters had been broken. My mind had loosened its grip on my heart, which seemed to be functioning superlatively in extracting defunct sentiments from its previous emotions. It was a weird and unfamiliar sensation.

I left to see Lili and her friends at Miraflores around 9 am. The gentleman, Lucas, a Peruvian who was taking us out on his boat lived in Miraflores. Lili knew him through one of her best friends in Lima, Neika, who at the time was dating Lucas. Both Lucas and Neika were very welcoming, and were glad to have Lili and me accompany them on the trip. The day on the ocean was to be the day that would define my journey as it really was.

To Sail

It was a day of freedom amid the vast sea,
with the eternal horizon turning my eyes from the
land toward the mysticism of what exists
beyond dreams.

The breeze carried the sails with my heart hoisting its colors,
embracing its fondness of light that shines upon the blue
to exhibit the hidden diamonds, that take us away from the
prisms of reality to the bliss of what the ocean contains.

෪ ෬

The sleepless hours and inundation of emotions combined with the whimsical ocean had a powerful effect on me that day, breaking all my undefined guards to make me realize that I was on a journey truly seeking my own version of truth, a truth that defined my purpose and guided me on a path that was rightfully mine. There was peace in accepting the wanderer's quest. Sailing away from the horizon and then back to the land of humans following the shades of orange emanating from the sunset, was a time to cherish that solemn understanding.

As I got in my taxi for the hostel in Barranco, I was glad I'd begun my Peruvian journey by working with an NGO, but I needed to leave Villa soon and solely focus on the prime reason I'd come to Peru. I couldn't help others, if I myself was in a state of helplessness. I needed to become truly aware of who I was and devote my entire energy to discovering my real path.

It was my last night with all the travelers from the group, and my mind had started to lose its ability to function after being awake for more than 60 hours. Eventually, I gave in to a bed in the dreamy dark with massively-induced melatonin in my brain till daylight hit the lids of my eyes.

I'd left Villa on Wednesday for couple of hours on a mission to combat fear and here I was on a bed in a hostel four nights later, overpowered by the events that had followed my successful conquest of fear. I embarked on my return to Villa with vigor in my heart, tears in my eyes, and a hint of joy in the hollowness within me.

ℰℭ

Resurgence

I had been burying myself under the ground.
It was time to emerge from the dark,
And walk the path I was born to lead,
To discover the purpose that would be mine.

VII. THIRSTY DAYS

COMING BACK TO VILLA was like waking from a dream, where my mind's perception of reality had been altered by the breakdown of all the guards fettering me. It was the most vulnerable I had ever felt in my life. It was a state of utmost divinity: change was at its peak and I had let go of myself to align with the process of renouncing every part of my old presumed self.

The new semester at the NGO began the day after my return to Villa, and a few new local volunteers and children showed up throughout the introductory week. The week was to consist mostly of educational field trips and end with the commencement of the Social Entrepreneurship course on Saturday. On the first day, I shared my preceding week's unforeseen events with Eve over lunch. As I was reciting the story delicately, she knew that it was time for me to soon continue upon my journey. She asked as I revealed my vulnerable self to her, what I was going to do next.

"I am not entirely sure, but I have decided to continue my journey from Villa to face the unknown and see where life takes me. I don't know what's going to happen or what I will do. But there is a blaze hidden in my core that needs to be freed and I won't stop until I find the purpose, which will help me unleash that eternal fire."

Eve totally understood and said that she fully supported my decision. "Just inform Emily, and then I will take care of the rest," she said. I thanked her for being so understanding, and said, "I really appreciate it. I'll leave at the end of next week after the second Social Entrepreneurship Workshop. That will also allow me ample time to finish the rest of the projects I have in mind for the NGO."

The news of my decision to leave Villa the coming week wasn't received very cheerfully by the local volunteers or Ana Maria and my host family. We'd gotten closer than I could have anticipated, but being understanding and wonderfully kind, they all respected my choice and accepted the reality that my time at the NGO was temporary. The next two weeks were dedicated solely to completing my projects and spending quality time with my host family, local volunteers and students.

The Social Entrepreneurship course began on the Saturday of the introductory week at a place on top of a hill in Oasis neighborhood, which had even more adverse living conditions than the area around the NGO's Community Center in La Encantada. Being on top of a hill, it offered a scenic view of the ocean which provided a calm learning space for the students. The first workshop was to get the students to focus on social problems in their community and to introduce them to the concept of Social Entrepreneurship. They were very receptive to the model, which could be used to solve a social problem with an entrepreneurial approach. They got passionately involved in discussing the social problems within their community, which they themselves faced daily because of a lack of education and opportunities.

The successful kickoff of the Social Entrepreneurship Workshop encouraged me to use my last week to complete more projects for the NGO. I built a rock garden in an unwanted space in the Community Center with waste material and re-developed the small garden outside the Community Center. These were projects, I didn't have an expertise or any prior work experience in, but it was so fulfilling to selflessly create something for the students who would have something better to look at than just areas filled with trash and dirt.

My time in Villa was to end on the Saturday after the second Social Entrepreneurship Workshop, at which Lili would give a guest lecture. I'd invited her to lead the workshop and share her journey as a woman entrepreneur, who'd built her own nutrition company in the U.S from scratch. It produced organic and vegan-based products for the market, while educating individuals to lead healthier and environment-friendly lifestyles.

The previous night had been my last night in Villa, and I'd spent it with my lovely host family. They'd been asking me to cook Indian food for them since my arrival, so I prepared my own unique chicken coconut curry, a mixture of Asian and Indian cuisines, as my way of thanking them for all their love and warmth. They had touched my heart with their hospitality, and I told them in my improved Spanish when we were all sitting together at the round dining table and about to begin eating, "*Estoy agradecio de estar aqui.*" That was followed with a hand gesture pointing at Nancy and saying, "*Eres similar mi madre, gracias por todo,*" to which, Nancy replied emotionally with, "*Ahhhh, Kartt!*", while Ana Maria, who was sitting next to Nancy had her eyes filled with tears of joy.

That dinner was not to be my last meal with the family as Nancy had told me earlier when I was cooking, "*Prepararemos el desayuno de mañana*", which I figured meant they wanted to prepare breakfast for me the next morning.

In total, I stayed in the district of Villa El Salvador for a little over a month with a bunch of strangers who, by the time of my departure, had become my family. A new chapter was to begin the next day. And even though I didn't know what was to happen in the future, the events from that first month had equipped my heart with an immense amount of courage to face anything and everything that was to come my way.

My last day in Villa began with a genial but nostalgic breakfast with the family. Nancy had prepared a classic Peruvian breakfast for the occasion, consisting of Peruvian brewed coffee and a *Tamale*, a little steamed corn dumpling, which is very popular in Latin America and is enjoyed as a breakfast delicacy. In my last few hours the breakfast allowed me to once again embrace a family, who had unbolted the screws in their hearts to treat me as their own.

ℰℛ

During my last week in Villa, Peru had been in a state of emergency because of flooding in the northern part of the country. Countless bridges had collapsed, many people had lost their lives and several homes had been destroyed. There was chaos and panic in the entire country. Even Lima had been dramatically affected by the floods. The water pipes to several regions of Lima had broken, which had resulted in no water supply for most districts in Lima including Villa El Salvador and Barranco. This had had a direct impact on every person in Lima, including myself.

I'd had to buy bottled water for everything and use the minimum possible, to make sure I wouldn't run out of drinking water if the situation got any worse than it was already. Even the shopkeepers were selling limited number of bottles to preserve it for everyone. It was an hour of water crisis with no declaration of its end. It was then I realized how we take everything for granted, especially a basic necessity like water.

A. If There Is No Water, There Is No Life

Instead of recognizing the importance of basic resources like water and air which we can't survive without, we spend trillions of dollars on investments that ruin the natural state of those resources. We need to build sustainable infrastructures to conserve the natural resources essential for our existence rather than developing temporary solutions. Long-term policies are required so that our institutions grow in consonance with nature. We, as a civilization should always be prepared to deal with natural disasters and emergency situations without politicizing matters that can result in the deaths of many.

The state of emergency had incited fear amongst Peruvians and even though there was chaos all around the country, Nancy motivated us to focus on life's positives and to appreciate our last meal together. I took that opportunity to tell the family once again how they'd touched my heart, because of how comfortable they'd made me feel in an unfamiliar environment.

సం భ

After an emotional breakfast with them, I received a call from Lili, saying she'd soon be arriving. Despite Lili being originally from Lima, that was her first time in Villa El Salvador, which presented a drastic change from the part of Lima she lived in, so it was my responsibility to make sure she felt comfortable in the new environment. This was quite ironic, given that I was the outsider in her country! Soon afterwards, I received her outside the house and we took a tuk-tuk to the place in Oasis where the second Social Entrepreneurship Workshop was to be held.

Lili had never addressed students before, and addressing a group of people of low socio-economic status would be different from her usual presentations in formal business settings to investors. Presenting to young students can be one of the most challenging tasks in the world, as you have to grab their attention. You have to convey your message in a manner they can relate to and facilitate discussion that encourages them to be alert and attentive to what you are saying.

The traditional teacher-centered educational approach of plainly talking at students while expecting them to grasp information is not very effective. It doesn't encourage them to be involved in a two-way interaction with the speaker, and thus subverts the creation of a healthy space to exchange ideas, thoughts, beliefs, and so on. But the birth of that space can change the students' mindset in order that they perceive the information in new ways, and absorb much more than they would have by simply having someone lecture them.

Lili addressed the students in Spanish, so I didn't completely understand everything she said, but she did a wonderful job of turning the workshop into a brainstorming session, where she combined her talk with incisive questions that propelled the students to be a part of her story. The enthusiasm she generated among them while reciting her journey as a female entrepreneur was clearly visible in their shimmering eyes. They were mesmerized by her devotion to her mission and inspired by the actions she took to build her company: her words were irresistible.

The end of Lili's presentation was also the end of my stay in Villa. It was time to say goodbye to the students, local volunteers and Eve, who were all very sad that I was leaving. Being a volunteer and a teacher at the NGO for that short period had taught me more about myself than I could have ever anticipated. When you are teaching someone, it's actually a two-way street: you learn substantially from the students and they learn from you. Students have so much to offer if you provide them with the means to bring out their best.

In terms of my whole life, I had a short stay at the NGO but it was enough for me to recognize how demanding the life of a teacher/ mentor can be, because of the immense responsibility resting on their shoulders. If used properly, their position of guidance can shape students to build a better world. Being there gave me insight into how important it is for our society to focus on developing a robust education system that revolves around providing quality teachers/mentors for the entire world's younger generation. A system built on the principle of providing a quality and wholesome education for all could solve most of the problems currently persisting in our world. It's the one thing that can bridge the gaps between humans produced by false ideas dividing us on the basis of countless variables that are insignificant in terms of moving our civilization toward a common goal of building a peaceful, healthy, sustainable, transformative, and enriched planet.

I left the facility with Lili, parting from the members of the community with a smile on my face and with words of optimism for them to continue flourishing and growing in their lives. Lili and I made our way back to *Avenida Jose Carlos Mariategui* from Oasis on a shared van-ride, when she told me that she hadn't been in one for years, to which I amiably smiled, "I love sharing these rides with the locals."

With our arrival at my host family's house, it was time for me to say goodbye to the family and end a defining chapter of my life. The entire family was waiting for me in the living room to see me off. They all stood up as Lili and I entered. I introduced them to Lili, and then quickly went upstairs to collect my backpack. As Lili and I were leaving I told my host mom in Spanish, "*Siempre estarás en mi corazón,*" to which, she replied modestly, "*Ahh Kaart, esta es tu casa y siempre eres bienvenido aquí.*"

I conveyed my feelings of appreciation to Nancy with assistance from Lili, thanking her and everyone in the family for all the love they had showered me with during my stay at their house. After all the hugs and kisses, we made our way outside where a taxi had been waiting for us. It was to drop Lili off at her father's house, in a beautiful large district called Surco, covered with many parks and some well-known universities, and also home for many families of varying socio-economic status. The car was then to take me to a house in Barranco where my friend Jack lived. I was going to start the new chapter of my Peruvian journey with him.

Departing from Villa stirred an abundance of unfamiliar and overflowing emotions in my body. I was content with what I'd done for my projects at the NGO but was saddened from having to say goodbye to my host family and all the wonderful individuals who'd welcomed me into their lives with open hearts. At the same time, I was excited about the new start.

‍ ‍

I'd entered a transition stage where one story had been completed and a new one was yet to begin. At that stage, my mind was utterly confounded by varied emotions, which in turn led to growing self-awareness and shed light on matters of my heart and also awakened deeply-wounding realizations. All the free-flowing electrifying charge in my nerves took me onto the next level of truth seeking.

The Desert

Stranded on a desert,
with no sight of an oasis and no soul to be seen,
was when I felt the heartbeat.

A dry throat,
with numb eyes and shaken lips,
was when I felt the touch.

Hell, it seemed,
but heavenly it pleased,
was when I felt the truth.

While I was sitting beside Lili in the back seat of our taxi, I was enshrined in the transition stage with no idea of what was to come. My heart was beating insistently and my body felt chilled in Lima's hot weather. Lili was studying me with compassion in her eyes, as she could sense the lawless discharge of sentiments from within me. As I continued breathing, my mind was dismantling the conditioning that was suppressing my sublime strength and preventing my in-built courage from perceiving the actual path for my heart to take so that it could sense its true self.

The taxi abruptly stopped... but it took me a second to realize that we had arrived in Surco, where Lili had to get off. Lili was leaving for the U.S. the next day, so it was another goodbye with a remarkable friend.

As she kissed my right cheek, I said, "Thank you for everything, Lili! I'm going to miss you, but I have no doubt in my mind that we'll see each other again." I also told her, "I'm so grateful to have you in my life and wish you the best for your company and all the exciting things that are coming your way."

Lili replied, "Thank you for letting me share my story with the students, Kart. I'm equally grateful to have you in my life! I'll pray for your journey and am proud of you for being so brave in listening to your heart."

Our reunion in another country ended with a tenacious promise that life would definitely have our paths cross again in the future.

VIII. THE INSOMNIAC WRITER

MY TAXI RIDE CONTINUED toward an address in Barranco where my friend Jack lived. He'd told me that I could rent out a private room in that house from the landlord at an affordable 25 soles (approximately $8) a night. I was sold on his offer as that was cheaper than sharing a dorm room at a hostel.

When I'd asked Jack for more details about the owner of the property, he had mentioned that the proprietor was an old Peruvian man, who'd resided in the U.S. as an illegal immigrant for decades only to be deported eventually and forced into becoming the landlord for his property in Barranco to sustain himself.

Jack had been staying there for several months and described the house as a mansion with innumerable rooms. He didn't even know how many people lived there! As the taxi entered Barranco, I messaged him saying I'd be there soon. He replied that he'd meet me at the door, and also that Louis, the owner, was drunk and had an escort with him – whom I was to ignore.

I was speechless after reading the message with no idea of what I was getting myself into. Still, I went with the flow and let life reveal whatever it had in store for me. Night was aspiring when the taxi stopped outside the house, which had a large wooden door with an oval-shaped curvy top. I caught sight of Jack's face peeking out the door.

He welcomed me as I parted ways with the taxi, "Let's go to the living room to see Louis and get you a room." I followed Jack through a sizable entryway into the living room. It was a gigantic house in Spanish-style architecture. I had Jack's warning in mind about the owner being drunk and in the company of a woman, as we stepped inside to meet him to get a room for my temporary stay.

Louis was sitting on a couch in the living room watching football and drinking rum with a skinny Peruvian woman sitting beside him and wearing a cheeky smile on her face. A sullen wasted voice was directed toward me, "Where are you from?" Louis's whopping belly, wrinkly face, swollen eyes and grey hair were clear indicators of his poor health and discontented life. "How long will you stay here for?" I answered that I wasn't sure, but would pay for four nights and let him know in advance if I decided to stay longer. He nodded his head in agreement, luckily not being too hard to deal with, and after a few other general questions he let me have a private room on the first floor of the house with a shared bathroom.

It had only been one hour since I'd left Villa, which had emotionally struck the core of my body, and having to deal with a drunken house-owner to get myself a room wasn't the most ideal situation to be in when my mind was in such a state of tumult. Changing locations during travel are accompanied by extensive mental development and bless an individual by numbing him or her to external stimuli. That way the traveler's mind is not unsettled and does not oppose the self's serenity.

℘ ℰ

The water crisis in Lima was at its peak with no water dripping through the taps even in Barranco. Jack as a journalist was very much aware of how the crisis was unfolding, and had kept me constantly updated about the worsening conditions in other parts of the country.

Soon after I dropped my bags in my little rectangular room on the first floor with a single bed, small window and plain white walls, he took me to attend a fundraiser being held for the flood victims. On our way, we bought tons of rice to donate for the flood victims and when we reached the building where the fundraiser was being held, I had a strong intuition that it wasn't going to be like any other fundraiser I'd attended ever before in my life.

It was invite-only and being held at a Barranco rooftop apartment only a few feet's distance from *Plaza de Armas* and the only way to get in was if you knew one of the organizers. Jack was friends with one of them, Ana (another individual with the same name as my musician friend from Argentina), a young Peruvian woman with a shaven head, resilient presence and heavily-spirited intentions that gave her the strength to stand up against government authorities and various establishments, who had stopped her own country's people from practicing their inborn rights as Peruvian citizens.

Ana was an activist, like most of the other organizers there, who carried out various campaigns all around Peru against the corrupt and stood her ground for people, who'd been wronged by the system. It wasn't a setup I usually found myself in, but thanks to Jack I was standing amongst the anarchists of Peruvian society so I could fathom the passion burning in their souls to make a stand against the wrong-doing of the powerful operating behind the curtains.

I met all kinds of people at the fundraiser and when Jack introduced me to Ana, she welcomed me with a firm clinch of my arms and also invited me on a group excursion with a bunch of journalists and activists, that was to leave the next day for southern Peru to interview people in the areas severely wrecked by the floods. I agreed to her offer, because it sounded like a great opportunity to witness with my own eyes the actual situation in the acutel damaged areas.

The remaining hours at the fundraiser were spent conversing with two Peruvian women, whom Jack and I met at the table where we sat down for the evening. They were smoking cigarettes, when I asked one of them, "Do you mind if we join you two?" "Of course," she replied and followed it with a hand shake while saying, "*Mi nombres es Gabriela.*" I noticed her piercing eyes, bloodshot lips and silky hair that slipped through the top of her neck.

Jack introduced himself to the woman seated next to Gabriela, whose name was Marisol. She was a beautiful woman whose skin was radiant in the dark, and eyes carried loads of kindness while her pursed lips blew out smoke from dragging on the burning cigarette between her fingers.

The two women shared an apartment in Barranco. Gabriela was an architect and Marisol worked for a Non-profit Organization. They were fascinated to find out that I was from India and had the typical Peruvian inquisitive reaction about the reason a man from India was in Peru. When Gabriela asked me what I had been doing in Peru, I told her unassumingly that I'd lived in Villa El Salvador for little over a month where I'd volunteered for an NGO. She responded with reverence in her voice, "When did you finish working there?" I smirked and expelled a chunk of air out of my nostrils: "A couple of hours ago! I've just moved to Barranco to the house where Jack lives."

Every time I told Peruvians from Lima's more affluent districts about my volunteering experience in Villa El Salvador, it always made them curious, as they wanted to hear more about my stay in Villa. Most of them had never been there and wouldn't even consider visiting because of its low socio-economic status.

Lima is an extremely polarized city. All its districts are based on income and social class, which engender a discordant environment where segregated communities of people live in the same city and bleed the same blood, but as separate entities rather than as a unified whole. The divide always reminded me of India, which has an unfathomable gap between the rich and the poor – their living conditions are on the opposite ends of the wealth spectrum. I'd witnessed a similar situation while living in the U.S., where the individuals living at the bottom of the food chain were afflicted by the powerful until their bodies had relinquished every drop of blood they could possibly yield.

It is a world of paradox where people say, "Every individual who is born on this planet has an equal opportunity in life", but that is absolutely false and is easily said by someone born into wealth. When I was working in the U.S., I would hear another statement from the wealthy too, "I have what I have because I worked hard for it and earned it myself." I don't think a person would utter such words if he or she was born in a disintegrated shack without a roof over their head.

This is not about comparing the rich and poor, or any sort of analysis, but simple fact: our world is not an equal place. Not yet. We talk about equality and make ourselves believe in the idea that everyone is equal, but the truth is that our world is far from being equal. The rich say the poor are lazy and don't work hard; the poor say, the rich have taken everything from us and there is no opportunity for us to escape poverty. And the vicious cycle of blame is made use of by the corrupt to stay in power and take advantage of people for their own selfish needs. We continue to live in our own little bubbles without being able to perceive our true path, which is what all humans have been given this gift of life for. Being human is a wonderful blessing and I really believe that we can do better than we do today. Deep inside the core of our humanity, there's a selfless self that can transcend the layers of our rapacious civilization and form an advanced civilization having magnanimous values central to its foundation, which will lead to a more unified and equal society.

The fundraiser was drawing to its end when Gabby and Marisol invited Jack and me over to their apartment in Barranco, where the entire night rolled by slurping red wine and listening to Peruvian classics. Throughout the evening, Jack and Gabby had an elevated discussion about Peru's political scene. Marisol retired early for bed and I merely listened to their symposium. The coming together of an insomniac journalist and a sprightly architect was a delight to my ears and also a political history lesson about Peru's transformation from the significant political events that had taken place there, and in South America over the preceding thirty years.

It was an eventful first night with Jack in Barranco on top of a long day of dealing with the emotions arising from the metaphysical changes taking place in my life following my departure from Villa and my sense of being hauled into a darkened tunnel with no sight of light.

The next morning, Jack had some unfortunate news, though. There had been a landslide on the highway we were supposed to drive on for the group excursion we'd been invited to by Ana. He doubted we'd still be able to go down south. It wasn't the most pleasant news to start off the day: the landslide was another natural catastrophe on top of all the flooding and had caused several casualties as well.

The ongoing water crunch in Peru had brought a halt to any possible traveling for the coming days, so I decided to stay in Barranco with Jack for a full week. That was also to be my last week before starting my two-week long pre-Ayahuasca diet prior to leaving for the jungle. I'd booked a flight for Iquitos based on the date my dear friend Katherine had arranged for my week with the shaman in the jungle, which was to be exactly three weeks from my first morning of waking up in the water-struck district of Barranco.

The two weeks of pre-diet for Ayahuasca involved following a strict regime of eating specific foods and living a disciplined lifestyle to help detoxify my mind and body of all the junk they had gathered over the years. Of course, two weeks wasn't enough time to get rid of all the amassed rubbish in my system, but it was a necessary period of mental and physical cleansing so that mind could nurture as much clarity as possible before completely surrendering to Ayahuasca on my journey to find my true purpose in life.

I wasn't going to the Amazon Jungle merely for the experience of doing Ayahuasca like many other travelers visiting South America. Something powerful was guiding me toward the source of Ayahuasca in the depths of the jungle, and every event taking place in my life was working toward my discovery of my true purpose in life. There was every reason to let go of my mental conditionings and follow my heart by listening to what was calling me from the Amazon.

I had complete faith in whatever was to come in the jungle, and I was willing to give everything to conquer fear and discover the truth about what ignited the fire in my soul. I had that deep-seated voice, which emerged in moments of despair to embrace me with the affirmation that the jungle was going to present me with the answers I had been looking for all my life.

The last week before the commencement of the cleansing process, was when I submerged below the sea-level and sunk into a bottomless ocean with no vision as to who I was and what I needed to do in life. Jack held my sinking body and brought it to the surface to bless my eyes with a ray of light. He became my mentor.

I deeply admired Jack for his dedication to and passion for his work. He provided me with guidance by inspiring a realization within me that writing was a core part of my life. That was why he'd become such a crucial character in my journey toward self-discovery. I stayed in his room for that week learning about different styles of writing, discussing numerous writers, reading all kinds of literary material, watching intense documentaries and observing his every move. I became his shadow for a week.

I didn't know it at the time, but that week with Jack was to lay the foundation of my path as a writer. At times, he'd ask me what I wanted from him and I wouldn't have a response, because all I wanted was to simply observe him and learn the intricacies of a writer's mind. As human beings, we want to transfer the beauty of the world we perceive onto a piece of paper and assert the power inherent in combining words.

Jack was undoubtedly a genius with an exceptional mind that had inexhaustible potential. His genius also brought a dark side to his personality, as many a time, he couldn't control his profound mind. Information would burst from him while he consumed substantial amounts of liquor to cope with his inexorable and endless thoughts. He described his drinking as a British cultural norm and rested the case with, "Alcohol works as a lubricant for my mind, and as there is already a cocktail going up in my head, I might as well deluge myself in it whole heartedly," which he uttered with an enchanting smile that exposed the innocence of his heart.

Jack had a daily evening ritual of drinking a bottle of red wine followed shortly after by the annihilation of a quarter flask of inexpensive rum. He also had an inconceivable capacity to work and was completely immersed in it. I asked him once what he wanted to do in life, to which he responded, "Exactly what I am doing right now."

He was one of the most interesting individuals I had ever met in my life and somehow, I admired his mind regardless of it being the reason for his vicious drinking, which I knew wasn't good for his health. However, I couldn't be of much influence as alcohol had become a part of his lifestyle and I had simply no control over his actions. I accepted Jack for who he was.

I could relate with Jack about many aspects of life, and even though we'd had totally different upbringings, there was a strong bond between us. Jack was so fervently in love with his work that being around him and just observing him was a constant inspiration for me. He was fearless and extremely driven. Every piece of his investigative journalism was based on extensive research and getting his facts directly from a genuine source to find out actually what had happened. His information was based on direct understandings from visiting the most dangerous regions in Peru and South America where no other journalists dared to go, because the likelihood of return was always a question of interest. His fearless attitude was what generated immense respect in my heart every time I saw him in action, which was almost all the time as he was the definition of action.

During that week, not much changed in Peru: it was still in a state of emergency. The water deadlock in Lima caused inflation in the prices of food and water. The demand for water and food exceeded the supply which caused more tension around the city. I had to continue sustaining myself on a limited supply of bottled water.

There were many days with absolutely no water in the house which meant we couldn't flush toilets. I had to comply with Jack's brilliant idea of using a plastic bag in the mornings when I dumped the debris out from my stomach and then walked out of the house holding the same plastic bag in my hands and wearing a smile on my face, until I found a dust bin in our neighborhood to dispose of the bag.

It was not till the beginning of the next week when the water crisis ended in Lima, after having lasted for more than a week. Living without water for such a lengthy time turned me into a conservative water user even after the water crisis had ended, and more importantly, made me appreciate water for its crucial purpose of sustaining life on our planet.

On the Thursday of that week, I decided that I couldn't keep residing at that house, until my departure time to the Amazon Jungle. As much as I wanted to keep living in the same house with Jack, I knew it was time for me to move on from Barranco and continue my journey with a sound focus on preparing myself for Ayahuasca. I thought that the best thing would be to find a local gig in Lima for couple of weeks at a peaceful hostel, where I could live for free in exchange for volunteering several hours every day. It would also be a great way of saving money on accommodation.

It was time to rekindle my canvasing abilities and go knock on every hostel door situated in Miraflores. It was a sunny Friday afternoon, when I commenced going door-to-door for every hostel with a confident mindset and accepting each rejection with a smile, reminding me of my days of working in Brooklyn as a door-to-door salesman. My whole day was consumed by rejections, and at dusk my feet came to rest at *Parque Kennedy*, a famous Lima landmark named in the honor of President John F. Kennedy who'd provided Peru with aid during his tenure as the President of the U.S.

The park was in the center of Miraflores, besides *Parque Central de Miraflores* and the prominent colossal structure of a Catholic Church called *Iglesia La Virgen Milagrosa*. All three attractions formed a triangular space at the heart of Miraflores, and offered visitors a surprising pool of calm among the craziness of the busy and prosperous district of Miraflores.

It was an enjoyable area where you could roam freely under the shadows of shady trees, sit on numerous stonework surfaces, marvel at the paintings by street artists and watch sporadic dance spectacles by the elderly. *Parque Kennedy* also hosted countless number of cats in its lush gardens, making the park a nurturing home for cats, who dwelt there and could be seen roaming around the area at all times.

As I sat down on one of the stone seats in the park with my face pointing directly at the enormous Catholic Church, while being saluted by the blustering breeze piercing through my clothes, I messaged Kofi saying I was in *Parque Kennedy* and that if he was around we could get together.

Kofi lived in Miraflores and sustained his life by working at Kaminu Hostel and offering private English tutoring to local residents, for which he had to move around the city all day visiting the homes of his students. When I messaged him, I wasn't sure if he was going to be in the area because of his active schedule, but I received a prompt reply saying, "I'll be at *Parque Kennedy* soon and will have thirty minutes before leaving for my evening class. Let's meet for a quick talk."

The half-hour with Kofi allowed us to pause during our exhilarating day of running around in Lima. It was a moment for relaxation where I let my lungs be satiated by sharing the art of smoking a cigarette with Kofi, a chain smoker. He'd finished teaching a young Peruvian boy English and only had a half-hour to spare before leaving to tutor another student.

I had a light-hearted and refreshing conversation with Kofi over a smoke, an unfamiliar activity for me as I'd never been a smoker but had found myself indulging in it several times since my arrival in Peru, as it was an extension of Lima's social culture. I'd decided to give up my search for a volunteer opportunity, but Kofi suggested I give it one more shot at a hostel named Puriwasi, which was situated further away from the triangular section past *Avenida Jose Larco* on the intersection of *Calle Manuel Bonilla* and *Avenida la Paz*.

Kofi told me as we were separating that it was a less commercial and more community-based hostel with a rooftop, and that they might just have an opening for me. After Kofi and I parted ways, I wasn't sure if I wanted to continue with finding a volunteer opening until I heard a voice inside my head saying "I've already been rejected by seven hostels. Why not try one more? Maybe they'll have something for me." So, I decided to follow Kofi's directions and try one last hostel.

Avenida la Paz was barely a five-minute walk away from *Parque Kennedy* and walking swiftly through *Calle Manuel Bonilla* had me standing outside the hostel's thick glass door in a fraction of a second. There was a black tinted text saying *Puriwasi* on the transparent glass door, with yellow-colored walls leading into the building. I walked through the glass door and followed the marble stairs, which complemented the yellow-painted walls. The stairs led to the second floor of the building, where a reception desk was placed past a narrow door.

A young Peruvian girl wearing sleek spectacles was seated behind the reception desk. Whilst walking toward her, I said "*Hola, como estas?*" She replied with a generous smile on her face, "*Hola, muy bien,*" and followed it with, "How can I help you?" I explained to her that I was looking for a volunteer opportunity, and a friend of mine had told me that this hostel hosted volunteers. "Is there any possibility that I could volunteer here for free accommodation?" With a dejected smile on her face she told me that currently their volunteer space was full, but if I really wanted to volunteer there I could ask the owner to see if he could accommodate me.

I said "*Buenaso*" cheerfully and asked if she could point me in the owner's direction. She advised me not to interrupt him for the next 30 minutes as he was sitting upstairs on the rooftop watching a FIFA World Cup Qualifier Match of Peru. She was very helpful and told me as I was about to make my way up the stairs that the owner was fanatical about football and would not appreciate any interference during the game. "I would recommend approaching him after the game is over," she said. I replied with a genuine smile affirming that I'd follow her advice.

As I was walking up the stairs to the rooftop, I thought to myself that only in South America would an individual not want to meet you because a football game was on. Football was loved by everyone in Peru and South America. It was more than just a sport, more like something sacred with a divine essence.

My feet pursued the marble stairway onto Puriwasi's illustrious rooftop, with its convivial vibe cherished by hostel visitors. It was uncovered in parts, and in other parts, covered. It was well designed for a free-flowing and open environment so that individuals felt comfortable sharing the space. Its walls continued with the yellow from the bottom of the building but with funky art giving birth to a pulsating and creative spirit. It had elegant but simple wooden furniture along with numerous plants promoting a green environment against the Miraflores backdrop.

Many individuals stood with their eyes intently focused onto what looked like thin air from where I was. I went nearer to the standing crowd to look in their direction of vision. A television with a live football game on it had their eyes transfixed. I quietly asked the fellow I was standing next to, "Who's the owner here?" to which he silently aimed his finger in the direction of a man seated on a chair, placed in the middle of the standing crowd.

The owner looked like an entranced king. His eyes were fixated on the television, intensely hoping to see Peru win the game. I walked inaudibly past the crowd to sit on a table with some travelers, that I could see weren't that interested in watching the game. I briefly explained my situation to them and then patiently waited for the game to end, wishing Peru would win as I thought that that would brighten the owner's mood.

The thrilling game ended in about twenty minutes with Peru winning, which made me feel cheerful about approaching the owner, who seemed to have dissolved into a state of delight after watching his country win the game.

I introduced myself and asked him if there was a possibility for me to volunteer at his hostel. His name was Sergio, a beefy Peruvian man who had an intimidating look that could turn gently chirpy with an authentic smile shining through his huge brown eyes. He was a very straightforward man, who didn't believe in small talk and got straight to the point unlike most Peruvians.

In just few minutes, he told me in his graceful but sturdy voice that one of the volunteers from Brazil, who'd been working at the bar was leaving the next day, so he could accommodate me at the bar starting the next day but there was one condition. "We require a minimum commitment of two weeks from our volunteers," he said. On hearing that I jovially responded, "That's perfect! I have exactly two weeks before leaving for Iquitos and have no problem starting tomorrow." Sergio then said that I could check-in the next day by 1 pm, and would be working at the bar from 9 pm till midnight on weekdays and 1 am on weekends. I was thrilled to hear these words and said, "*Gracias amigo*! See you tomorrow."

We shook hands, and with that, the decision to go to one last hostel had paid off!

In a span of thirty minutes from parting ways with Kofi at *Parque Kennedy*, the mission I'd set out with for the day had been accomplished. Not letting the rejections from other hostels affect my intention to keep pursuing my goal was what resulted in completion of my mission. It was a reminder of what I used to say to my sales team in New York, "Every 'no' is one step closer to a 'yes', all you have to do is keep moving forward with a courageous mindset."

Little missions like finding a volunteer gig to larger dreams like changing the world can be fulfilled, if you truly believe in bringing your ideas into reality. No dream is inconceivable, if you have the strength to pursue it for every second and incessantly work toward it. Every little aspect of your life needs to be aligned with a never-give-up mindset; only then can life greet you with honest and extraordinary experiences so that you can morph into a free-flowing state like the waves of a cosmic ocean.

I got a taxi from Puriwasi on *Avenida la Paz* for Barranco to go meet with my musician friend from Argentina, Ana. I messaged her as I got in the taxi that I'd found a volunteer opening at a hostel in Miraflores and suggested that we meet that night before I left Barranco.

Ana had been working part-time at a vegan café in Barranco to support her traveling. It was situated beside *Plaza de Armas* and was only a ten-minute walk away from where I'd been living. I'd mostly go see her in the evenings, when she'd finished working at the café; we'd stroll from there through Barranco to end up at the park beside *Malecon Paul Harris*, which had been officially agreed upon by both of us to be our favorite spot in Barranco.

Ana and I even shared the same birthday and with her being the younger one, she'd been instantly decreed to be the "little twin sister". From that Barranco cliff top, we'd be hypnotized by Lima's coast line and surrender to the ebb and flow of the waves of the superlative ocean. Every time we'd become slaves of peace by fusing with the ocean. We'd place ourselves contentedly on the grass spreading across the flat surface at the dome's head and reflect upon our lives.

That was to be the second last time when Ana and I were to meet at our beloved spot in Barranco, as I was to start volunteering at Puriwasi Hostel in Miraflores the next day and her travel plans were to change in the coming week. My hours preceding our meeting were spent at my residence in Barranco with Jack, who was extremely thrilled to hear that I'd found a volunteer gig at a spunky hostel in Miraflores.

Jack and Ana had met one another for the first time earlier that week at a local Peruvian bar, with a frontal view of *Plaza de Armas* on *Avenida Almte Miguel Grau*. In their first meeting, it didn't take them long to be fully stimulated by each other's charisma, which combined their well-equipped nerdy minds and fearless demeanors. Their re-meeting in Jack's chamber, which was really less of a room than a sanctuary with book-towers on its floor, only encouraged their natural inclinations to be involved in studious discussion.

I couldn't have asked to be spending my last night in Barranco with better friends than Jack and Ana, before commencing my journey's next chapter by volunteering at a hostel. It was a memorable night for me. It played out in front of my eyes as I sat on a chair in the corner of Jack's room with an appreciative smile on my face and thankfulness in my eyes to be the sole observer of their dialogue, covering topics ranging from theoretical physics to diverse theories about the functioning of the human brain.

While they were enthusiastically engaged in their discussion, I was thinking how grateful I was to have had both of them introduce their spirits into my life and that if I hadn't taken that momentous step of leaving New York and surrendering myself to the world, I wouldn't have met them or been embraced by their honest friendship at my time of utmost vulnerability.

Their kinship fed me with resolute strength and rugged courage to deal with the changes that were splitting apart my deep-rooted fears. It was a night of pure confidence for my soul, which was ready to enter the next stage of my journey when the sun cast its polished shades onto Lima's teal sky the next day.

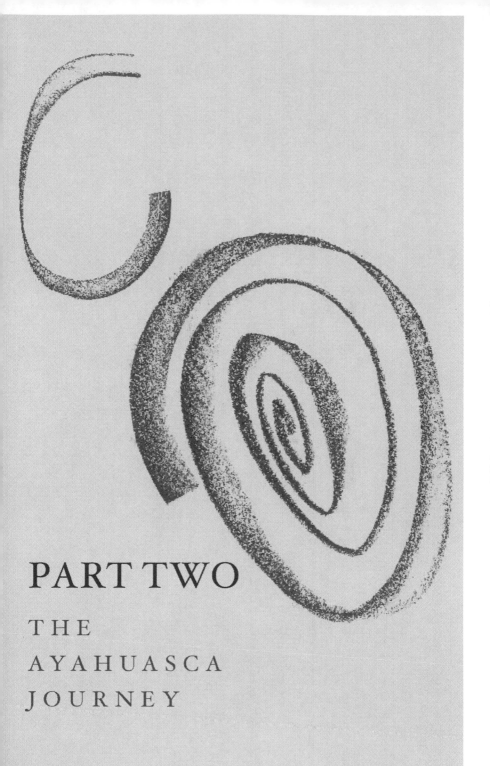

PART TWO

THE AYAHUASCA JOURNEY

I. A TRAVELER'S ABODE

*I*T WAS LATE MORNING when I called myself a taxi for Puriwasi. Jack was writing an article on his computer. I thanked him for guiding me through that week. "Best of luck mate... we'll see each other soon", he said pensively as he stood up to furnish me with a huge hug.

I left Jack's room to find Louis and hand in the keys for the room I'd stayed in. He was seated at his usual spot on the couch of his living room when I thanked him for letting me stay in his house and dropped the keys into his far-reaching hand. I went out to position myself at the curb of the street where I patiently waited for several minutes for my taxi to arrive. Backpacks on both sides of my body were strapped on my shoulders, but as I stood unattended on that vacant ashen street I beheld the emptiness in my heart.

A taxi ride signifies the end of one story and promises the beginning of a new one so I entered a self-reflective space in the momentary time-lapse of the ride. Every event from my preceding story, streamed in front of my eyes like a movie in which I played the role of a leading actor. The time-lapse terminated with the taxi stopping in front of Puriwasi Hostel at *Avenida la Paz*, and the movie's exclusive streaming concluded as I got out, grabbed my backpacks and walked past the glass door of the hostel to follow the marbled stairs up to the reception desk.

A different girl was seated behind the reception desk, Peruvian but slightly older than the previous one, who'd been very young and worked part-time for some extra cash. I had to introduce myself to the new girl, whose name was Ximena. She was to become a good friend during my stay at the hostel and was an absolute help whenever I needed it.

Ximena was a whimsical woman in her late twenties, who lived in Miraflores and had been working for Sergio for several years. She had an eccentric and bright personality, and an engaging physical appearance that seized attention with a shimmering piercing planted just below her full carmine lips and a few artworks floating around on her skin. She was aware that a new volunteer was to come in that day, which made it painless for me to check-in straight away and have a bed allotted to me in a typical eight-bed dormitory with bunk beds, which dropped the cost of a bed for backpackers traveling on a low budget.

I'd been assigned a top-bunk mattress for no cost as part of my volunteering, and the dormitory had a tiny private balcony, which overlooked *Avenida la Paz* and the rest of Miraflores. There was a comfortable chair on the balcony, which was to be predominantly mine for the next couple of weeks. I knew right away when I saw the balcony that it was going to be my sacred space while I stayed in the hostel.

The two weeks I was to be there before departing for the jungle were the two weeks I was to be on the pre-Ayahuasca diet. I had begun it earlier that day. The hostel was quiet and placid, which attracted wonderful travelers and I couldn't have asked for a better place to be at for that time.

It wasn't till late evening that I had to start working at the rooftop bar, so I took the opportunity to figure out how I was to use the approaching two weeks to prepare myself properly for my encounter with Ayahuasca in the jungle. I'd planned to follow a general Ayahuasca diet, which I'd found online through one of the Ayahuasca web communities. It was very comprehensive.

While on it, I was not to consume any alcohol, salt & pepper, fried food, sugar or artificial sweeteners, caffeine, animal fat, dairy products, hot spices/chilies/pepper, carbonated drinks, dried fruits, citrus, fibrous fruits, vinegar or pickled fruits, onion or garlic, spinach or tomatoes, or oil (except for using coconut/olive oil very sparingly for cooking). Nor was I allowed any recreational or prescription drugs. Sexual activity, including masturbation was banned too.

There were some general restrictions too. I was to avoid unnecessary socialization and any sort of negative interaction with people.

By that point of time, I was certain that Ayahuasca was one of the crucial aspects of my Peruvian journey, and the inner voice that had been guiding me throughout had only strengthened my willingness to respect the whole Ayahuasca process. I was ready to prepare myself whole-heartedly for my Ayahuasca excursion into the jungle.

In addition to the dietary regime, I'd decided to ban myself from using technology and the internet for those two weeks and focus my entire attention on detoxifying my mind from any sort of external stimulus that bolstered my mental constraints and skewed my brain away from developing clarity about the actual purpose I should live for. The only time I'd use the internet was to message my family about my whereabouts and my decision that I was staying away from internet.

It was to be a fresh start, wearing new shoes in a setting that was alien to me, while my mind would occupy itself for the approaching days by meditating earnestly, painting freely, writing expressly about what I was possibly seeking from life, volunteering smoothly at the hostel and remaining an aloof part of the traveler's community.

Fortunately, the hostel had a small kitchen installed in the intimate rooftop space, which would allow me to prepare my own food and establish an easy-to-practice meal cycle that would help me eat food containing all my body's essential meal-building components while completely harmonizing with the Ayahuasca dietary restrictions.

For breakfast, I ate things like boiled eggs with fruits like apple or watermelon. For lunch and dinner, I ate lentils or chickpeas or kidney beans in combination with steamed rice and vegetables – but without any extra flavoring of any sort. I had bananas, apples, pears and *grenadine* (a delicious Peruvian fruit) for snacks.

It would be challenging indeed to adhere to such a restricted food regimen for a total of two weeks while living in one of the most passionate of foodie cities, but I was determined to stick with it and not stray from the path I'd chosen for myself. Undermining the whole Ayahuasca process for any momentary sensual pleasure was just out of question!

I didn't know on the first day of starting the Ayahuasca diet that those two weeks prior to going to the jungle would herald a radical process of change. My solidarity in sticking to the strict diet while living in a hostel among travelers in vivacious Miraflores, was to show me the value of discipline and self-determination regardless of the countless distractions that surrounded me.

Life in Miraflores and *A Traveler's Guidebook to Lima* feature experiencing local culture by trying various delicacies, engaging in the city's night life and drinking heavily while actively socializing with the crowd – basically, everything I had to refrain from for those two weeks! The thing I told myself when I began the diet was that living in such an environment and still choosing to not indulge in any temptation would only strengthen my mindset toward my mission, and would also mightily help me during my time in the jungle.

Those two weeks can be broken down in two parts, as each week played a distinctive role in preparing my mind before its time in the depths of the Amazon Jungle.

A. Week 1: Shield of Warriors

It was late in the evening around 8 pm when I went up Puriwasi's marbled stairs to the cozy rooftop space and began my work at the bar. Ximena had told me that I would find Julian, the bartender, upstairs and that he would train me in the work I needed to do there.

I'd never been a bartender before in my life but had always wondered what it was like to serve drinks from behind the bar counter. My curiosity was about to become reality, as I was to learn a new skill and try something different for a short but a very crucial period of my life. It was ironic that I would be working in a bar at the same time as dedicating myself to the unexciting detoxifying Ayahuasca diet, but luckily it was a very low-key bar that wasn't open to the general public and only served the needs of hostel guests and their friends.

Puriwasi, being a comparatively small hostel with maximum capacity of thirty-six beds, didn't have an image as a party hostel. It catered to a niche of more amiable and relaxed travelers, who weren't simply drifting around South America to party but were grounded in reality of exploring more of themselves and the world.

The rooftop, which was vacant at the time, in striking comparison with my preliminary visit during Peru's FIFA qualifier game, seemed to be coiled in silence. Only one man could be seen. He was wearing a yellow-colored Puriwasi shirt designed to match the yellow walls of the hostel, a definite sign that he was the bartender, Julian.

Julian had a lean physique and was just behind a black marble slab at the front of the tiny bar. The black-colored front was approximately four feet high and separated customers from the bar. People came there to order drinks. There were three bar stools for individuals who wanted to be at the bar, so that they wouldn't have to stand around or sit at other tables further away if the bar was busy.

Julian was cleaning some utensils behind the bar. I said to him as I reached the tiny setup, "*Hola amigo. Como estas?* I'm the new volunteer here," to which he replied briskly, "*Hola amigo*, my name's Julian. Where are you from?" I told him I was from India and would be volunteering there for couple of weeks, before leaving for the jungle.

Julian was a young Peruvian in his early twenties, who was studying at a university in Lima and worked at the hostel part-time for some extra cash and to meet travelers from all over the world. He was a light-hearted man, with a neat hairstyle that complemented his shaven burnished face and ornate brown eyes. He was an easy-going Latino I became friends with right away and knew immediately that I was going to be very comfortable working with him.

The bar entrance was a tiny door, that required a person to enter like a midget to reach inside its rectangular cozy space. It had a multifunctional usage: operating as a bar at nights and preparing breakfast in the mornings. Julian straightaway trained me about the bar's functioning while we exchanged life-stories. In just a couple of minutes, we were at ease with each other and it was obvious that we got along well. After getting properly acquainted with him, I told Julian about my intention of going to the Amazon Jungle and doing Ayahuasca in a few weeks. He was aware of the Ayahuasca diet and asked me if I'd been following the required diet. "Yes, I began it this morning to prepare myself before leaving for Iquitos." He thought it was good that I was doing it properly.

Ayahuasca had been declared a part of Peru's cultural heritage, but in general it wasn't very popular with Peruvians, who treasured it but also feared the consequences of doing it, and rightly so as it was considered something that required a demanding effort from the individual pursuing it. It primarily lured travelers, who visited South America. Julian himself had not done Ayahuasca, but because he worked at a hostel he'd come across few travelers, who had and that's why it was easier for him to be very respectful and supportive of my decision. He could comprehend the spiritual significance attached to it and appreciated my willingness to do it for the sake of seeking something of real value and true significance in my life.

The first day of working at the bar was low-key as the hostel wasn't much occupied, because the floods in Peru had caused a temporarily halt to the influx of tourists into the country. This was financially bad for the tourism industry but the halt was expected to overturn in couple of weeks.

It was stimulating for my mind to begin working in a new environment while using my every second to be more conscious and aware of my thoughts and thus constantly purify my mind, at the same time support my body with the Ayahuasca regimen. My whole daily routine that I'd worked out that first day was instinctively systematized to stimulate change in my core as time progressed.

That week consisted of working with Julian at the bar and developing other worthy relationships with two remarkable individuals, one of them being the other volunteer, Landor, who was in the same dormitory as me. Landor, or Leo, as I called him, was a traveler from Argentina, who'd been staying at Puriwasi for almost a month and handling the breakfast shift. He'd been intrepidly riding alone on a classy motorbike all around South America for thirteen months until his arrival in Lima, where he'd found himself a volunteering spot at Puriwasi – which led to our meeting.

Having an exemplary companion like Leo during my stay in Puriwasi, couldn't have been of more substance. He was also planning on attending an Ayahuasca ceremony at a place near Lima just before I was to depart for mine, which of course, brought us even closer: both of us were in a similar head-space and getting ready for our renaissance as humans. Having him around during the day time at the hostel, allowed us to share our reasons for doing Ayahuasca and what was it that we were looking to do with our lives.

Leo was a handsome man with an athletic body, lengthy chestnut-colored luxurious hair above his tanned forehead and a face draped in a chunky long beard. He had a rounded metal piercing in his left ear that matched his sizable generous smile, while his hazel-tinted eyes delivered messages of respect. His appearance perfectly fitted with the image of the adventurous biker, who'd conquered the streets of South America all by himself. He started his Ayahuasca diet in the middle of my first week on the same diet, and that allowed us to share many of our tasteless stodgy meals together.

℘ ☙

My first week of volunteering at Puriwasi was going to be Julian's last week of working at the bar. He'd mentioned that on my second day of assisting him. When I asked him, who was to replace him, he told me he'd got Sergio to hire his best friend, Franco, for the job. Franco was to start working the next week and his training was to begin at the end of the current week.

Franco was the second individual after Leo, who entered in my life as a special person in Puriwasi. I was to deem him my best friend in Peru at a later stage of my story, for the kind of unimaginable connection we shared as individuals.

The synchronicity of wavelengths from Julian, Leo, Franco, and I was perfect, and that led them to becoming my brothers for the all-embracing period I was with them, when I was in a state of utmost vulnerability.

The other travelers I met while working at the rooftop bar couldn't believe that I'd only known these three for such a short period of time. That was the week when I realized that in life, some people are meant to enter your life and hold a special place in your heart with their selfless desire, loving attitude, honest speech, compassionate gestures, kind soul, understanding nature, and trustworthy manner. Their vigorous spirits secure your chest with supportive arms and a regenerative touch to rekindle the divine fire within you.

It was incredible how simply having them around me during the entire course of being submersed in the Ayahuasca process provided me with so much support.

Franco and Julian never pressured me to drink, smoke, or take part in any activity that would interfere with my Ayahuasca diet. For instance, Franco had trained as a body builder at one point of his life, and he said to me at the end of the first week, when I was craving for a sip of beer because I'd seen a bunch of travelers drinking and having a good time, "You don't need to drink alcohol to have fun," which resonated very much with me when I was extremely tempted to drink.

It was a moment of weakness that was quickly grabbed by the evil in me to do something that wasn't right for me in the long run, but thanks to Franco, I reminded myself that the craving was temporary and it would pass with time. Giving into it even once would have certainly affected my ability to sustain the Ayahuasca diet.

Franco was a kind man with a heart of pure gold, who came in my life like a Peruvian messiah. He always bore a large smile on his alluring face, while his curly hair whirled over his shiny temples. He had a commanding demeanor that always reflected a sense of ardor, topped with an exquisite body that seemed to have been carved by a sculptor to portray him as the perfect man.

Franco had not done Ayahuasca before, but told me when I'd first told him about my intention of doing it that he would doubtlessly do it in the future, once he was certain he was ready for it. He honored my decision of going to the jungle to pursue my life-quest. I thought to myself how blessed I was to have Julian, Leo and Franco pierce my heart and act as my zealous warriors to nurture me with courage, at the same time as demonstrating the importance of the selfless love that can exist among humans from distinct backgrounds. I was to them what they were to me, and that's what made the bond pure.

During that first week of volunteering, I experienced a fluid transition because of Julian, Leo and Franco standing firmly by my side. They became influential characters during my Peruvian voyage, and their demeanor deserves a proper honoring in this story.

ॐ ॐ

In the middle of the first week, I decided to ask Sergio to move my shift during the second week from working night-time at the bar to preparing breakfast in the morning. I wanted to start waking up early and completely avoid the late-night bar scene before leaving for the jungle. Leo's shift was going to end that week and he would be simply staying at the hostel for a couple of days before leaving for his Ayahuasca ceremony.

So, with Leo finishing his duties at the start of my second week, it was possible for me to move to the morning shift. As much as I loved working at the bar with Julian and Franco, preparing breakfast and having a quiet time in the evenings resonated better with my Ayahuasca preparation.

At first, Sergio didn't accept my request because he thought I was well-suited for the bar, and my social skills were good to keep travelers entertained. So, I had to really explain the situation to him, "Sergio, I love working at the bar but after my second week I am leaving for the jungle for Ayahuasca, and working at the bar is a little distracting for me as I need more quiet time." He replied sympathetically, "OK... I'll move you when Leo finishes." Happily, I said, "*Gracias amigo*! I promise you that when I come back from Iquitos, I will work at the bar with Franco and will do my best to make it the finest it can be."

At the end of the first week when I told Franco and Julian about my decision to change my shift for the second week, they were in complete agreement with my choice. I promised Franco too about working at the bar after I returned from Iquitos.

My last night of working at the bar was also Julian's last night at Puriwasi before handing over to Franco, who'd be the sole person managing the bar from the beginning of the next week. I would get to meet Julian in the future at regular intervals, as he'd still visit Puriwasi occasionally, but I'd be seeing Franco almost every day during the second week as he would be working only a staircase away from my room.

With that night's extinction, I made a resolute decision for the upcoming week to completely focus my mind on the specifics of what I wanted to get out of Ayahuasca. There was nothing else for my brain other than its participation in the Ayahuasca procedure, which was to become a bruising reality in the course of a week.

B. Week 2: Internal Struggle

Breakfast preparation began at 7 am on Monday morning with Sergio, who showed me how to set up a conventional hostel breakfast. It comprised of preparing cloth-filter hand-drip Peruvian coffee, boiling hot water for tea bags, buying freshly-baked bread, cutting fruit, pouring milk in a glass jug and storing cereal in a large bowl. It was not an extravagant breakfast and usually required preparation time of about thirty to forty minutes, including the time for getting the newly-baked bread rolls from a local bakery around the corner from the hostel.

The bar counter was used as a platform for all the breakfast items. At the end, Sergio asked me, "Easy? Huh?" to which I replied, "Yes I'll be able to do this from tomorrow without any problem."

Breakfast hours were from 8 am to 11 am. So, I reconfigured my mornings to start with a deep meditation in the presence of the rising sun around 6 am. The aim for my second week at the hostel was to construct a lifestyle that would support the detoxifying process beyond what the Ayahuasca diet did and exterminate deep-seated impediments in my brain. I had put my phone on airplane mode for an indefinite time-period and wasn't going to read any material or even use my laptop for the entire week. I was to fully attend to disconnecting myself from the needless turmoil of the external world.

The only activity I was to indulge in, other than working at the morning shift, was writing a daily journal to help me exercise my thoughts and clarify my mind to further assimilate my reasons of pursuing Ayahuasca. I limited my conversations with people even more during the second week and, because I wasn't working at the bar anymore, that was easier to do.

The major difference between working late nights at the bar and preparing breakfast early mornings, was the energy of the customers. At night, every one's energy was always upbeat but in the mornings, it was the total opposite. Most of them even struggled to open their eyes then. It was intriguing to stand behind the bar and simply observe the crowd, which was mostly busy looking at their phones while sluggishly shoving food in their mouths.

Only a few seemed lively in the mornings and tried to engage in conversation with the people around them. The contrast from night to morning was intriguing. Most travelers were heavily involved in meeting new people during drinking hours, but wouldn't even look at their neighbors in the mornings. There was this hysterical contradiction every morning, which I reckoned at first was because most of them were not morning people, but then I asked myself if it could also be that many of them were dependent on alcohol to generate the confidence to start a conversation with a stranger.

When I was previously living in the U.S., there'd been a huge trend among the young generation to be dependent on alcohol to loosen up for interacting with strangers in social settings. It's a vicious cycle that many people fall into, where they think they need alcohol to be able to talk to strangers.

As well, all around the world and in every social setting people are always immersed in their smart phones rather than being engaged with the people around them to share moments of raw emotion. Speaking to strangers doesn't have to entail the selfish intention of getting something out of the other person; it can be purely selfless in nature based on just sharing the integrity of what makes us human.

As a result of these observations, I theorized that nobody is born as a morning person or a night person. Their subconscious mind makes them identify with one or the other based on how the atmosphere at a particular time of the day makes them feel. When the group of people came to the bar at night time, they had the clear intention of meeting other travelers, which set up different behavior in their personalities. The same group did not have a similar intention in the mornings, which resulted in distinctively different behavior. Both situations show altered behavior, and which one is the true reflection of the individual is not for me to say, but they clearly suggest that we humans are programmed to function based on what a particular situation demands from us and the environments we usually find ourselves in.

We never try to question, let alone be aware of the actual reasons for our behavior in specific scenarios, because of how strictly governed we are by the programming deep in the subconscious levels of our mind. This, of course, makes it extremely difficult for us to break out of the cycle in which our reactions to external stimuli put us at the mercy of what happens outside us without being able to investigate what is truly waiting for us inside instead.

ॐ

The second week of my pre-Ayahuasca diet went smoothly and I focused on the introspective array of waves floating within my mind and body.

Meditation helped me keep my mind balanced and the disciplined clean diet showed its positive effects on my body; my energy levels were increasing and my body felt rejuvenated at regular intervals.

No unnecessary contact with the outside world gifted my thoughts with more lucidity and helped me concentrate on my motives that deserved more attention. Every day of journal-writing assisted in materializing my motives by strengthening my understanding of their implications. I was certain that having prized reasons tightly gripped at my core were only going to help me deal with my testing time in the jungle, and that a clear mind would support me in staying engrossed in matters of deep significance.

The last few days before leaving for the Amazon Jungle seemed to be the lengthiest days of my life. Even though I was trying to stay patient and calm about the whole Ayahuasca thing, I was wrestling with not being consumed by anticipation of what was to come.

Leo left Puriwasi to hit the road on his motorcycle in the middle of that week for his next destination. This was soon after his return from attending a single Ayahuasca ceremony with a shaman somewhere on the outskirts of Lima. He'd been shaken apart by it, and I could feel the avalanche of emotions through his eyes when he tightly embraced me right after his reappearance at Puriwasi. When I asked him how it was, he told me in a low voice, "*Muy, muy intenso.*" He was seated on the couch on our dormitory's balcony. His statement was brimming with overwhelm about what he'd seen in the ceremony, and for me it was a testimony that a storm was coming my way. It was tough to see Leo leave Lima on his journey in such a defenseless state, but I wished him my best when he took off on his remaining ride through South America.

My day to leave for the jungle was approaching, which seemed to generate curiosity among other travelers when they found out what I was going to do. As much as I tried to limit my conversations with others, it was difficult to stay mute while living in the hostel, which, after all, is a base for socializing with travelers. Some travelers expressed negative thoughts about it based on their perception of Ayahuasca from the internet but many were inspired by my dedication. It was always a mixed bag of perspectives stemming from various thought processes, but my primary objective was to maintain a balanced mind, that wouldn't get affected by any statement regardless of it being positive or negative. I would always remind myself of why I was doing, what I was doing, and not let my decision be affected by anyone's words.

℘ ℂ

The Power is in You

If someone tries to take you off your path of finding your purpose,
never let them win over your mind;
it's not their journey but yours.

No one can tell you how to walk on your path except your heart,
which is always right and takes you where you truly belong.
Keep listening to your heart.

Surround yourself with individuals who are encouraging resources
during your journey.

There is no need to invest your energy in dealing with people,
who can't appreciate you for who you are.
There's no need to even react to their words;
just smile and not react.

Your smile is the strongest weapon you own.
Use it wisely to deal with individuals whose words don't resonate
with your dreams.
Thank them for their kind words and affection that come from the
deep-rooted fears they have hoarded within themselves.
Remember: it's not their fault,
because their words are derived from anxiety and insecurity.

You, on the other hand, are the master of your own destiny
and no person can come in the way of you achieving your dreams or the
purpose you are willing to surrender everything for.

In surrender lies the real strength.
In you is the power.

℘ ℂ

The hours of anticipation had finally passed to welcome the day, when I would embark on a new journey. A journey that was going to change me and my life forever, the Journey of Ayahuasca.

I had let go of all expectations and over time, had only grown in harmony with my decision to take on that expedition. My belief in something stronger than myself had become fiercer than ever before, and I had no doubt that it would get me safely through the jungle.

It was an unknown path that possessed no surety of return, but I was convinced that I had to walk on it to risk everything I could to discover my true purpose in life. I didn't tell my family where I was going; all I said was that I would be unreachable for at least a week. The only people who knew I was leaving for the jungle were the staff of Puriwasi Hostel.

II. THE STILLNESS OF MIND

I ARRIVED LATE AT NIGHT in Iquitos, the city known as the gateway to the Amazon Jungle. I took a taxi from the airport through the city's minimal late-night traffic to a hotel in less than 15 minutes. The jungle city seemed to have a sense of placidity in its air. The receptionist was asleep when I got there, and I had to wake him up to get my room for the night. The hotel seemed unfilled and my ears couldn't hear any noise at all coming from the rooms. Coming from Lima, where I'd stayed next to a busy street in Miraflores, I was used to waking up to the clamor of traffic every morning, so the silence awakened my senses to an extreme degree of alertness. I was able to detect a noiseless drop of water from the tap in the basin of one of the bathrooms. If I'd been in Lima, my consciousness wouldn't have even considered grasping that particular sound, because it would have been busy processing all the other background noises.

To reach my room, I had to walk through a dark passage and wasn't aware of a single soul. The silence brought a sense of relief to my mind and had me ready for the next day of navigating deep into the jungle. My Peruvian friend from Lima, Katherine who'd helped arrange the week in the jungle for me had told me that a woman from the jungle would pick me up from the hotel reception the next day at 9 am. Having come so far from the default world, there was no skepticism of any sort in my mind anymore and I thought of that person, who was coming to pick me up as a carrier to the source, whose chore in my journey was to take me to my *Moirai*, the Greek Goddesses of Fate.

I lay down on my standard bed in my simple hotel room with the same impression of stillness in my mind, a validation from my spirit that I was to walk on an unknown path as the sun hoisted itself upon Iquitos. There was no surety about what was to come next, but I was certain that the inconceivable energy that had brought me there would continue to take care of me every step of the way like a mother, who cares for her child with all her fondness and warmth from the day she senses the child's first movements in her womb, and mentors her child with all her devotion, until it is equipped with all the indispensable learnings required to face the world.

A. Into the Jungle

Watching my breath with eyes closed and an awakened mind, the night went by with no awareness of time and I awoke with the same stillness in my mind. I quickly got ready and was waiting for the hotel staff to tell me when Jazmine, the woman from the jungle, arrived to take me to a village in the jungle, where a shaman conducted Ayahuasca ceremonies. I was to find out later from her that she was the daughter of the shaman but she lived in Iquitos and was the link between the village and the people from the outside world, who came to the Amazon searching for an authentic shaman.

The shaman had built the village to preserve the legitimacy of Mother Ayahuasca, which is how the indigenous communities of the Amazon referred to Ayahuasca's divine aspect. Mother Ayahuasca herself had conveyed the message to the shaman to establish this village. It was the shaman's pure intention that kept the village running smoothly, and also presented the jungle villagers with an opportunity to welcome outsiders into their mystical world. Becoming a shaman is not a job you can search for on the internet. This shaman had gained all his knowledge about shamanism from his father; it was a legacy that had followed in their family for generations. His son, the other shaman, had been trained by the elder shaman himself in a continuation of that tradition.

The immense commercialization of Ayahuasca in recent years has resulted in many locals calling themselves shamans for financial reasons to take advantage of outsiders visiting South America, who yearn for some kind of a fun experience from Ayahuasca, but it is not for that. These practices have resulted in some fearful stories about Ayahuasca, because if a person uses it without the required minimal understanding, he or she is using it for the wrong reason and putting his or herself into a serious situation. That applies to everything in life really. It's crucial to question the why and have a solid reason for your actions because every cause has some kind of effect in the long run. Having a strong reason makes you search for something authentic and you don't fall for someone who is trying to exploit you.

If a surgeon in a hospital, for example, is not competent, well-trained, proficient, and knowledgeable about a surgical procedure, but still operates on patients who are defenseless and in need of a surgery, the results can be very damaging for the patients. It's similar for Ayahuasca, though it's not a physical surgery of your body but a mental surgery of your brain. To have it conducted properly, you need genuine guidance from a shaman who is wise, knowledgeable and experienced. Under the influence of Ayahuasca, you put your life into the hands of the shaman. It's not a fun drug to trip on with your friends, but something potent that brings out your evils from behind the locked doors deep within your mind. On Ayahuasca, you need to be able to trust someone with your life, because you can be in a situation when you need the shaman to assist you combat the darkness within you.

୫ ଓଃ

I was meditating in my room when I heard the knock at my door, and went to the reception where Jazmine stood waiting for me. Her facial features were sharp, and she had a dainty body with a gleaming dark skin, undoubtedly a person who belonged in the jungle.

"*Hola, como estas?*" she said with a comforting smile on her face. I replied with a firm, "*Muy bien,*" and then continued with "*Mi nombre es Kart… Mucho gusto, Jazmine.*" She smiled again and told me that a vehicle was waiting outside to take me to the city's riverside.

The automobile was a classic three-wheel metal structure built to accommodate no more than two passengers. I could see its old engine beneath the sitting area. The vehicle ran on oil and ejected dense clouds of dingy smoke while operating. I placed my backpack at the rear of the vehicle and sat at the front for my ride toward the Iquitos riverside.

Jazmine told me that after I reached the riverside, I had to take a boat ride to go deeper into the jungle and then take a swampy path to reach the Ayahuasca village. As vague the instructions were, I still replied with a confident, "I've got it" and signaled the driver to move.

That drive was my last interaction with civilization, as the boat trip was to take me away from Iquitos into the jungle, where I wouldn't hear any sort of man-made jangle. On reaching the local harbor, I was introduced to another man who was to accompany me on that leg of the journey.

"*Como estas, amigo?*" he asked, to which I replied, "*Muy bien, es tu?*"

He was an older man, who straightway nodded his head and introduced himself by saying, "*Muy bien. Mi nombres es Manuel, soy de Mexico. De donde eres?*"

"*Mi nombres es Kart. Y soy de India. Tu hablas ingles?*" I responded.

He replied in English and we continued our conversation in English.

Manuel told me that he had been to that village which obviously aroused a few questions in my mind.

I asked him how his encounter with Ayahuasca had been, to which he said, "I stayed in this specific place a year ago, and it transformed my life forever."

Manuel was a very kind man, who'd previously struggled with alcohol and drug abuse, which badly affected his relationship with his wife and children. Ayahausca relieved him of his addiction and led him to a much healthier lifestyle. He was a short man with minimal hair on the crown of his head, but a glistening face that was a true reflection of his healthy living.

Having a mature and experienced companion like him with me on the boat, encouraged me in many ways to feel lighter and less worried by thoughts about the unexpected. Even though this kind of journey is to be walked alone, the individuals who join forces with you in the grueling process and grant you their downright love and support can be of tremendous assistance in battling through all the suffering that comes along with it.

Incredible individuals from various parts of the world were going to join me the next day for the entire week in the jungle. I didn't know it then, but they were going to play pivotal roles in my journey. They were on their own paths, seeking their own versions of the truth to find inner peace and somehow, we were all going to have substantial impacts on one another's lives.

The voyage into the abyss of the Amazon Jungle was scenic and picturesque. On our way, we passed many small villages located at the edge of the river where the tribes had built wooden huts over the water that stood on extended logs rooted into the river bottom. These huts had a mini dock at the front for the inhabitants to park their boats, which they used to transport themselves to the mainland. Their lives were artlessly integrated with the ecosystem of the wilderness.

After twenty to thirty minutes, Manuel and I reached the boggy land we had to walk on for about thirty or so more minutes to reach our final destination. Walking on it in the nihility of the Amazonian Jungle, I reflected upon my past that now had me heading toward the Ayahuasca village. I'd followed my inner voice beyond everyone's rational understanding to embark on my truth-seeking journey, and it now seemed unreal to be taking the final steps to the village.

My mind couldn't comprehend the reality of this final moment. I felt like a spectator in my own dream without knowing the coming revelation. I had left everything behind to be where I was at that moment and every bold stride roused my heart beat, as my mind got quieter. And that's when I heard a voice.

It was Manuel who said, "There it is. We've arrived."

The months of traveling and journeying had come to a stop. I had reached the destination that was awaiting my presence. The Amazon had called me for a reason and it was time for the reason to materialize.

We walked along its clear entrance-way with trees shading our steps from both sides flawlessly and making the path into the village striking.

Manuel became an unofficial guide and started giving me a tour of the place. The path led to the *maloca*, an enormous round wooden hut-like structure where the Ayahuasca ceremonies were held. It was considered the most secure place in the settlement as the shamans protected it from the evil spirits. We were later told by our translator that leaving the *maloca* during an Ayahuasca ceremony is not advisable, as we could put ourselves into a dangerous situation.

Past the *maloca* was the dining area and next to that was the kitchen, where food was cooked in compliance with the Ayahuasca diet. Two walking tracks originated from the dining area, one which led deeper into the jungle to the visitors' residences, and one in the other direction toward a majestic natural pond. The visitors' residences were elementary wooden hut structures, *tambos*, built to accommodate a single person each. The pond was an oval-shaped basin filled with natural unblemished water. It was also surrounded by millions of trees, making it irresistible for human eyes to be mesmerized by its beauty. Looking at it, I had to pinch myself to make sure that I wasn't dreaming or upended on a movie set. It was a surreal vision that had become a part of that chapter of my story.

Manuel, who remembered most of the folks from the tribe from his prior visit there, was busy embracing them with hugs. Being fluent in Spanish, he was able to communicate proficiently with them. All the Amazonians there had a noticeable gleam on their faces and gentility in their smiles. Their hearts transmitted kindness, which an individual from the outside world didn't need a degree from a prestigious university to acknowledge – earnest receptiveness was enough. We were soon shown the way to our residences. Occasionally, we had to walk over clapboard planks to cross little streams, which meant the *tambos* were constructed short distances from one another.

As Manuel and I were early arrivals, we were allotted *tambos* situated right at the end of that route, which allowed us to scout the entire area while passing by all the other *tambos*, where the other visitors were to stay. Soon we reached our *tambos*, which were constructed on top of log-stumps. My *tambo* was ringed by trees, which created a natural environment for it in the jungle. It had a single bed, a timeworn table, and a toilet which was flushed out with a bucket of water. There was no technology whatsoever in the *tambo* and I was far away from any of the conceivable sound transmissions our civilizations offered.

All the basic facilities in the jungle were more than enough for me to feel content with what I had. I was joyous because I'd found that incomparable endemic village in the jungle. There was one more night to sleep with the thought that I would become one with Ayahuasca, as that was to happen in the first ceremony in the *maloca* the next day. I used the remaining hours of that day to practice my usual mental exercise of gathering my thoughts and clearing my mind of all unnecessary distractions. It allowed my mind to center my attention on important thoughts and be really firm about the questions I wanted to ask Mother Ayahuasca, during the limited time I would access another reality.

B. The Inevitable Union

Sleeping through the jungle choruses and waking up to the humming of birds at the start of my second day elevated me with an uplifting sensation throughout my body. An hour of meditation, followed by breakfast with Manuel was a virtuous way to hail my first sunrise in the jungle. That evening was going to commence the unification with Ayahuasca that I had traveled thousands of miles for.

During breakfast, Manuel told me that our group of Ayahuasca seekers would get larger by 10 am, and that we would have our first gathering as a group in the *maloca*. He also explained that the translator/helper would be the link between us and the elder shaman, and would confer the necessary information about ceremonies upon us when we assembled in the *maloca*.

The time from the breakfast to the arrival of the rest of the Ayahuasca seekers went by briskly. At one stage, I was ambling around the kitchen area, when I noticed some individuals walking straight toward me. A girl with an ivory-shaded skin and curly amber-rich hair was leading them.

She halted in front of me and, gazing straight into my eyes, said, "*Quien eres tu?*" I understood, she didn't know I was one of the outsiders. So, I replied by saying, "*Mi nombre es Kart*, I came here yesterday with Manuel." She nodded her head, indicating she knew then who I was, and said, "My name is Mia and I will be your translator for the week," which I thought was great.

She told me to be at the *maloca* by 1 pm for our first gathering. I received this information with a sober smile and then moved away, to let her continue with the other seekers. As they passed by me, they shook my hand one after the other, not knowing I was one of them.

Before our first gathering, I had the opportunity to introduce myself to some of these pursuers of truth. They all seemed to have come from lands far away seeking something of their own from Ayahuasca, and shortly after conversing quietly with some of them it was time for our first gathering as a group in the *maloca*. As per Mia's instructions, we sat in a circular formation with her supervising. She was accompanied by another translator, Roy, a man from an Amazonian tribe located deep within the jungle. He had been drinking Ayahuasca for several years now. His skin was as shimmering as the rays of the sun and just seeing his tranquil face made me feel at peace.

Mia, an Argentinian woman, with a voice as melodious as a nightingale initiated our first gathering by introducing herself. She outlined her and Roy's responsibilities for the week, following which, she laid out the rules we had to follow during our time in the jungle. She gave specific instructions about the Ayahuasca ceremonies that were to be held in the evenings, and then asked each of us to share our reasons for coming to that place with the entire group.

As each person spoke about their reasons, I saw how each and every one of them sitting in that circle was weighed down by their own unique set of ordeals. Some spoke with tears in their eyes, some with sadness and some with pure determination, trusting in the Ayahuasca plant to help relieve them of their agony and find internal peace. At the beginning, I didn't understand the significance of these gatherings, which were to take place every day. But slowly as the days went by with us experiencing the enhancing supremacy of the Ayahuasca ceremonies, I understood their importance.

Ayahuasca ceremonies are no less than deep surgical operations on the mind, which leave an individual defenseless and vulnerable to an indescribable extent. Therefore, genuine love and encouragement from fellow group members during that profound healing procedure is priceless. That circle was a ring of trust and a no-judgment zone where everyone in our group could share about their Ayahuasca ceremonies, without being scrutinized or looked down upon by anyone else. In that first gathering we were all strangers, but a week later, we were to become a family after dealing with our excessive loads of heavy stuff together.

As the gathering continued, we were told that the first Ayahuasca ceremony would begin at 7 pm with the twilight. It was going to be everyone's first encounter with Ayahuasca except for Manuel, so we were each to be given a small shot to begin with to test our body's response to the medicine, as it affects every individual differently. There is no way to know the right amount for a person without that preliminary shot. The best approach is to start with a minimal dose and increase the amount based on how each person's body responds to the brew.

During that hour, we were also presented with *mapacho*, a pure form of tobacco that is grown in the Amazon Jungle. It is considered a very scared plant by the indigenous people and is used as a medicine in shamanic practices for its numerous benefits. If used properly, it can ameliorate the healing process. It is not even close to commercial tobacco, which is filled with hundreds of chemicals and is severely unhealthy for the human body. *Mapacho* is a wild and naturally-grown tobacco, commonly used around Amazonas by indigenous people for its healing properties. Mia explained to us that everything nature provides us, if used for healing in a skillful manner under the guidance of a knowledgeable person, can be very beneficial for a person's health.

Our first gathering ended with solemnity in the air as all of us had now assimilated the gravity of the situation we were in. In our first time coming together as a group, most people got past their superficial guards, and as they weren't bothered about the consequences of the words that came out of their mouths, they were able to share their intricate reasons for coming to the jungle.

It was then that the first sign appeared to me of how Mother Ayahuasca benevolently calls upon her children to connect with their inner selves.

C. The First Ceremony

The afternoon went by with a sense of urgency in my veins. I meditated most of the time to keep my nerves at peace with the surrounding, and soon enough the digits on the clock reached the number six. That was when most of us met outside the *maloca* to talk with one another while smoking rolls of *mapacho*, and fully seize mental clarity before entering the *maloca*.

As it was the first ceremony, none of us knew what to expect. I was trying my best to walk in without any expectations as to what was to happen. To not have expectations is the best preparation for your mind, as every Ayahuasca ceremony is different and it's impossible to predict what's to come. Having no expectations suits the process of purification.

That applies in life as well: we are trained to have expectations from people and places, which can lead to endless disappointment or dissatisfaction. We don't acknowledge that constantly having expectations can be treacherous for maintaining the balance of our mind, which is the most important thing in life, because that is what drives us to attain our purpose.

The time had come for us to enter the *maloca* and place ourselves on the mattresses that were distributed around it in a loop-formation. A bucket was positioned next to each mattress, provided for the specific purpose of purging. Purging during an Ayahuasca ceremony is a vital part of the healing process.

Mia had explained to us earlier that traditional healing practices like Ayahuasca and Ayurveda focus on cleansing the body of physical ailments naturally and purging is an essential part of that cleansing process. It expels the somatic impurities collected in the body to heal and restore the physical structure.

The sun went down inviting darkness into the sky, the commencement of the ceremony, and summoning Mother Ayahuasca to exhibit her arcane powers. Earlier on, Manuel had said, "The time chosen for merging with Mother Ayahuasca is purposely set during the night in the presence of the moon, because that's when she is the most dynamic and effective."

It is in the darkness when you see the light that is hidden deep within yourself.

The *maloca* was utterly enshrined by the gloom of the hour, with only a single candle placed on a tiny wooden slab in the middle. The two shamans and the wife of the elder shaman were sitting at one end of the *maloca* and away from the burning candle. We were instructed to walk toward the shaman in succession, starting from their right side to receive our Ayahuasca shot. The procedure began in silence, as no words were to be spoken by any person. I was seated on the third mattress from the person who was to drink the first shot. The wooden floor of the *maloca* echoed in response to the footsteps of the person, who strode toward the shaman to receive the shot. The light from the candle blended with the darkness in the *maloca* portraying the shadows of the creatures walking back and forth from their mattresses.

Receiving the Ayahuasca shot began slowly and I keenly observed the people who went to take one before me. They unhurriedly walked to the elder shaman, who was sitting on an elevated structure looking like a jungle tsar. Each recipient sat on the floor next to Mia, in front of the elder shaman. The elder shaman then picked up a shot-glass while his wife, who sat next to him, poured Ayahuasca brew into it and held it in front of the elder shaman. He then inhaled a puff of his rolled *mapacho* and blew the smoke from his mouth onto the shot, while uttering some words in his native language. The shot was then handed to the recipient who drank it in his or her own time. After swallowing the entire shot, the recipient walked back to their mattress and the next person continued the procedure. As the shadow, next to me was coming back from receiving his shot, my heart started beating overpoweringly. Even though I felt calm, a biological reaction still took place in my body and aroused a little nervousness.

The moment of unification with Ayahuasca had come and as I walked toward the elder shaman, my heart started beating at an increasing rate. I walked across the *maloca's* vibrating wooden floor closer to the elder shaman. The nearer I got to him, the more of his shadowy figure I could see. He was wearing a white outfit and appeared to look like a Messiah of Mother Earth, who was going to guide me on the journey of finding my purpose in life. I sat down next to Mia, who told me that as it was my first ceremony they were going to give me only a moderate quantity to see how my body reacted and if desired I could always have another shot later during the ceremony.

The elder shaman handed me the shot after doing his ritual. I stared at the brew and before drinking it, I asked the plant spirit of Ayahuasca "to help me find my purpose in life," and declared, "I am completely surrendering myself to you with an indisputable belief."

I gulped down the shot without any hesitation or doubt. Its taste was unique, not comparable to anything I'd downed before. It was very thick, in between solid and liquid states. The taste was a mixture of sweet and sour with a pungent aroma. I'd been told before that some people are disgusted by the taste of the brew and feel like vomiting right after swigging it, but it didn't matter to me as years of unnecessary alcohol intake during my time in America had trained me to drink any shot regardless of its aftertaste. Straight away after drinking it, I walked back to my spot and sat down on the mattress sealing my eyes to focus my absolute attention on the window beneath the nostrils to observe my breath. My heart was pounding as if it was going to rip out of my chest into my hands. I could feel the medicine spreading its roots in my body, and my heart was reacting to it in an obnoxious manner. I thought I was having a cardiac arrest, until I realized that it was a response created by fear. My heart kept pummeling like a pneumatic drill, but I persisted in maintaining my mind's serenity by focusing on my breath.

Soon, everyone had drunk a shot of Ayahuasca and the ceremony officially began. The shamans started by playing Icaros, powerful music in which shamans combine vocals, whistling and humming to guide the ceremony. They use these mighty songs to connect deeper with the spirit of the Ayahuasca plant and to guide all the people in the *maloca* through their spiritual journeys.

At that point, I was still battling with my uncontrollable heartbeat. Eventually, I realized that I couldn't fight Ayahuasca but needed to completely submit to it. There was a change instantaneously, and I dropped down onto my back with it. My heart gradually started beating at a normal pace and as I marveled about my mind with closed eyes, I was taken into an alternate world. The buzz of the jungle became exponentially louder and I felt more alive than ever before. Usually when you close your eyes, all there is to see is blackness but this was something else and I had not experienced anything like it before. My eyes were closed to the outside world but a new world had unveiled within my mind. The space in my brain had become extensive, without any confinement whatsoever. The only part of my body still in my control was my breath. I was now in another reality that existed in my subconscious mind.

A bright light was prominent throughout the space, beaming altering colors comparable to the special effects in a Disney movie. The transition from my heart throbbing out of my rib cage to that state of extreme illumination was inexplicable. Innumerable tinted lights blended together in a prism-like wave and flew upwards through the new-found space in my brain. The wave was crowning at its peak, but suddenly I felt a tingling sensation in my stomach, a clear indication to get up and grab hold of my bucket.

I purged into the bucket without holding anything back. I had vomited before in my life but this time was distinctive: I didn't feel nauseous afterwards, but lighter. No food came out in the spew as we'd drunk the Ayahuasca on an empty stomach. It contained impurities from my body and purging them cleansed my body from years of accumulated rubbish. As I finished throwing up the last bits of defilements from my body, I lay back down on the mattress to return to my inward reality. Ayahuasca takes full control of the mind after the purge and submerges you further into a new reality. On closing my eyes I was back with the prism-streaking lights, but their velocity had increased rapidly and the colors had become much more exuberant and prominent.

Suddenly, I heard a voice that came from the direction of the celestial source where the lights were going. I was amazed at hearing the voice, and asked myself "Is this the spirit of the Ayahuasca plant? Could this be Mother Ayahuasca herself?" The voice didn't have its own character, but spoke to me through my own subliminal voice. At the beginning, I wasn't sure if it was Mother Ayahuasca, so, to be absolutely certain, I asked her questions about life I didn't have answers for. She was able to answer them, and delivered them through my own deep-seated voice – and thus confirmed her appearance. I could easily differentiate between the two voices inside my head: one voice was my conscious mind questioning Mother Ayahuasca, and the other deep-seated voice was enlivened by her to answer my questions. Till that moment, whenever I'd asked these questions there'd been no answers to find, but now she showed me what I needed to see, rather than what I wanted to see.

That was our grandiose introduction to each other. Mother Ayahuasca told me, "I have called you here for a specific reason. It is not a coincidence that you are here. I have brought you here to uncover your true path so that you can walk on it and serve your purpose in the world."

For us to get familiar with each other, we indulged in an inquisitively extensive dialogue. She showed how important it was for humans to build a life in conformity with nature, and also revealed to me the marvelous and wondrous beauty of my family and friends. Mother Ayahuasca explained to me how it was indispensable that I quit my job in New York and walked on an unknown path, to discover the real meaning of life. She comforted me with tremendous conviction that it had been predetermined that I go on the journey of seeing the world through a new set of eyes, and that no one could have come in the way of that predetermination. As the dialogue continued, my understanding of that unseen reality, my questions for her became more detailed and intimate, leading to 'why' she had called me to the jungle and 'what' my purpose in life was. She responded by requesting me to patiently hold the rest of my questions for future ceremonies.

Mother Ayahuasca declared that she is an unadulterated component of Mother Nature, which is the mother of all and the reason behind this planet's existence. She unveiled the significant respect demanded of human kind for nature if our species is to survive in the long run. She revealed the prodigious strength of motherhood and brought my own mother into the equation by showing her compassion and love for me. Graceful visions of my mother and her eternal spirit were displayed to me by Mother Ayahuasca, who also exhibited the happiness that endured in my life because of the astounding people who were a part of it. She unraveled a stirring spectacle of my mother's absolute, unmitigated and ethereal love for me, and how that was the quintessential contributor to my strength in the world. With the dosage of Ayahuasca fading, the visceral voice of Mother Ayahuasca became more distant and I knew it was time for me to end the first ceremony, sated with contentment.

At that point, I felt a tap on my left shoulder. It was Roy, who asked me, "Do you want to drink one more shot?" I turned it down as I'd been advised by Mother Ayahuasca to not drink any more as we were to reunify again in the coming ceremonies, and that was enough for today.

I accepted her advice and just remained with the after-effects of uniting with her for that first time. I couldn't think anymore but stayed with the exotic feeling of what I had just experienced. I gently raised my upper body to sit on the mattress, while resting my back on the wooden surface behind me. I lit a *mapacho* and inhaled its smoke deeply to let it discharge through my throat into my body and aid my mind in returning to that reality and attaining a blissful state. Soon, the ceremony ended with the sound of Icaros submerging into the darkness and the shamans exiting the *maloca*. Slowly gaining control over my senses, I raised my body onto my feet and walked out of the *maloca* to seat myself on a wooden bench thirty feet away, holding a *mapacho* between my fingers and leisurely blowing smoke out of my mouth in time with my breath, while admiring the full moon that was beaming out of the blackness from the hovering sky.

My first ceremony had begun with fear that energized my heart and then incited a petrifying reaction at the start of the ritual. Overcoming the distressing fear and transitioning into an experience of love of motherhood concluded the ceremony by nourishing my soul with everlasting gratitude. Mother Ayahuasca is extremely erratic, nobody can predict what she has in store for you. What started out as fear transformed in an instant into something extraordinary, leaving me wordless and stupefied by the end of the ceremony. It brought me into a zone, where I was thoughtless and felt tremendously beholden to having become one with the plant spirit of Ayahuasca.

As I was smoking the *mapacho* while being mesmerized by the luminous moon, other seekers gradually started coming out of the *maloca*. Most of them went straight past me immersed in themselves, not ready to exchange stories with others. Some sat next to me, feeling amazed, baffled or startled by what they had just witnessed.

Ron, an American, sat next to me and lighting a *mapacho* expressed his sentiments to me. Stirred by his finding that time is so relative in an Ayahuasca ceremony and staring at the moon, he said, "Time is so funny..." and kept looking at the moon with a perplexed look on his face.

During the ceremony, you lose sense of time. Hours can go by like seconds and at intervals, seconds can feel like a lifetime. It's truly exceptional how time, which we consider so valuable in human civilizations cannot be quantified in an altered state of reality. As both Ron and I were staring at the moon, totally bewildered by our ceremonial experiences, another fellow of our group, Daniel, a Canadian who'd traveled out of the North American borders for the first time in his life, joined us amidst the nocturnal shade of baffling darkness.

Having these men from distant parts of the world sitting next to me and going through vivid and obscure emotions in that moment of time, made me understand something truly compelling about humanity. Sharing our vulnerabilities and being empathetic about them with one another is what human experience is all about. What brought us together in that moment was our common purpose to walk on a free-path and our aspiration to break away from the synthetic constraints inhibiting us from discovering the truth. The beauty of Ayahuasca is its tremendous capacity to teach individuals the art of being honest and receptive with all humans, and to assist them in building connections that are genuine and emboldened by selfless values. As our *mapachos* burnt further with every inhalation, we became more aware of our surroundings. The moon was bright enough for our eyes to see and appreciate the jungle around us. It was a moment of stillness, followed by the walk back to our *tambos*.

The breeze piloted us through the silence of the jungle. Ron's *tambo* was the first we came upon; mine and Daniel's *tambos* were next to each other at the end of the trail. We walked through the quietness with emotions overflowing from our cores, ready for respite after our first encounter with Mother Ayahuasca. On reaching Daniel's *tambo*, I embraced him with all my compassion, and then continued walking. I entered my *tambo* still trying to process the first ceremony, lay down on my bed and shut my eyes. I was looking forward to the coming ceremonies, as I knew that the first ceremony was just an introduction, merely a trailer... The unforeseeable events of the imminent days were going to play a pivotal role in shaping my entire life's journey.

III. DAY 3: REBIRTH

*T*HE THIRD DAY BEGAN with the familiar avian melody and the sun-god reflecting his rays through the green encasing my *tambo*. I made my way toward the dining area to have breakfast with the entire group, after a morning meditation session reflecting upon the first ceremony from the preceding night. There was a sense of lightness in my body as I floated along the walkway to reach my destination, a sure sign that the mysterious healing process of Ayahuasca had begun and I had started feeling its effects.

When I entered the dining area, I could hear many voices exchanging their ceremonial experiences from the night before and as I sat down next to them, an-easy-to-recognize New York accent sailed in my direction in the form of a question, "So… your turn, how was it?"

A man named Jorey had asked me that question. He was a lanky-looking guy, who seemed to be in his mid-forties with many loose wrinkles on his face and curly hair that had turned grey. He sported a discolored-white stubble and wore thick-framed glasses to see clearly through his sizable hazel-green eyes. He gazed at me closely waiting for a response to his query, when I firmly smiled at him and said, "It was nice." He kept looking at me hoping to get more of a response, but I had nothing more to say as I was still processing it all. I would speak of it in detail during our group's second gathering in the *maloca*, which was to take place shortly after breakfast and was the appropriate setting to share about the ceremony with everyone at once.

It was going to be our first gathering as a group after drinking Ayahuasca and uniting with Mother Nature. What was truly special about Mother Ayahuasca was that she presented everyone with their own unique spiritual journey to help them discover their own version of the truth for their own specific lives.

Shortly after breakfast, we assembled inside the *maloca* in a circle to begin our first gathering to share our ceremonial experiences. Mia led the gathering again, but there was a conspicuous change in everyone's energies compared to when we'd first met as a group the previous morning. The change could be sensed by every individual sitting in the circle, and undoubtedly correlated with the first ceremony, which had had some sort of arcane effect on every member of our newly-formed group.

The first ceremony was simply an introduction to Ayahuasca and was purely for us to get acquainted with how Ayahuasca works and what it does to our bodies; it was also crucial for us to figure out the amount that was suitable for our bodies.

Listening to everyone regarding their experience from the first ceremony, it was evident that every member of our group was going to up their dosage of Ayahuasca brew in the second ceremony, which was to be held that evening. It was only after the second ceremony, when things were to get serious.

Mia announced during our gathering that there would be a one-on-one meeting with the elder shaman that afternoon after lunch in the *maloca*, for each of us to discuss with the shaman the specifics of our reasons for doing Ayahuasca. Mia and Roy were to sit in during the meeting with the shaman as translators to facilitate proper communication.

Our first gathering after attending an Ayahuasca ceremony ended after that announcement with a revitalizing spirit that galvanized me to not hold anything back for the second ceremony.

A. The Second Ceremony

I slowly made my way out of the *maloca* after the end of our morning gathering and installed myself on the wooden bench outside, where I lit a *mapacho* to inhale its sacred raw smoke.

Quite a few members of the group joined me on the bench, which could easily accommodate about ten people at a time. It was to turn into a cherished spot for our newly-formed group during our stay there. That bench was where we would share our heartfelt feelings with one another while pacifying our minds by burning *mapachos*.

The one-on-one meetings with the head shaman began shortly after lunch. I was seated next to Manuel in the dining room, where we both waited as we were the last ones on the list. We were conversing about the first ceremony and, Manuel being a wise and compassionate man, was sharing with me how his first ceremony had been entirely about his wife and children.

It was always very comforting to speak with Manuel, as he was very understanding and was conscious of the potent energy of Ayahuasca because of how his life had dramatically changed since he'd first drank it. It had been a year since his last ceremony, and he told me that every Ayahuasca ceremony is a new ceremony, not necessarily a continuation of the previous one, and most of the time it is about an entirely new episode of your life-story. "There is no way to know what is coming."

It was then my turn to see the shaman in the *maloca*. He was sitting on a chair at a right-angle from the entrance about twenty steps away. Roy was seated next to him on the floor and Mia wasn't to be seen anywhere. I sat on the floor across from Roy and in front of the shaman, while greeting the shaman with "*Hola*" in a soft voice. I'd been told earlier by Manuel that the elder shaman was in his late sixties, but when I saw him up close in the day-light, it was difficult for me to believe that: he could have easily passed for a man who was still in his forties.

His eyes were glowing in a manner, I had never witnessed before. They were almost alien-like and just looking into them my entire body felt numb for several seconds without any thoughts arising in my mind – as if it had been hypnotized by his stare. I felt as if the shaman had extracted all the information about me just from that one direct gaze into my eyes. His presence was enchantingly tranquillizing and looking into his eyes admitted me into a stage of nirvana. The skin of his face was ablaze as he sat there peacefully in silence.

Roy asked me, "Do you have any questions for the shaman?" Bringing myself back into the moment, I told Roy, "The reason I came to do Ayahuasca is to find my true purpose in life as I feel extremely lost in my core." Roy conveyed my message to the shaman in some tribal language, who after listening to Roy's words shut his eyes and turned his head toward the sky for couple of seconds.

He then slowly turned his head back toward Roy to deliver a message while gently opening his eyes. After carefully listening to the shaman, Roy tried his best to translate the message in his broken English and told me, "The shaman says Mother Ayahuasca calls everyone for a reason. She knows the best for you and will show you the path that is yours if you let her." I replied with an OK and Roy continued, "The shaman has prescribed a herbal medicine for you to take during your stay here. It will assist you in calming your mind and will work as a stimulus to go in-depth during the Ayahuasca ceremonies. Drink this medicine every morning and evening on an empty stomach."

I said, "Gracias" to the shaman and to Roy and then made my way out of the *maloca*. Meeting with the shaman gave me some kind of sublime fortitude to deal with the coming ceremonies, which I somehow knew were going to be all-embracing. I went to the dining room to let Manuel know it was his turn to see the shaman and then left for my *tambo* to meditate and mentally prepare myself for the second ceremony.

ℰℬ

With the sun sliding down behind the tall sturdy trees and the turquoise sky fading, the *maloca* beckoned me for the second ceremony. I went via the medicine room to drink the medicine the shaman had prescribed for me. All the medicines were brewed from herbs that naturally grew in the jungle and had been tested by the elder shaman himself to determine their specific healing properties. A local guy from the jungle named Rahelio greeted me. I gave him the paper containing the name of my prescribed medicine. He then offered me a shot of a green-colored fluid and signaled me to gulp it. It had a very refreshing aftertaste to it which eased the task of consuming it for the rest of my stay.

I continued walking toward the *maloca*, only to stop at the wooden bench outside the *maloca*, where I joined a fellow seeker,

Emilian from Canada for a round of *mapacho* before entering. I asked him as I sat down next to him on the bench if he minded if I joined him for a smoke. "Sure," he replied and passed me a hand-rolled *mapacho*. I asked him if he was ready, to which, he replied, "I hope so."

As I ignited the *mapacho* and inhaled my first puff of white smoke, Emilian asked me if I was ready for the second ceremony. "Yes, but I have no expectations from it whatsoever." He smiled at me and said, "That's probably the best way to go about it."

We conversed briefly about our families over that single roll of *mapacho*, and when they'd burned themselves out, Emilian uttered, "It's time for us to go inside the *maloca* and be part of the second ceremony." I threw away my *mapacho* and swiftly raised myself up from the bench to follow him into the *maloca* for our reunification with Mother Ayahuasca.

I sat on a different mattress for the second ceremony, one installed at the other end of the *maloca*, directly opposite to where the shamans would be seated. As darkness fell upon the *maloca*, the second ceremony began with a similar ritual to the first ceremony's, with each individual quietly going to the elder shaman to receive their Ayahuasca shot.

There was no more nervousness in my body or mind. I was ready to reunite with Mother Ayahuasca, and as soon as the person next to me came back to his mattress after drinking the shot, I unhurriedly carried myself to the other end of *maloca* in front of the shaman and next to Mia, who asked me as I squatted down, "Kart, do you want to increase the dosage from the first ceremony?" Without any uncertainty in my mind I replied with an assured "Yes." After performing his customary smoking ceremony over the brew, the shaman handed me an enormous double shot of the Ayahuasca brew. It was much bigger than the one I'd swigged in the first ceremony, and it took me two rounds of gulping to devour it. I went back to the mattress and lay on my back to shut my eyes and welcome my pilgrimage into an awakened macrocosm with Mother Ayahuasca guiding me.

₭ ℛ

With time losing its essence, my mind broadening and my senses increasing in awareness of all the distinctive vibrations surrounding me, Mother Ayahuasca came to life in my being and greeted me with illustrations of totally different lessons from my first ceremony.

She presented to me with insightful visions of all the natural spectacles that constitute our world. I was shown the immeasurable dynamism of the ocean and the actual course of development of our planet from the beginning of time, when it was merely a tiny particle and how it developed into a grand globe of a planet through the exponential multiplications and re-multiplications of those tiny particles over the ages.

Mother Ayahuasca showed me nature's supernatural prominence and declared that nature is what provides humans with everything essential to their growth and self-development. The particles that created this planet are essentially what form us and for us to understand the true purpose of life, it's crucial to submerse ourselves with nature. When we establish a pure connection with nature is when we gain the strength to look within ourselves and become aware that our being as a material body is solely governed by the laws of nature. There is a universal energy, which comes from a source deep within our planet to keep us alive. That energy is kindled in all of us and no existential living being dies. Instead, it transmutes from one physical structure to another by liberating itself from having to enclose its limitless powers in a physical form, which is preordained to decease with the dusty land.

As the visions were getting more astounding and unbelievable, I had a similar tingling sensation in my stomach as in the first ceremony, a clear signal that it was time for me to purge again. After having undergone the purge in the first ceremony, it was easier to go through it again and I actually began to appreciate it for removing the seriously-imbedded impurities from my body.

While I was purging, I could hear a few of the other seekers laughing energetically in the background. Mia had told us in our morning gathering that Ayahuasca could trigger any sort of emotional release – crying, laughing, happiness, sadness, joy, love and so on in the process of bringing up the ingrained horrors from a person's body.

It was crucial to maintain the sanctity of the ceremony by letting the release fully unfold so that our minds could be unleashed from all our controlling repressions. I gradually lay back down on my mattress after the purge to return to Mother Ayahuasca, resolutely ignoring the laughs of the other seekers in the background. I centered my senses on the chanting of Icaros, which guided me back into the transcendental world past the measures of time and space to converge with Mother Ayahuasca again.

The Mother provided more insight into the meaning of life, by exhibiting a prolonged vision of the evolution of our earth throughout the anomalies that prevailed during earlier ages. The teachings continued with revelations of when our species was born from tiny particles into the development of our civilizations. She carried me through the various civilizations to demonstrate how with time, we humans lost a sense of ourselves and got separated from our true identities to live in illusions disconnected from nature and the concrete values of life.

My mind was blown away from obtaining Mother Ayahuasca's revered knowledge. It was more than I could have ever imagined, which only led to the idea of taking another Ayahuasca shot to go deeper into the journey. When I considered that, my body was already strongly under the influence of Ayahuasca. I was certain that if I drank more of the brew, my body wouldn't be able to handle it and I would be pushed beyond my capabilities. For that reason I wasn't able to let go of the idea of drinking more of the brew. I surrendered my decision to the mercy of the Mother, who uttered the words, "Drink it" as her voice faded away into the dimness and vanished with those last words.

৯০ ৫৪

In that moment, I couldn't understand why Mother Ayahuasca told me to drink more of the brew even when she was aware that my body wasn't suited to handling more. But instead of doubting her call, I decided to follow her instruction. I got to my feet to slowly move in the shaman's direction, who was taking a moment's rest from orchestrating the Icaros. I asked Mia for one more shot, knowing in my heart that I was pushing myself beyond my limits.

On being offered another shot by Mia, I obeyed the Mother's declaration and swallowed it without thinking about the after-effects. I went back and lay down on my mattress hoping to hear the resounding voice of Mother Ayahuasca, but she didn't emerge. Instead the stinging sensations returned to my stomach, getting me to purge for the second time in that ceremony. It was a more thorough purge this time, and pushed my bodily limits to spark a transition, with my tumbling down on the mattress.

My heartbeat immediately escalated and the visions transformed into a horrific sequel. The floor beneath me started shaking and the *maloca* swirled in front of my eyes at an unprecedented velocity. My mind lost control and the only thing holding me to reality was my breath, which was continuingly only halting.

My eyes opened in an attempt to ground myself to actuality, but everything tangible around me evaporated and I was borne into a distorted reality with innumerable dimensions fluctuating around me with nothing concrete for my eyes to center their attention on.

I'd been invaded by all my evils; they'd swept me into a dark place where my mind lost control over everything. Unable to cope up with the dark spirits, my physical structure was being ruptured which caused my heart itself to stop. I was in urgent need of aid and if I wasn't able to get immediate assistance, I didn't know what would happen.

With all my inbred determination, I managed to get to my feet and make my way toward Mia, whose mattress was at the other end of the *maloca*, next to the shamans.

The tormenting situation demanded my mind make sense of where I was, but with every breath it was losing cognition. My heart was giving up and my mind had lost its awareness. The only thing keeping me alive was my innate desire to live.

The distance from my mattress to Mia's mattress could normally be covered in less than ten seconds but in those moments, getting there was the most difficult walk of my life. Every step robbed me more of the last bits of vitality left in me and decelerated my heart closer to shut-down. The tenacity for living had me reach Mia's mattress, only to find her not there. At that point, my legs lost the ability to stand and my body plummeted straight down onto her mattress.

Even though I was trying to deeply inhale air, my lungs didn't respond anymore. I knew I was dying but couldn't do anything to save myself.

I used the last bits of the verve left in me to move my neck and see the shamans, who were barely ten feet away from me. It was to be my last attempt to save myself. My only chance at survival was to somehow reach the shamans, who were submerged in the act of guiding the ceremony with Icaros.

My legs had given up on me and didn't contain enough strength for me to rise again. With my last breaths, I drew together all the power I possibly could from each part of my body to crawl punishingly in the direction of the shamans. Exhaustingly, I placed my arms forward to painfully move my body nearer to the shamans. Tears were streaming down from my eyes.

My ego was savagely tossed aside and I felt helpless all the way down to the core of my being, while I silently screamed, "*Ayuda mi... ayuda mi...* help me ..."

The younger shaman quickly came to my rescue as my breath ceased after uttering those words before outright collapse. In that last stage of grief was when I really accepted being completely helpless and having no control over my life anymore.

The younger shaman was telling me to breathe, holding up my body so that my lungs could function again. But it was too late...

My heart had entirely stopped beating, my lungs had been thoroughly crushed and my mind had lost all its awareness. I was dying and stuck in another reality with no getaway. There was no love, no family or friends in that dark world. If someone were to describe hell: that was it – an inescapable reality I had become an eternal part of.

No more oxygen was inhaled, resulting in a sudden black-out. It was the end of my life. I had died.

80 03

Like a lightning beam over my lifeless heart, the image of my mother appeared on the blackness of hell that had overcome me. Her selfless love ignited the soul of my heart to bring me back to life. The shaman was pounding his hands over my chest to get my heart beating again. I was coming back to life by excruciating breath. I was being reborn, my whole body shaking with desire to resurface from the depths of hell.

In that moment of truth was when I purged my veins out. The shaman quickly handed me a bucket in which I continued to purge endlessly, shoving out whopping blobs of evil that had been concealed in my body over its lifetime. All the evil contained in those chunky blobs was shrieking at me in agony because of their desire to stay inside my body, but regardless of how traumatic it was, I kept expelling them.

I purged my soul into that bucket to acknowledge my rebirth after confronting my own death. All my evil came out in that process of immense suffering, and I was rescued from what had seemed an inescapable reality.

When it wasn't materially possible for me to purge anymore and seeing as the bucket contained such malicious evil, I tried to push it far away from everyone with the infinitesimal amount of energy I could muster in my arms. I thanked Mother Nature, who would accept that evil with open arms, like all the other vile things we give her, only to forgive us each time because of the greatness of her being.

Tears were streaming through my eyes and my shadowy surroundings were still bleary, even after my rebirth. I was trying to focus all my attention on the image of my devoted mother, whose measureless love had brought me back from the dead.

My body was still in a horrifying situation, and all I wanted was to tell my family and friends, how much I loved them and that I would do anything possible to see them once more.

It was a form of pure suffering. Whatever I had learnt in life till that instance had been permanently flushed out of my system and brought me to my knees in a state of pure devotion toward a superior power. I prayed for it to save me from the ultimate stage of human suffering,

Until that moment I used to believe, I was the strong one in my family and that it was my strengthened personality that had provided me with an edge over others, but that illusion was unquestionably shattered on that occasion of immeasurable pain. All my pride and ego evaporated with my every fresh breath.

It was the love of my family and friends that had kept me alive and brought me back from the dead. The younger shaman was still continuously working on me; asking me to breathe and circling around me chanting prayers and puffing *mapacho* smoke onto my body to release me from the foul spirits that had amassed throughout my entire mortality.

The elder shaman, who had been orchestrating the entire ceremony with Icaros during that time, soon halted the singing briefly. That was when Mia, who had been assisting the younger shaman, carried me in her tender arms to place me in front of the elder shaman, who ignited a roll of *mapacho* and then heavily blew its sacred smoke over my skull to begin the healing process in cooperation with the harmonizing Icaros chorus.

To keep myself within the reality of the physical world, I held the elder shaman's feet with complete devotion to his powers and asked him to save me. Countless tears were still flooding down my face as I tried to focus my attention on the Icaros melody, and unceasingly thank my loved ones for all they had done for me throughout their lives.

I apologized to everyone I had ever hurt. All I wanted was for that torturous moment to end; it was the most painful thing to have endured. I was suffering physically, mentally and emotionally, and I told myself that if I survived this, my entire life's structure was going to change forever.

My every cell was depleted of energy from breathing through hell. By that point, both the shamans were engaged in their sacred rituals to help me get out of that state of supreme agony.

I had never actually prayed in my life until that span of terror, but I sincerely surrendered myself into beseeching for my life from every god I could think of. Pleading with them saying, "Save me … save me… I want to live…" All I wanted was to hug my family and friends, tell them how much I loved them. I didn't want my life to end there.

Eventually, I reached a stage where I started embracing the totality of the suffering and found contentment in the idea of death, burning away all the residue of fear. That's when I felt all the evil spirits leave my body. The shamans were still revolving around me, chanting their mantras and blowing smoke onto my body to get every single evil life-force to perish from my being.

All my pride had collapsed from having my life completely dependent on someone else. The shamans had saved my life and my hand was still placed on the elder shaman's leg, to provide me with some relief and security in evil's blaze of sovereignty.

Shortly, I lost the sense of physicality in my body and all that was left was a steady flow of energy from top to bottom. All the evil had departed, and my mind and body had harmonized. I felt light as a feather as if someone had just lifted a mountain from my shoulders. I had given my everything, and there was nothing more left in me to give.

Mia, who had been supporting the shamans during that immense cleansing, asked me how I was feeling. I had regained my ability to comprehend a question, so I responded with, "Better." She looked into my eyes with empathy and said, "If you are feeling better, it's important for you to continue the ceremony at your original spot as the shamans have to carry on the ceremony for everyone in the *maloca*."

The bleary shadows around me had disappeared and I was coming out of the distorted place my mind had been in. It was very comforting to have been able to hold the shaman and I thanked both of them for saving my life.

I complied with Mia's request to continue the ceremony on my own, when she told me that I didn't have to be physically present with the shamans to feel secure, as they knew who was going through what at all times and their spirits were powerful enough to guide me on my journey from a distance.

It was quite possible that someone else might require the shaman's assistance so to protect the sanctity of the ceremony, I asked her if she could help me stand up. Rising to my feet after my rebirth was like being a child walking for the first time. Mia unhurriedly accompanied me back to my mattress, while I was still recovering from what had transpired in the most impactful moment of my life.

℘ ℭ

As we reached my mattress, I firmly hugged Mia. I was extremely grateful to her and the shamans who had brought me back to life. It was a moment of enormous relief after burning through hell. My body freely dropped on to the mattress in submission to gravity to greet another transition.

A cosmic voice emerged... the return of Mother Ayahuasca, who'd resurfaced to bless a new-born with her sacramental teachings. All my illusory constraints had been demolished in the process of battling my own death. My mind was relieved of all the preconceived notions I'd been brainwashed into believing all my life, and finally learned about my true path.

I thanked Mother Ayahuasca for telling me to take the extra shot, as what came from it had absolutely transformed my being. Facing my own death and living through hell had detached me from my fears, death being the ultimate fear of them all.

In that final transition, Mother Ayahuasca blessed me with visions of my reason for existing. She told me to lead a life founded upon the mission of spreading selfless love, kindness and compassion to fellow beings: the real purpose of my life was to serve others.

Just about then, the shamans began the closing rituals of the Ayahuasca ceremony, in which they trooped around the *maloca* to position themselves in front of each of us, who were sitting in a prayer-position while waiting. The shamans performed a ritual of blowing the sacred smoke onto us in addition to chanting the Icaros. They did that by blowing *mapacho* smoke with a piercing "ssshhhooo" over our head, hands and entire body. Then they put our hands into a prayer position, so that they could conclude the holy ritual by blasting the smoke onto the hands.

When the younger shaman completed performing the closing ritual on me, I devotedly held his feet in appreciation, "*Mucha mucha gracias,*" for what he had done to save me.

Soon, Mia announced that the ceremony was officially over and the shamans exited the *maloca*. Even after the end of ceremony, which was post-midnight, I was still in tune with Mother Ayahuasca, whose voice was gradually distancing from me. She was encouraging me to acknowledge my rebirth as the start of my new life by being eternally true to myself.

Eventually when her voice disappeared, I continued lying on my mattress so that my body could gain enough energy to walk again, as I wasn't sure it was strong enough to take me back to the *tambo*: I was exhausted in a way I'd never been before.

I had broken past all my limits and given beyond my everything. The battle to rise against my own death in a frightening endeavor to get the humanely devils out of my body, had consumed the last bits of energy from every cell in my body.

After the enormity of that night, my body arose leadenly from the mattress and sluggishly guided my feet outside the *maloca*, where I heard the voices of some of the group members coming from the direction of the dining hall.

The skin on my face was tight from all my tears over the course of many hours. My mind wasn't able to formulate any thoughts, as it was overwhelmed by the years of experiences and teachings in just several hours, and my body was still moving listlessly. If someone from the outside world had seen me in that condition, they wouldn't have known what to make of me.

I followed the voices inside the dining hall to carry myself to the presence of some of the seekers, seated at one of the tables listening to a person from Germany tell his ceremonial experience. A man named Richard, was one of the individuals who'd been laughing outrageously during the ceremony, was simply bursting with uncontrollable energy.

Richard was a very talkative man and a wonderful story-teller, who could speak for hours without gasping for a single breath. He was an animated individual, who could have become an actor. He had a bulky physique that he used effectively along with his large eyes to depict many characters and narrate entertaining stories to a crowd. He was sharing his discovery from the ceremony that he was the Monkey King and no one around him could stop laughing at his comical depictions of himself. He was in a manic state while I, on the other hand, was at the opposite end of the energetic spectrum.

When I entered the dining facility, seeing the reaction on all their faces clearly indicated that they had figured out I was wholeheartedly shaken up from my ceremony. I sat down quietly across from Richard next to Daniel. All the individuals along with Richard slowly quietened when they realized how enduringly unsettling my second ceremony was.

Daniel along with Jorey empathized with me and soon we followed Richard out into the open space, where the moon was beaming out of the black sky to illuminate the pond with its vitality.

Richard was out of control and expanding upon his finding of himself to be the Monkey King, when Roy came by to suggest to the rest of us to get some rest. I was in no position to walk by myself to my *tambo*, as I was still struggling to get a hold of relative reality because my mind was still under the influence of Ayahuasca. So, Daniel, Roy and Manuel (who had just come out of the *maloca*) accompanied me all the way till my *tambo* and gave me enormous hugs to express their unconditional love and support.

On entering my *tambo*, I fell to my bed as if it was my grave and gradually closed my eyes thanking my mother, loved ones, shamans and everyone whose love and kindness had helped me get through the most excruciating night of my life. It was a night that I won't ever forget, even if I really wanted to. Mother Ayahuasca had given me a new birth, which in the process, had taken everything from me. I ended the night only wondering if I would unite with Mother Ayahuasca once more.

IV. THE ULTIMATE TEACHING

A. Day 4

AFTER SPENDING THE NIGHT in a state of exhaustion, my eyes opened with the first rays of sunshine. I woke up realizing that the night before wasn't a dream but the most real thing I'd ever been a part of. It had affected me in a manner that I couldn't comprehend and I knew my brain would need time to process everything.

The day started with the usual rituals, but I felt different. Something deep within me had changed after I'd confronted all my shrouded fears, and with my resurrection during the night I'd evolved into a new creature, freed of all his shackles.

I made my way toward the dining hall, cautiously walking along the muddy trails that had been swamped by the early morning rain, while still in a state of unfamiliar mental awareness that was continuously flooding my emotions past my heart's broken barricades.

The first individual I happened to come across on the trail was the elder shaman, making his way between the huts positioned next to the kitchen. He looked in my direction and instantly recognized me, obviously because of what had happened the night before and instead of entering the hut, he stopped on the path to smile at me and inquire, if I was OK.

I held his secure hands to reply with a respectful, "*Estoy bien*," and thanked him once more for what he had done for me. He smiled and entered the hut with sparkling eyes, leaving me with a comforting presence that made me feel at ease. It seemed as if the meeting had been scripted to take place at that particular moment to help me start my day with blessings from the spiritual leader of the Amazon.

The dining room had a different atmosphere compared to the preceding days. Unquestionably, things had gotten serious last night and I wasn't the only one who'd been through a powerful transformation. The emotional flow silently echoing in the room could be easily felt. No one was keen to hear about someone else's ceremony, but just wordlessly understood its contents. In just three days, there'd been a drastic change in the entire group because of the intensity of the Ayahuasca ceremonies.

The post-breakfast gathering went on for an indefinite period, as the second ceremony had shaken up the group members in a manner they'd never experienced before. By then, the importance of those group gatherings made sense to all of us: going through Ayahuasca ceremonies was extremely challenging and having people around you, who could relate to you at that time of utmost susceptibility, unquestionably assisted in processing the intensified material in your mind.

Listening to other people's experiences boosted my mettle to share my experience, which was an immensely crucifying spiritual journey on its own, that nurtured a pure bond among us. By the end of that gathering, there was more empathy, humility, love, compassion, and kindness being offered from everyone, which I was very grateful to have become a part of.

The gathering ended with an announcement from Mia that there'd be no Ayahuasca ceremonies that day. A tribe from a nearby village would visit us in the afternoon to display their locally-crafted accessories and perform a tribal dance. And the next day, we would not have our morning gathering after breakfast, as the elder shaman would be taking us on a tour of his farm.

Afterwards, most of us smoked rolls of *mapachos* and conversed at our wooden bench outside the *maloca*. Everyone's encouragement certainly helped me get through that unbelievably arduous day, and till we reconvened again in the afternoon to see the local tribe's artworks, most of us spent rest of the morning sharing and talking about our lives. It was incredible how easy it was for me to feel so comfortable around that group of seekers, who'd found their way to the Amazon to deal with all their fears.

The tribal dance performance was originally supposed to take place at the space around the pond, but because of the rainy weather it was held inside the *maloca*. It was an opportunity for the tribe to showcase their art and culture to people from the outside world. But what was really special was that it was the tribe that Roy, one of our translators, came from and he was the one who'd invited them to perform for us.

Roy had originally been a jeweler, who'd sold his artwork to tourists in Iquitos. That was how he learned his English. He was only in his early thirties but had five children, and had told me that one of his sons was also going to come along with the tribe to showcase the ornaments they'd created together. On hearing that, I'd promised him that I was going to get one of his pieces.

Roy was such a kind and honest man that getting a necklace from him was the least I could do to support his family. He had dedicated his life to serve others by assisting the shamans in the Ayahuasca ceremonies, which was a truly demanding undertaking. So, taking something back with me to the outside world that had been created by an individual of such an exceptional character was the best way to honor Roy and the indigenous tribes of the Amazon Jungle.

֍ ֎

The visiting tribe showcased their artworks before staging their dance performance. I entered the *maloca* with Roy. We went around the *maloca* greeting the various members of his tribe, who were all dressed in their traditional white-colored attire for the dance sequence and finally reached the spot where Roy's young son was sitting with all their hand-crafted jewelry.

Roy introduced me to his son and showed me the necklaces that had taken him months to produce. I intently gazed at the necklaces and was startled by the details contained in them. They were simply exceptional. I was particularly entranced by one necklace, which featured "the tooth of a jaguar" attached to a polished fossil of the Ayahuasca plant. I asked Roy, "Is this the tooth of a real Jaguar?" To which he replied, "Yes. I roamed around in the jungle for almost six months before I came across a Jaguar skeleton, from which I acquired this tooth."

Jaguars are symbolic of strength and courage for indigenous tribes of the Amazon Jungle and with an added fossil of the Ayahuasca plant, that necklace was an impeccable depiction of what uplifted the Amazonians. I told Roy that it was perfect and it would also be a constant reminder of my time in the Amazon Jungle even after my return to civilization.

The afternoon after receiving that necklace from Roy was consumed by intermingling with the divine and cheerful tribal people, who after showcasing their artwork performed their folk dance. The men of the tribe played rhythmic music using their local instruments, while the women moved their bodies elegantly around in circles in perfect concord with the drumming of the upbeat music.

The women taught us their spirited dance moves and all of us joined the dance performance after a point. The *maloca's* wooden floor shook wildly, almost to breaking point from all the jumping, and brought a sense of worry to Mia, who was trying to calm down the elated tribal women.

The whole tribe really brought a recharging life-force into our lives before leaving us with an important teaching about being happy in the now. It revived me so I became more aligned with myself and felt prepared for the following day's ceremony. By night, I'd decided to drink Ayahuasca in my third ceremony. It was a decision made with full confidence in myself and Mother Ayahuasca, as the voice within me told me that there was more for me to gain from her.

I went to bed that night with no doubt in my mind about drinking Ayahuasca for the third time, and even though I'd given my everything in the second ceremony, that day ignited a fire in my core that generated a genuine belief that there was more left in me to give.

B. Day 5

The day for the third ceremony began with me listening to the artless hymn composed by the rain drumming on the roof of my *tambo*, surprisingly with no water leaking into the rough wooden structure. It was an even gloomier morning than the day before, but there was something about the rain in the Amazon that created a pleasing atmosphere in which all living beings could subsist harmoniously with nature, and effortlessly be a part of a self-sustaining ecosystem.

I was excited about the tour of the farm that was to take place after breakfast. It was a usual breakfast, but something noticeable about it was the constant majestic change in each person in our group. Ayahuasca as a medicine had become a part of our systems, resulting in constant healing of everyone without our conscious awareness of the sweeping transformations that were happening subconsciously.

It was shortly after breakfast when the elder shaman magically appeared to take us on the tour of his farm. Most of us were sitting outside the *maloca* at our usual spot, smoking rolls of *mapachos* in the drizzling jungle.

He arrived with his customary harmonious walk, joyful appearance and sparkling eyes. Our entire group was forever fascinated by his eyes which were always a topic of discussion. Staring into his eyes was like looking through an infinite other-dimensional space.

He took us on a delightful tour of his farm that he had built himself over the years in the jungle. Mia translated his commentary, delivering the complete story behind the development of all the innovative natural methods he'd incorporated to grow all kinds of organic food, while using the resources provided by Earth sustainably.

It was a prime example of permaculture farming, where everything was designed for what was necessary in an ingenious ecosystem within the jungle. Mia told us that he'd built the farm to grow various types of grains, vegetables, fruits, and herbs in accordance with the environmental surroundings while preserving the richness of soil, eliminating waste, preventing the use of chemicals and simply reflecting nature.

His innovative and fruitful methods were able to grow crops faster than any industrialized farm, which extinguishes natural farming and is also extremely detrimental for a region's biome and the local agricultural economy.

Most of the food consumed in the village was cultivated on that farm, and all the Ayahuasca feasts we'd been devouring were mainly prepared using ingredients that originated from it.

The village was exclusively independent of the food industry because of his efforts to build a self-sustaining farm, so they weren't forced into consuming poisonous packaged foods, supplied by the unregulated large food corporations that have a hold over the world's entire food industry, which allows them to indulge in many malpractices: from abusing farmers in developing worlds, to causing inflation based on demand for a particular food item, to the demolition of ecological communities and... the list goes on.

Touring around the elder shaman's farm and learning about his natural, innovative and self-sustaining agricultural methods that balanced the surrounding environment, had me thinking. We, who live in so-called civilized societies think of ourselves as better off and more advanced than these indigenous tribal people and look down on them. But we overlook the possibility that with their ingenuous ways of living, these individuals could radically supersede us by attaining supreme consciousness and living with more awareness about themselves than we could ever achieve. They are doing lasting work for our planet at the ground level, while we are living with an ignorant mindset and fail to recognize their genuine efforts because we are so engrossed in our privileged bubbles and in desperately trying to manifest our egos.

These so-called backward people practice self-sustaining harmonious living in complete agreement with nature. We are controlled by the corrupt, who condition us with selfish motives that benefit the top few and create a possibly irreversible imbalance in the world. Climate change, vast unemployment around the globe, destructive forms of farming in the name of development, local businesses bankrupted because of globalization, oceans poisoned, youth manipulated by advertisers, terrorism, income inequality, immense gaps in wealth distribution... it's an endless list.

Basically, this imbalance has compelled us to lose touch with humanity and led to a chaotic world. We need more awareness among humans than ever before to come together as one species and unite to stand for truth, to find the purpose we are born for and live in a manner that doesn't harm others or our only planet, which is currently bleeding from our hurtful actions.

Hearing Mia recite the story of the elder shaman building that phenomenal place from the ground up was truly inspiring. Mia told us that Mother Ayahuasca herself had guided the elder shaman and delegated him with the responsibility of building such a place that could nurture a healing environment, where seekers from the outside world could visit in order to reconnect with themselves while tuning into nature to lead their self-transformation and walk on a peaceful path.

The remaining hours of the day, until the moment of sitting outside the *maloca* and smoking a *mapacho* before the commencement of the third ceremony, went by with me recollecting all the impactful moments of the previous Ayahuasca ceremonies. By then, I had let go of any thoughts or expectations, especially after what had surfaced in the second ceremony.

I hadn't even thought about how much of the Ayahuasca brew I was going to drink, and completely left that decision to my heart, which would make its appeal when Mia asked me how much I wanted.

C. The Third Ceremony

The grey sky expired into the shadows and signaled us to enter the *maloca* for the third ceremony. My Ayahuasca journey resumed itself, as somehow, I found myself seated on the mattress situated at the same spot as the previous ceremony.

The weather conditions were theatrical during the ceremony. Wind was pounding with full force, lightning striking the instrumental chords of the enraged clouds that were blessing us with holy water as the jungle surrendered itself to the Gods who were reigning their wrath upon us.

The ceremony began in synchronicity with the musical composition being performed by the gods themselves. Our feet in rhythm with the god's composition, we silently trod the wooden floor of the *maloca* to receive our magical shots.

In no time, I was sitting in front of the elder shaman, when Mia asked me the much-awaited question of how much I wanted. With no previous thought to the amount, I said without a doubt in my mind, "Give me the big shot," in an assertive declaration from my heart.

I got back to my mattress after downing the shot and straight away lay down sealing my eye lids. It took longer than usual for Mother Ayahuasca to arrive, but she saluted me with her presence by fusing my spirit with the composition being performed by the gods in the thundering sky. I was discharged from any sense of physicality and into an illustration of colorful patterns, originating from a combination of the medicinal hymns of Icaros and the musical utterances of the skies. These transmuted into the teachings of Ayahuasca about how to thrive.

From my previous Ayahuasca ceremony, I'd gathered that Mother Ayahuasca used a three-level system. First, she demonstrated her teachings to me. Second, she tested me based on what I'd learned from those teachings. Third, she provided me with an overview based on my actual self-realizations acquired in applying her teachings to meet the test challenges.

I'd already demonstrated and tested about an expanded range of Mother Ayahuasca's teachings that had taken me through a journey of many lifetimes.

With chromatic patterns moving in synchronicity with the musical performances of nature and the Icaros, Mother Ayahuasca exhibited her ultimate teaching to me through a theatrical show that revealed the importance of achieving inner peace and harmony in life.

She declared to me that real peace and harmony within myself required innate strength, determination and patience. My ultimate pursuit, as it is for all of humanity, is to keep transforming myself to find that contentment within that resonates with the pure harmonious voice of peace.

It was a revelation that made me realize how we need to connect with nature and our inner selves to find true happiness. Materialistic and sensual pleasures are nothing but mere illusions, distractions that divert us from the truth that can't be found looking outside. The possibility of experiencing what is true only occurs when we close our eyes to the deceptive external world.

The breathtaking theatrical performance came to an end with a break in the Icaros. A transition occurred with a new wave of Icaros, and the extensive amount of medicine I'd consumed earlier took its full effect on my body to transport me to a similar hellish confinement as the one in the second ceremony for a last face-off with the deep remaining evils.

The visions soon went out of control forming a distorted reality where I felt seized by the horrors of my psyche, but having dealt with them before, I knew I didn't stand alone. The shamans were with me. I had the love of my mother, family and friends. But most important of all, the strength I'd gained from facing my fear of death in the second ceremony had toughened my spirit to face any arising evil.

I raised my body into a meditative posture and concentrated on the chanting of the Icaros.

My heart beat was rising again, while a lethal fire ignited in my brain. The pounding of my heart and the blazing in my brain mounted dramatically second by second: it was a battle between my mind and my heart. Mother Ayahuasca was helping me fight that glorious battle with the evil that dominated my mind, while my heart actively pursued it to eliminate it.

The battle took its course and reached a stage where my mind was entirely in flames and my heart had broken past its bodily limitations. Throughout the battle, I held the Jaguar necklace on my neck that I'd received from Roy the day before. It kept me grounded and my bravery blossomed: Jaguars do not let the mind win over the heart. Mother Ayahuasca, Icaros and my loved ones reinforced my heart with the courage it required to fight that battle, as my mind was about to spiritedly explode.

Suddenly, the wave of Icaros dropped and I purged the burning flames into the bucket, expelling the remaining evil out of my body. My heart had won the battle in expelling all the fear from the deepest roots of my core, to relieve me of my bondages and free me of my own deeply existing darkness. It was the most testing battle I had ever fought but conquering my mind liberated me from the fears that had contaminated it for years. The battle concluded with that final purge...

The consummate transition occurred with the purge, guiding my ceremony to its last stage with illumination from twinkling divine lights throughout my mind. The gods of all religions mirrored brightly among that luminosity to bestow celestial blessings on me. My eyes floated in tears not of sadness, joy, pain, anger or suffering but pure devotion. My entire life's journey from the moment I was born till that moment of salvation was flashing in front of my steady eyes.

The ceremony was coming to its conclusion, with the younger shaman standing in front of me performing his closing ritual of blowing smoke over my head, as I continued in the liberating state that had finally freed me from my pain and suffering. I had become a complete devotee of the shamans. Streams flooded through my eyes with a feeling of immense gratitude in my heart for everything Mother Ayahuasca and the Amazon had provided me. He ended with his traditional ssshooo sound to mark his last blast of smoke to alleviate me of evil spirits – if there were left any.

I firmly held his legs before his leaving saying, "*Mucha gracias*", while innumerable tears still rolled down my face. His shadowy contour, which was almost invisible in the darkness accepted my appreciation with an assuring smile that conveyed he knew everything I'd been through.

I lay back down on the mattress, physically exhausted but mentally relieved. The ceremony officially ended with the shamans exiting the *maloca*, but I did not move an inch from my mattress. The endless flow was still running down from my eyes, as I felt extremely grateful to Mother Ayahuasca for endowing me with such a powerful transformational journey. She had given me much, much more than I'd ever imagined and I was absolutely certain in that lasting moment that my life could not be the same after breathing through these Ayahuasca ceremonies.

Hours went by after the third ceremony ended, but I did not move away from the mattress, until I heard the chords of a guitar. I'd stayed there under the influence of the medicine, which was assisting me in soothing my sorrows. The chords were being strummed by a villager, who came to the *maloca* after the end of every ceremony to play and sing melodic hymns for the people, who remained there after a strenuous ceremony.

I gently strolled in the direction of what had my heart quivering. The villager, whose face was shimmering in the dim light that had been turned on after the ceremony, was sitting beside Mia who was solemnly seated on her mattress with her back resting on the *maloca's* wooden wall.

I sat down next to the kind man without uttering a word, but he saw the magnitude of loaded emotions gushing through me and unrolled his lyrical tongue to sing for me in his angelic voice. It was the most melodious voice I'd ever heard in my life, and fully incorporated the weight of all my Ayahuasca ceremonies.

It sparked an act of release in the form of full-scale weeping from my whole heart to let go of the entire collection of emotions I'd experienced over the span of those few days in the Amazon. I cried from my heart, body and soul. The tears weren't just dropping from my eyes, but were ascending all the way up from beneath my roots like a fountain liberating the darkness that besieges our world.

The flooding resolved with the termination of his performance, and I was finally brought to peace in that eternal moment. I acknowledged his tender-hearted smile and then whispered, "*Mucha gracias*," as I kissed his gracious hands with love from all my heart.

I reached back for my mattress only to fall on it with the last bits of energy left in me, when I heard Mother Ayahuasca for one last time, "Rest son. Just rest now.

"Tell others the story of the Amazon when you go back.

"It's your duty as my messenger to remind people of the importance of living in connection with nature, and to nurture the values of compassion, kindness, humility, appreciation, respect, and love for all beings. People have forgotten how to live peacefully and harmoniously.

"Remind them of the strength that holds humanity together.

"To serve them is your purpose and to lead them is your mission.

"Help others find their true purpose in life, as you have found yours.

"Be generous and live a life of purity and kindness.

"Be the voice for people, who are weakened by the corrupt and stand up for what's right.

"The change is in you, and your acceptance of the change moves the world a step closer to the change.

"Thank you for your complete surrender.

"I have blessed you with all my teachings and now it's your responsibility to spread them to the world, so it can come together and unify in these times of darkness. The current situation demands the people of the world work as one and protect the world for future generations. They will look to their leaders in hope that they are leaving a better and more peaceful world.

"But now, it's time for you to rest. You don't need to drink more of me. I will be with you at all times. Rest son. Rest…"

Her voice disappeared with those last words echoing in my ears and I thanked Mother Ayahuasca with tears of indebtedness, throughout our final goodbye.

She'd told me not to drink anymore Ayahuasca brew, as I had given her everything beyond my potential for which, she'd blessed me with a lifetime worth of teachings.

There was no more energy left in me to be able to stand again and my body's cells dozed off in agreement with my mind, which went into a place of pure serenity.

My third ceremony, the last one where I was to drink Ayahuasca, concluded on the mattress inside the *maloca*, and with no conscious ability to adhere to any thoughts, my brain disconnected from the planet in the deep realm of the subconscious mind.

The third ceremony had gifted me with a new life, which was to begin with the sunrise. I would commence walking on the path shown to me by Mother Ayahuasca, with a purpose that was only going to get fiercer with time.

V. FINAL MOMENTS

A. Day 6

MY EYES OPENED IN the early morning to the rowdy crowing of roosters. I was lying on the same mattress where I'd begun my third ceremony. I'd been beached for almost twelve hours there, the most crucial twelve hours of my life, through which I was sanctified with a lifetime of teachings.

Some villagers were quietly cleaning the *maloca* when I woke up, trying their best not to disturb me.

I consciously brought my awareness to various parts of my body to awaken them so that my physical structure would start functioning again, and eventually got my body to stand on its own feet and leave the *maloca* to make its way into the dining room.

Some of my fellow group-members were having breakfast when I entered, and they acknowledged my presence with their affectionate smiles. I hugged them with care and passed on my feelings of gratitude. That morning I felt like a new man, who'd received more than what he'd come looking for, which made me appreciative of everything that had transpired during that week.

The breakfast stretched out until our group's morning gathering in the *maloca*. Everyone seemed to have been affected dramatically by the third ceremony. That day's gathering went on for hours, with every individual sharing their life-changing experiences. Ron, the American guy from Washington had got stuck in a despicable black hole with no escape during his third ceremony, comparable to my terrifying second ceremony experience. His face turned pale and tears streamed down his face as he narrated facing his fears that had taken him to a dark place, which he described as "hell".

For me, it was my mother's love that had saved me; for Ron it was his daughter's love that got him out of that horrific reality. Listening to Ron's experience brought goose bumps to my body, as I could relate to the terrifying state he'd been in with so much empathy.

Our gatherings had become such a special part of the Ayahuasca journey, as they truly fostered raw human connections. Listening to some of the other transformational incidents had my heart generate immense amounts of happiness for them. The gatherings taught me to get past the surface-level stuff while interacting with other humans, and really acknowledge the good that resides within every being.

I also learnt that an important aspect of connecting with other human beings at the core level is to not be afraid of showing your true vulnerable self. That doesn't mean you're weak; it proves you are a human like them, and can be susceptible at times. It opens a window for others to share their dormant feelings without fear of being judged.

At the end of our gathering, I was prompted to thank every person in the group including Mia and Roy, who'd done so much for me during my entire healing process. I told the group how I wouldn't have been able to get through all the ceremonies without their unconditional love and support.

Some other group-members and I decided that we would simply attend the fourth ceremony but not drink the brew.

It was my last day in the village, as I was to leave for the outside world after breakfast the next day with a few of the other group members. A new adventure awaited.

The last day there was spent swimming in the natural pond, creating memories with my group-members and cherishing every fruitful moment that presented itself. The day went by as quickly as the blow of a whistle.

B. The Fourth Ceremony

The sun slowly drifting away into the horizon indicated it was time for us to informally assemble outside the *maloca* and indulge in our traditional ritual of smoking *mapachos* for one last time. The last Ayahuasca ceremony was to begin soon and for me it was to be about self-reflection and support for those of my fellow group members, who would be drinking the Ayahuasca brew. Manuel, Ron and I were the ones not drinking, so we decided to sit next to one another close to the exit door of the *maloca* to separate ourselves from those who were. Our intention was to not interfere with their processes, and just pass on our positive energies for others to have a significant last ceremony.

The shamans initiated the surge of the Icaros soon after everyone had consumed their Ayahuasca brew and even though I hadn't drunk any of it, I knew the medicine had become a part of my system too. So, I lay down like the others and entered a mindful-stage listening to the Icaros while bridging gaps with Mother Ayahuasca.

I didn't know what happened after arriving in the mindful stage, but my brain completely disconnected itself from everything and went beyond the deepest stages of sleep to just fully shut off.

The way Mother Ayahuasca functions is purely remarkable; she always provides you with what you need rather than what you want, ultimately assisting you in maturing into a loving human being. After enduring the previous intense Ayahuasca ceremonies, which had extracted every last bit of energy that my body and mind could deliver, disconnection from my organism was exactly what I needed so that I could be fully recharged before leaving the Amazon. And thanks to Mother Ayahuasca that's what I got!

ॐ ௸

I came back to consciousness with possibly the only horrific scream that could have woken me up, a scream from the roots of pure evil. It was Jannicke, a beautiful girl from Norway, who was a blossoming flower in our group. Her affectionate lush eyes reflected the purity of her wise nature, and her warmhearted smile could melt hearts.

As admirable as she was, Jannicke was struggling with depression as she had been treated very badly by some people in her past, but instead of feeling sorry for herself she'd decided to leave Norway and travel to South America in the hope of uncovering her true potential to lead a happier life. Mother Ayahuasca had healed her tremendously during that week in the Amazon and the previous three ceremonies helped her feel the worthy spirit of love and kindness within her.

Those preceding ceremonies were also a preparation for her to gain the strength to face the heinous terrors unveiled in the fourth ceremony.

I will never forget that barbarous, cruel and bloodthirsty scream in my life, unmatched by anything I'd ever heard before. It was a materialization of evil in its extreme form, which required both shamans, Roy and Mia to assist her in fighting. She was yelling, "Get out of me," ferociously as Mia and Roy held her body and the shamans conducted their rituals upon her while tirelessly chanting their mantras.

Even though every individual in the *maloca* was going through their own Ayahuasca journeys at the time, in that primal moment when Jannicke was torturously engaged, everybody's human spirits merged into one to stand against the absolute darkness that consumed her, in hope that she would see the day's light with triumph over her fears.

℘ ℭ

It was an unimaginable sight - the younger shaman was blowing smoke on her stomach while using his hands to extract the evil from inside her body. The elder shaman was reciting his prayers and circling around her body to relieve her pain. Roy tightly held her hands, while Mia concentrated on securing her feet to restrain her.

If I hadn't witnessed it with my own eyes, I might have not believed it to be a true story but seeing Jannicke go through that suffering was unbelievably gruesome. Her hellish cries were to echo in my ears for eternity. It went on till Mia announced the official end of the fourth ceremony at midnight. The intensity of Jannicke's screams had lessened by the time ceremony concluded, but the shamans kept on with their rituals. I prayed intently for Jannicke during the entire ceremony.

Ron, Manuel and I were the first ones to exit the *maloca*. We went to the dining hall straight away, where we began discussing what Jannicke was going through and how it had been for us to sit in the ceremony without drinking the Ayahuasca brew. Some of the others joined us shortly and by that time no more screams were to be heard, which was a relief for all of us who'd been collectively praying for Jannicke to be relieved of her immense struggle.

It was the end of our last ceremony and I embraced everyone for completing their Ayahuasca journeys, which brought a unanimous sentiment of humility among us. I passed my last night in the jungle sitting in the dining hall with some of my fellow group members, feeling extremely gratified for all that had happened. In the middle of our conversation, the dining room door was opened, presenting us with Jannicke's lively smiling face.

There was absolute silence in the room, and not a word was uttered by anyone, as she gently advanced toward the table where we were seated. All of us jumped out of our seats at once to hug her for battling through it all. We told her how proud we were of her for dealing with the most torturous moment of her life and were elated to see her finally smiling with ease. She sat among us in a cheerful state next to Roy, who had accompanied her to the dining hall as a safeguard.

Seeing Jannicke so ecstatic generated a truly extraordinary sentiment of contentment within me, providing me with a significant amount of true meaning in life that no sum of money could ever produce. Suddenly though, Jannicke screamed again. Holding her stomach, she cried, "There is something inside me."

Roy quickly grabbed her in his arms and carried her to the *maloca*, the most secure place in the facility. She was then worked upon by one of the shamans who'd been quickly called by Mia on hearing Jannicke's scream. The shaman continued performing his rituals for extracting the formless evil from her body, and she was kept in the *maloca* for the entire night.

All of us were confident that Jannicke would be perfectly alright by the morning as she was in secure hands. With that assurance in our minds, we made our way back to our *tambos* to get some rest.

I lay down in my *tambo* for one last time to conclude my Ayahuasca Journey, while thanking Mother Ayahuasca for revealing to me my selfless purpose of serving others, and entrusting me with the immense responsibility of being a messenger for the Amazon Jungle as well as the emphatic duty to deliver Mother Ayahuasca's message to the outside world.

C. Day 7: Adios Amazon

My eyes opened with sun drawing its light through the *tambo's* windows. I arose with a rejuvenated sense of belonging and made my way toward the dining hall for my last meal in the village.

On reaching the dining hall I came across Manuel, who was standing outside the dining facility with his backpack on the ground. He was leaving early for Iquitos as his flight to Lima departed in the afternoon. Manuel was the first member of our group to leave the village, and after everyone offered him their goodbye hugs, he was soon hiking on the trail leading toward Iquitos.

Watching Manuel walk away reminded me of the first moment when I'd met him exactly one week before. He was the first person I had met from our group of seekers and, as I observed him becoming more distant, the thought surfaced that my whole being had been transformed since that first interaction with him on the riverside. I knew it was going to take time to process everything that had happened in the Amazon, as a week in the Ayahuasca village was equivalent to many lifetimes.

I was to leave for Iquitos after breakfast with three other members of our group and Roy. I was to have a whole day to myself in the capital city of the Peruvian Amazon, as I didn't have to be at the airport till late at night to board my flight for Lima, but I had three tasks unequivocally in mind to complete there in Iquitos.

First: Get a tattoo from a local artist depicting that week in the Amazon. I'd asked Roy if he knew a good tattoo artist in Iquitos, as I had an idea that would portray my Ayahuasca Journey, which undeniably deserved to be carved on my body. I wanted to get the tattoo done in the Amazon, as I felt only a local artist could express the idea with absolute authenticity. Roy had told me he knew just the guy for me and that he could take me to him.

Second: Go to an Internet café to message my family and friends and thank them for everything they'd done for me and convey my message of love in terms of their significance in my life, and that if it were not for them I wouldn't have actually survived my time in the jungle.

Third: In the third Ayahuasca ceremony, Mother Ayahuasca had visually illustrated to me what I needed to do in the future to walk on my real path. One crucial segment was that on my return to India, I needed to go to the Himalayas. It was a very specific and insistent insight, which had my heart absolutely keen on signing myself up for a Vipassana meditation course in the Himalayas as soon as I returned to Iquitos. Going to such a course was essential for me to access the depths of my mind so that I could process that week in the Amazon, and further continue my life's journey in the heights of the mighty Himalayas.

These were three very explicit tasks for my first steps in Iquitos. They inspired my heart and cheered my mind, which harbored clarity like never before.

With the end of my Ayahuasca Journey, three of my group-members, Jorey (the New Yorker), Cohen and Tommy, and I plus Roy began our stroll back along the path that led to the riverside, where we could get a boat for Iquitos.

Cohen was a graceful man originally from New Zealand, who lived in Barcelona, Spain. Just before coming to the Amazon, he'd completed the famous *El Camino Santiago* Pilgrimage in Spain. After his merciful unification with Mother Ayahuasca, he planned to continue journeying from Peru through other South American countries and onto the United States, fly to New Zealand to see his family, and afterwards return to Spain to start working again. His work as a ship's captain allowed him to travel during the time he was not at sea, which was most of the time. He was a wise leader and a knowledgeable man, well-traveled and an astonishing individual to simply talk to, as he had abundance of knowledge to share.

The third group member, Tommy was a tall, skinny, dynamic, and a charming individual, with long curly brown hair, large amber eyes and glossy whitish skin. Tommy was a Brit with a lovable smile, who'd backpacked across the world through dozens of countries confronting extreme conditions while basically doing anything he could to sustain himself. He was a spunky, confident individual with a breezy, empathetic and jovial disposition, which combined with his eloquent British commentary skills, made him a pleasant person to be around.

The stroll to the riverside with those wonderful companions made me want to treasure forever those final moments in that village. My mind was calm and my body felt lighter as we got on the boat for Iquitos. I wasn't sure how I was going to react with the outside world after such an eventful week, but I was looking forward to walking around on the streets of a city.

The boat ride back to Iquitos was serene and the still water only complimented the tranquility of the scenery. On reaching the riverside at Iquitos, we parted ways in two separate motor rides. Roy, Jorey and I left together in one, while Tommy and Cohen left in the other but decided to meet later for dinner with an open invitation for whoever could join.

Roy and I dropped Jorey at a hotel and straight away left for the tattoo studio, where the tattoo artist worked. The artist was available, a dark-skinned young man with facial features native to the indigenous communities of the Amazon. He wore thick-framed glasses, stubble on his face and radiated a casual vibe. He obviously didn't speak any English, so Roy had to translate my idea to him.

The three of us started discussing the design of the tattoo and somehow, I just knew he was the right guy for the job. I conveyed to him that I wanted the tattoo to depict my Ayahuasca journey with its crucial elements, the shaman, Ayahuasca itself and Icaros. We came up with a rough sketch for the tattoo and then he asked us to come back in thirty minutes to look at the design, and only if I approved the design, would he do the tattooing.

Roy then directed me toward an Internet café and told me that he had to take care of some work and would be back in about half hour. At the Internet café, I took care of my other tasks. I sent messages of appreciation and love to my family and all my close friends, and then registered for a ten-day Vipassana course in exactly two-months at Ladakh, known as the land of high passes, which is situated in the Northern most part of India, and shares its eastern border with Tibet. The course couldn't have been scheduled at a more suitable time! In the months to come after my arrival in India, I was to intently start practicing and studying Tibetan Buddhism at the sacred Buddhist monasteries of Ladakh, eventually making me into a devoted Buddhist practitioner for life.

By the time these chores were completed, Roy had returned. We then headed back to the tattoo artist, who had a design ready for us to look at. I looked at the design and in just a mere second of looking at it, I knew that was it. He couldn't have designed something more flawless and truthful to the experience. I instantaneously approved of the design and asked him to begin the inking. The tattoo was drawn as a painting to be carved on the outer surface of my upper right arm from just above the elbow to the top of my shoulder.

In a matter of few minutes he'd begun. I was seated on an elevated chair, which made it easier for him to have an aligned view of my arm. It also provided his hands with a comfortable angle to work on my arm easily. After imprinting the design on my arm, he started the inking.

Looking at the size and complexity of the design, I thought the tattoo was going to take at least five to six hours but that man was extraordinarily talented. I had never witnessed anyone tattoo like that before. His eyes were fixed on my arm and his eye-lids didn't even seem to blink once the entire time he was painting on my arm, which had become a canvas for his work. He finished the whole piece in just two hours and fifteen minutes without even breaking for a second. It was preposterous; it was difficult for my instincts to comprehend his talent as he was just a simple man from the Amazon with no brand sponsoring him or any internet presence but was blessed with an extraordinary gift. He was a rare artist of a caliber unparalleled to anything I'd seen before.

The whole time, my eyes were shut and in sync with the artist's meditative state for painting on me, which led me to completely relax my arm for him until his final strokes ceased.

I opened my eyes to look at the artist, who was silently observing the tattoo after its completion. He didn't utter a word, but I knew it had been completed. Shortly afterwards, he pointed toward the mirror for me to look at it. I stared at the painting that was inscribed on my arm forever. Tears started dripping down from my eyes as I gazed upon that emblematic piece of art implanted on my being.

Roy was standing next to me with an overflowing smile on his face that mirrored the sensations arising in me. I thanked the artist for creating such a spectacular work and told Roy that I was going to be forever in his debt for taking me there.

෧ ⊗

The tattoo artist had completed his work so swiftly, that it left many hours at my disposal before dinner. So, Roy and I decided to go to the hotels where Jorey and Cohen were staying, with the intention of collecting them for dinner. Tommy had told us earlier that he would be spending time with his fiancée who was supposed to be back in Iquitos that day from visiting other regions of the jungle.

The hotel staff told us that they had gone to a restaurant called the *Dawn on the Amazon Café*. It was a lively hunt for Jorey and Cohen, which ended with us riding on a tuk-tuk toward the restaurant, which was at *Malecon Maldonado*. On our arrival, Roy told me that he wouldn't join us for dinner as he had to go see his family. It was time for another goodbye and I was brimming with nothing but gratefulness toward him for everything he had done for me and the others during that whole week. I told Roy to take care of himself and his family and after a touching goodbye, I made my way inside the restaurant to link with Jorey and Cohen, who were at a table still getting a hold of everything that had just happened in the jungle.

Returning to civilization from being in a village shimmering under the influence of Ayahuasca for a week, was like waking up from an elongated dream where our brains didn't quite know how to react to external stimuli. We accepted that it was going to take some time before we'd get used to the outside world and were just taking life a second at a time.

As the wheels of the clock turned, the hour arrived for me to leave for the airport. It was an early morning flight for Lima, so I had just decided to spend my night at the airport. It was a benign and brief *adios* with Jorey and Cohen, as we would reunite again in Lima.

Tiredness from my first day in the civilized world kicked in when I was headed toward the airport. My arm was tender from the new tattoo and my mind was emotionally drained from all the goodbyes. I slept on a chair in the soulless waiting lounge of the airport for approximately six hours, until the boarding announcement of my flight to Lima.

The person who'd arrived in Iquitos a week ago had died in the middle of the Amazon to have been born as a new human being. I really didn't know what was to come next, but I was ready to face every challenge that life had to offer with an unflinching and undying spirit of love and compassion. My path had been revealed by Mother Ayahuasca and I had found the purpose I'd risked everything for. It was the beginning of a worldly journey to keep discovering myself and unearthing the universal truth that resided within my being.

After hours of sleeping on a chair in quietness of the airport, I somehow managed to drag my body to the boarding gate only to doze off again as soon as I settled down in the airplane. The plane flew above the Amazon Jungle into the misty clouds of Peru into a new space for the next phase of my journey.

Freedom

There is a fire that is asleep in the abyss of our being;
We live our lives in an illusion of being free.
Freedom cannot be taken, or granted, by anyone.
It can only be experienced when that fire is re-ignited.
Real freedom can only be won by battling the evil within.
External reality is only a distraction taking us far away from freedom.
To be really free is to break away from the chains that have bound us in this physical form.
When we taste real freedom, every other sensory object becomes futile.
No one can control this freedom of ours but us.
To be really free is to walk on the path of ultimate truth.
Truth pertaining to reality beyond our imagination.
Imagination that has no figure attached to it.
Only an awakening that can carry us from this world, to the one beyond.
Once that fire starts burning again.

PART THREE

DRIFTING
MODE

I. REDEMPTION IN LIMA

MY EYES OPENED TO the pilot's announcement that our flight was going to shortly land in Lima. A week in the jungle had metamorphosed me into a new being and it was time to experience the world from an altered state of mind.

It was early morning when I arrived back in Lima. The plane landed just in time for the sun to rise and brighten the day. By the time I found myself outside the airport, my consciousness had completely aroused. I waited in the parking lot for the Miraflores-airport van to pick me up. I was going back to Puriwasi Hostel and was to work there for the rest of my stay in Lima as planned.

Soon, the van arrived at the parking lot, but Lima being a gigantic city, it was going to take some time to reach Miraflores. Fortunately, there was Wi-Fi in the van, so I could call my parents. I'd been unable to call them from Iquitos, because of the time difference between Peru and India. As the van cruised to Miraflores, I had a video call with my parents. I briefed them about my week in the jungle, which they'd been unaware of, and then opened my heart to them about my unification with Mother Ayahuasca.

I told them how grateful I was to have them in my life, and that if not for their unconditional love I wouldn't have been able to get through that week as it was the most challenging week of my life. I could see my parents' hearts melting through the phone's screen and my mother was unreservedly in tears.

It had been a difficult month for her as her father had recently passed away, and her only son had disappeared somewhere in the Jungles of Peru. I couldn't imagine how difficult it must have been for her going through all that, so to finally be able to see me and hear my voice must have been very touching for her.

The gratitude I expressed to her for being such a wonderful mother, brought about an even more emotional response from her, so I continued the call with my father who was also struck deeply. He asked me to tell exactly what had happened in the jungle and I told him that I'd tell him the entire story in person as it would take hours to explain it all. My father agreed without any hesitation to listen to the story once I returned to India, as he knew instantly that it was something powerful and couldn't be recited over a phone call.

So much evil, ego, negativity, pride, and arrogance had been drained out of my system in the jungle that all my interactions with family, friends and even strangers instinctively became fluid: Mother Ayahuasca had assisted in opening my doors of compassion, gratitude, kindness, and love for all. That further allowed my fellow human beings an opportunity to open their locked doors and express what they truly felt about someone. It's incredible how by simply changing yourself, the world around you too starts automatically changing. That was when I completely understood the saying, "Change starts from within".

We are normally so focused on the negatives in others that we forget that the person in front of us is merely reflecting what's in our own being – whatever thought arises in our mind about the other person is actually a thought about our self.

Once you break out of that old cycle, your mind becomes a strong tool, which you can use to create your own reality and your own world. It's unbelievable what the mind is capable of, and that week in the jungle had emancipated my mind to scent its limitless potential. I was aware of my every sense and there was an inconceivable flow of energy in my body, which allowed me just a taste of my mind beyond its impurities.

It wasn't an end, but really the beginning of a continuous process where I could develop and grow more into a person who can eradicate suffering from within. To be walking on a path where your impurities are lessened with each stride forward grows your wisdom and cultivates your compassion, so that you can constantly improve and become a better human being.

I ended the video call with my father as the van entered Miraflores. It was time to begin the post-Ayahuasca Journey. It dropped me at the same parking lot on *Avenida Ricardo Palma* where I had gotten the ride for the airport a week before.

It was a two-minute walk to Puriwasi from there and I walked peacefully on *Avenida la Paz*, inhaling Lima's sunshine on the way. It felt terrific to be walking up Puriwasi's marble stairs once again. It was still quite early as I found myself standing in front of the reception, where a familiar face greeted me with a relieved smile. It was Ximena.

Her eyes were twinkling with happiness as she welcomed me back. The first words that came out of her mouth were, "You are alive!" To which I responded with a big smile on my face. She then asked me the obvious question, which I was going to hear numerous times in the coming week. "How was Ayahuasca?" I responded with the honest answer that was going to be my reply every time anyone asked me about my time in the jungle.

I gently moved my upper body near her face and staring into her eyes I whispered, "It was life-changing." My bed wouldn't be available till noon, so I used the available time to walk around *Parque Kennedy* and treat myself to a refreshing breakfast on that first day back in Lima.

I threw my luggage in the Puriwasi storage room and left to wander around the streets of Miraflores, only to realize after strolling around for a while that it was early Sunday morning, which had the prominent triangular region of Miraflores in a deserted condition. It was probably because most of the city was still under their bed covers hung-over from drinking excessive amounts of *Pisco Sours* the night before.

Even most of the breakfast spots were closed, but I continued strolling down *Av. Jose Larco* until I came across a local Peruvian café, located across from the famous grey-colored aged church, *Iglesia La Virgen Milagrosa*. I ordered a freshly-brewed Peruvian coffee, my reward after three weeks of following a strict Ayahuasca diet where no caffeine intake was endorsed.

As I sipped the freshly-brewed coffee after being completely detoxed by the diet and physically cleansed by innumerable purges, my brain instantly felt the rush stimulated by the caffeine. Simultaneously an intuition arose: the coming days in Lima were going to be immensely fruitful.

True power lies in developing oneself to reach a stage where we synchronize with time naturally. How we measure time in our civilization has no real significance, because once we become attuned with time in its own terms, it becomes purely relative. Seconds, minutes, hours, days, weeks, months, and years become irrelevant and breaking past them helps the mind process information faster and learn beyond its previous capabilities. Continuous practice evolves, where an individual explores the depths of his or her mind to break past its own concocted perimeters.

A. The Awakened Soul

I walked out of that café after eating a delicious breakfast and surveying my coming days in Lima, twelve days, to be exact, as I'd booked a flight for Cusco while in that café. Cusco is a city situated among the Peruvian Andes, and a prime tourist destination because of Machu Picchu: an ancient mystical Inca citadel built in the fifteenth century, located among the gods above the Urubamba River Valley.

As I strolled past the streets of Miraflores to make my way back to Puriwasi, the clocks stopped ticking and for the next twelve days, time as a measuring unit ceased to exist in my life. It was time to be detached from time and start living my life with the purpose that had been revealed to me in the Amazon.

I arrived back at Puriwasi and ran into Sergio, whom I had promised to work for as soon as I'd returned from the jungle. He was pleased to have me back and asked me to start working at the bar assisting Franco from the day after.

Even though I wouldn't have been against beginning to work at the bar that day itself, it was superb to have my first couple of days back in Lima solely to myself. Jorey and Cohen were supposed to be back in Lima from Iquitos that day as well.

So, after seeing Franco that evening at the bar, I later had dinner with both Jorey and Cohen, who were staying in Miraflores very close to Puriwasi. Spending time with them after coming back from the jungle was a remarkable way of getting myself acquainted with civilization again as we were all kind of in the same boat. Jorey was to leave for New York the next day and Cohen was to leave for Columbia the one after.

A Nameless Walk

Life seemed at ease with mind in motion and heart in spheres.
Dreams were in looks, when eyes became dear.
The truth was in sight with time losing its spite.
A path was found, as I got drowned.
In the midst of a city, was where I heard the deity.
Lost in my walk, was when I learned to talk.

ℛ ℭ

On the evening of the next day, I took Cohen on a walk around the *Malecon* area of Miraflores. From there we flowed all the way to Barranco, while discussing various aspects of leadership, the superficial lifestyles humans (including ourselves) get stuck in, the differences in us post-Ayahuasca because of realizations we'd had during our ceremonies, past relationships, traveling, human behavior, philosophy, our integration back into the civilized world, etc.

In Barranco I took Cohen to *Hosso Casual Nikkei*, the gastronomy restaurant where my coordinator from the NGO in Villa El Salvador, Eve, had taken me on my first visit to Barranco. Cohen and I continued our dialogue seated in its vibrant atmosphere over a platter loaded with appetizing sushi. It was the first time in three weeks that I'd treated my belly with one of Lima's delicacies.

I was glad to be spending my first two days back in the civilization with a member of our venerated group of seekers from the jungle. It dramatically assisted my mind in easing back into the default world, as only an individual who had been through a similar campaign could understand the electrifying changes my mind was going through.

While we were relishing the last portions of our meal together, Eve unexpectedly arrived along with a friend of hers. Our eyes met as soon as she entered through the door, which got Eve gleefully walking in our direction while enthusiastically roaring, "*Hola.*" I stood on my feet to gently hug her and meet her friend Charlotte, who was visiting her for a week from the U.S.

During my stay in Villa El Salvador, I'd briefly mentioned my intentions of going to the jungle to Eve, so when I introduced her to Cohen and told her that Cohen and I had met during our Ayahuasca journeys in Iquitos, and we'd just recently got back, she was obviously very curious. I asked Eve and Charlotte to join us at our table, and our evening rolled on with the four of us.

Neither Cohen nor I could fully address Eve's curiosity about what had happened in the jungle, because we still hadn't processed the whole thing ourselves. So, I just told Eve that it was an intense and life-changing quest, which was going to take some time to process. Cohen agreed with a consenting nod of his head. We simply weren't in positions to say anything about it and could only silently smile at the question.

Eve's friend, Charlotte told us during our talks that she was moving to Pucallpa, another city in the Peruvian Amazon situated on the eastern front of Peru with the Ucayali River, later that year for work and was very much interested in pursuing Ayahuasca once she moved there. I simply advised her that wherever she did it to make sure it was under the guidance of a shaman she could trust. It was a very powerful process and it was essential to do it with a worthy shaman who knew what he or she is doing. "Yes, definitely," she replied.

I also recommended her not to think of it as a fun experience, because it isn't. Ayahuasca is a potent healing force that could bring her deepest and darkest fears to the surface, so, it was crucial to drink it with a shaman in a safe environment, and if her intuition told her not to drink it, she'd be better off not drinking it. It was important to surrender her entire being to the healing process, or else she'd just be battling with Ayahuasca, which was a battle she could never win.

As our night continued, we moved to a jazz bar called *La Noche* where we listened to some local talented musicians forming a rhythmic pattern for their spectators to lose themselves in to the melodic waves emerging from their shiny instruments.

When Cohen whispered in my ear, "I'm going to leave for my hotel after the end of this piece," I decided to exit the bar with him for another goodbye. Eve and her friend also decided to leave for Villa El Salvador.

Cohen was to fly for Columbia the next day, so I wished him my best for all his future travels. I said goodbye to Eve as well, thinking I was going to see her again in future, but it turned out to be the last time. I also gave my best wishes to Eve's friend, who was to begin a new life soon. And after that classic nomad encounter, we went on our independent paths to our own exclusive destinations, mine being the one in Miraflores.

On my taxi ride back to Puriwasi, I thought about my plans to go on a hike the next day with Franco in Surco, the district where he lived. There was a mountain in Surco that could be hiked up, not an actual hike, but something of his own creation discovered by him and his Lima college friends. "The view from the top is breathtaking and it's a perfect place for grasping the socio-economic divide in Lima." I was sold on Franco's offer. It would also provide us with enough time, when I could tell the story of my Ayahuasca Journey to an outsider. I was glad for Franco to be the first person I'd narrate the whole story to.

II. SLIDING AWAY

THE NEXT DAY, I WOKE up to the usual clatter of traffic in Lima and left for Franco's house. The day went by as intended. We went to climb the craggy mountain at Surco while the sun was robustly shining over our heads, and I recited the story of my time in the jungle.

One of the main reasons I wanted to recite the Ayahuasca story first to Franco was because he really understood me well and knew it was difficult for me to find the right words for the compelling emotions that arose from thinking about my time in the jungle. It was crucial for me to start telling the whole story as I really wanted to share it with everyone, and I was certain that with consistent recital over time, the story would just flow out of my heart.

I'd been given the responsibility by Mother Ayahuasca to share the story with everyone, so I had zero intentions of keeping it private, even though it's almost impossible to fully describe such an experience in words. It was to be narrated with the hope of tearing down the layers of hiding and duality that consume human nature, and keep us in mindless prisons, in which we lose our real selves and forget the rawness of our true selves.

As I was reciting the story to Franco, I knew that I was going to articulate that story for everyone willing to listen, because I told the story with a voice directly linked to the source of energy in my heart.

The Amazon chronicle ended as we reached the top of the mountain, from where we could appreciate the whole of Lima. Franco didn't really have anything to say after listening to the story, but received it with the most genuine smile. Then we sat down on a giant rock to contemplate the vast expanse of the ocean effortlessly raging past the structures erected by humans on Lima's many districts.

෨ ෬

No sound. No human could be seen from the top of that mountain, which divided Lima's poor from everyone else. Just the turn of your head and you stepped into different worlds: palaces on one side and roofless shacks on the other. The two distinct realities transported me around the world to fathom the instability and absurd wealth gap that exists all over the globe.

It made me wonder if humanity will ever get free of its polarizing and segregating mentality. It might seem like the fundamental nature of humans because of our tendency to label everything from where a person is born, to their intellectual capacity, knowledge, social status, net worth, appearance, political beliefs, religious choice, norms, mindsets and so on.

The labels are endless as every person wants to feel that they belong somewhere. There is nothing wrong with that, but at the end of the day what we like to identify ourselves as doesn't really matter as it's just downright conditioning by our societies. We focus on the differences between us rather than embrace our similarities, but we are more similar than we think, and the differences are inconsequential. In loyalty to our beloved labels, we are dragged away from walking on a path that is liberating, nurturing and truly captures the spirit of humanity.

৯০ ଓଡ

The best part of climbing a mountain is the coming down again. Nothing can be more satisfying than running down like an unstoppable force even though most accidents happen coming down a mountain freely. It's a liberating feeling to run down a mountain where your blood pumps and you move along with the wind. We sprinted down after spending some time on the top. The climb up had been physically demanding, but running down was equally as demanding; it transformed into an organized landslide. The momentum from the run continued even afterwards allowing us to quickly reach Franco's home.

Franco's parents were delighted to welcome me to their house, even when we were both entirely covered in dirt. Her mom happily told us to shower, and later served a large delicious home-cooked Peruvian meal. I thought I had time-traveled back to my childhood. Of course, our minds then desired a holy *siesta* and our eyes only reared back to wakefulness a half-hour before we were supposed to open the hostel's bar.

It was peak hour and the traffic-swamped streets of Lima were the last place we wanted to be on. Franco rode the scooter like a racing driver cutting through little streets, outstripping other automobiles and creating his own routes with short cuts that were decidedly not meant for any vehicles, and got us to Puriwasi with a minute to spare before the designated opening time of the bar.

හ ෬

Working at a bar in a hostel was an unexpected life event that I happened to fall in love with for its simplicity and its offering of solidarity between all kinds of humans. It wasn't the bar aspect of the work that kept me so enthusiastic about being at Puriwasi, as both Franco and I hardly drank liquor, but the rejuvenating spirit of a community-based living, which acted as a savior for all kinds of distinct and exciting travelers out in the world exploring and seeking more than the usual with only limited sums of money. They were willing to share a space on the grounds that people from different backgrounds and cultures can exist together peacefully and happily, if they desire to do so.

A. Ten Days

I had ten more days in Lima, before my intended departure for Cusco and for the next ten days I would simply be assisting Franco and another co-volunteer, Carlos, at the bar. The three of us got along really well and eventually tagged our crew as the 'super trio'. It would turn out to be the bar's most profitable month during the functioning of the hostel over the years. We rotated our tasks according to the needs of the bar with the goal of creating an extremely pleasant and vibrant atmosphere for everyone to be at. Carlos would primarily take care of music and assist Franco at the bar. My prime responsibilities were to socialize with travelers, connect them with one another, and make sure they were having a good time.

By the end of my stay, Puriwasi was much more for me than just a hostel because of all that transpired on that cozy rooftop by the time of my departure. From subsisting during my pre-Ayahuasca weeks, when I was heavily involved in my diet and restrained by my mind's disarray, till the coming days when I would begin writing this book in the safe haven of the hostel rooftop – by the end of it all, the place cinched a memorable place in my heart forever.

℘ ℘

My first night of being back at the rooftop bar standing behind its black-colored shining platform, marked the beginning of the ten-day long informal gatherings of specific unique individuals, the world's outliers who dare to think differently and live to risk everything for what they truly believe in. They don't shy away from death but welcome it with their fearless eyes. They are the creators, innovators, authors, artists, visionaries, explorers, leaders, philosophers, entrepreneurs, thinkers, revolutionaries of the world who can't be identified merely by using our human measures of race, religion, ethnicity, background, country, place of origin and so on. Somehow, Puriwasi had become a place for the informal gatherings for such outliers, and in the coming ten days it was to host more of them who were to temporarily anchor their ships at that tiny island while exploring the vast ocean.

It wasn't a busy night and I was walking around the rooftop, while Franco stood inside the bar when two of such outliers entered the rooftop, Benjamin and Gro, a Norwegian couple who were out exploring parts of South America and Asia for four months and had just arrived in Lima.

Benjamin was born in Oslo to an Italian mother and a Norwegian father with Viking heritage. His Viking genes complimented him with a large physical structure and the Italian could be seen from his tanned skin, frizzy hair and brown eyes. His voice was rusty and masculine in nature but it was his genuine smile that brought humility to his being. His eyes were the mirror to his soul and a prime source of communicating with him. His partner, Gro, a beautiful woman born to Norwegian parents came to life only after her sculpture was chiseled by an exceptional craftsman. The top of her exquisite crown was decorated with silky golden hair. Her moon-like face had been engraved with crystal blue eyes and velvet red lips. But it was her diamond-like heart, which was crafted in a workshop with kindness as the prime element of its design configuration that made her an exceptional woman.

An unspoken bond was created among us instantly, and the next ten days with them were going to be one of the major highlights of my time back at Puriwasi. They'd originally planned to stay in Lima for couple of days, but ended up extending their stay for the time I was there and we spent almost all of that time together. Our days began late in the morning on the rooftop and continued the entire day and night while exploring Lima, only to drown with the sunrise early next morning on the same rooftop.

A couple of days after meeting Ben and Gro, I began writing this book. My purpose was intact in my heart and I had a solid determination to write something every day. I knew some days were going to be good and some bad, but I focused on one day at a time and stayed true to my calling. The key factors in completing the book were consistency, determination, persistence, and patience.

When I started writing, I had no doubt in my mind that I would finish the book, as I wasn't writing it for myself but something much more than what I could have ever conceptualized. I had an irrefutable faith in the elusive forces that had guided me to that moment and would continue to provide me with the constant inspiration, realizations, growth, and strength to complete the project.

The hours working on the book had my eyes intently latched onto my laptop screen, and when my eyes left the screen I would be in company with Ben and Gro, in particular with Ben. He and I sat on the rooftop all day and talked about everything. His sense of humor was brilliant and whenever I came up with one of my intense theories, he would listen to me seriously, lift a straight face and make just one comment in his macho Italian voice at the end of it, "Man, you are too intense," and then we'd just start laughing like maniacs at the absurdity of it.

With the days cruising by, more of such outliers joined us. The ten days in Puriwasi with Ben, Gro, Franco and the other outliers were to be a time of reward for the weeks of pushing through a piercing and stormy healing process, which, by the end of it all, had changed me as a person, and enabled me to tell others that I walked out of the Amazon Jungle as a transformed human being.

The change in me was drastic: my mind had more clarity than ever before; my self-reliance arose from humility, not ego. I was honest, objective, respectful, non-judgmental, and genuine in what I said and did. I had started walking on the path that had been shown to me during my time in the jungle, a path of spreading love and happiness, which was to thrive upon the seedlings of kindness and compassion.

Those ten days were a celebration of the precious gift we have for assuming the life form of a human. Most of the time we take it for granted and forget to appreciate the cardinal blessing of existing in a state that can be progressively transcended.

I became an active member of the traveler's community at Puriwasi, granting me with an opportunity to share about my time in the Amazon with other travelers.

I fell in love everyday with life and was fortunate enough to share that ecstatic feeling with remarkable individuals from all around the world. I understood the real value of bringing people together to build an environment where everyone can be empathetic toward one another and applaud the comfort of peacefully subsisting cooperatively as one community that fosters learning and growth for every individual as a human being.

Just before my last day of leaving for Cusco, I met with my dear friend Jack and also my Peruvian friend Gabriela whom Jack and I had met for the first time at the flood victim fundraiser. We got together at a local café near Puriwasi. It was an afternoon for a heartwarming *adios* with Gabriela, and spend lovely time with Jack, who later joined me and the other outliers at Puriwasi for our last time gathering together before we up-anchored the following morning with the sun winching up its colors.

I'd never thought before leaving for Peru that I'd end up working and staying in a Lima hostel and become comfortably part of a community where people would accept me and see me as one of their own. But when I did attain that comfortable stage at the hostel, it was a green flag for me to keep moving and not let the learning-curve plateau.

It was essential to begin a new learning-curve by putting myself in an uncomfortable scenario again. Not shying away from difficult stages, where new learning curves are created as you challenge yourself to face your fears, and cherishing the sight of the unknown turn every second of yours into a transfiguring element in your life.

In the evening of our last day together at Puriwasi, Ben and Gro were to fly for Asia. They stood in front of the reception with their backpacks strapped to their shoulders, eyes coated with mist and smiles touched with sobriety. Ben said, "It's not a goodbye. We will see each other again." I agreed and said, "We sure will. I am sure of it." We carried an assurance in our hearts that life would bring us together again.

My flight for Cusco was to leave early morning next day before sunrise, and I had reserved the same van-ride to the airport as last time. It wasn't my final good goodbye to Puriwasi as my flight out of Peru was from Lima, so I would return to Puriwasi for one more night. Later that night, Franco warned me, "If you don't see me again, I will never talk to you." I also had to take that threat into account, because I certainly didn't want to be on the bad side of a Latino man!

I managed to leave Puriwasi for the airport with all the lively memories from the past ten days floating through my head onto the icy window of the van. The preceding ten days in Lima were phenomenal and I was certain that my time in the Amazon Jungle had had a significant role in my uncovering that transformative state, where I was living my every moment completely aware of my breath and in peace with myself.

III. MY VOICE AMONG THE INCAS

M Y FLIGHT FOR CUSCO was on time and it flew with the sun gaining hold over Lima. I reached Cusco in a blink of an eye, only to find myself being greeted by showers from the godly sky. The heavens were grey and misty, and the breeze biting through the drizzling water was chilly. Before leaving for Cusco, Sergio had told me that they had another hostel in Cusco, and I could stay there for a reduced rate.

It was late April of 2017 when I arrived in Cusco and certainly felt the drastic drop in temperature compared to Lima, as Cusco is among the Andes mountains at an altitude of approximately 3,500 meters. The mountains were concealed beneath the sky's misty conditions, and the rain certainly didn't foster any warmth, but I loved the shift in my perception fashioned by Cusco's ghostly-looking environment. It provided my eyes with some gorgeous mountains to look at and my body relished the agreeableness of nature.

Cusco is a small city, so it didn't take more than 15 minutes before I arrived at Puriwasi, Cusco, near the central area of the city on *Calle Cuychipunco*. The Cusco hostel was built quite differently from the one in Lima. It had a sliding wooden door at the entrance of the building, which was erected upon a hefty rock foundation. *Calle Cuychipunco* was assembled out of beautifully imbedded brick-shaped stones like most of Cusco's streets, not concrete-based.

There were no stairs leading up to the reception as it was placed right beside the entrance door with a young Peruvian man standing right behind it. I said, "*Hola*," and followed with details about how I used to volunteer at Puriwasi, Lima whose owner, Sergio, had told me to come here. The young man happily received me but told me that they could only check me in a little later as it was still early in the morning, and then he guided me toward the living room situated on the floor above, the highest floor in the facility, which expanded horizontally not vertically.

He told me that I could relax there till check-in-time. It was a tiny living room with a television mounted on one wall and several bean bags in front where I lay down to doze off till check-in-time. I woke up in couple of hours to find myself in the company of two other travelers lying next to me. One of them was sleeping and the other was watching television.

Samirah greeted me amiably and so began another friendship. Samirah was born in Germany to a Thai father and a German mother, her facial features being a clear indicator of her genetic heritage. She was an astoundingly benevolent woman, who spoke in very lyrical tones with her lustrous pink lips making the air around us tranquil. She'd been in Argentina for quite a while, before starting to move around in South America and joining forces with her friend from home, Sveah, the girl sleeping next to her. Sveah was a shy but a very sweet girl, who didn't speak much but whose infrequent words were very genuine. She always tied her golden hair back onto her head tightly, and seemed to enjoy beautiful moments with amiable individuals, which, preciously, could be noticed in her verdant eyes.

A couple of minutes into the conversation, Samirah said, "My friend Sveah and I arrived in Cusco couple of days ago and don't have any plans as to when we are going to leave." Then she asked me, "How about you?" and I wasn't sure either. Samirah and I were going to become good friends by the end of our stay in Cusco, and our paths would somehow keep crossing on our journeys.

After I talked with Samirah for a while, the young Peruvian man from the reception came to the living room to inform me, "You can check in now." I said, "See you later," to Samirah and followed him to the reception.

He gave me a bed in a twelve-bed room dormitory for a rate of 25 soles (around $7.50) a night, which was quite affordable. After weeks of residing in Peru for no cost, 25 soles a night wasn't a bad deal for a traveler. I took a quick warm shower at the hostel, and when I left for *Plaza Mayor de Cusco* it wasn't raining anymore. The sun had now emerged from behind the leaf-clad mountains to radiate over the beautiful city of Cusco, which used to be the capital of the Inca Empire in the earlier centuries until the Spaniards conquered it and developed it with their colonial architecture. The city was embellished by excellent stone work; everything in the city was created from it.

Ten minutes into my walk on the stone-imbedded *Avenida El Sol*, after passing all the banks lined up in sequence and observing the locals, I arrived in the central plaza, *Plaza Mayor de Cusco*, the heart of the city, an astounding architectural achievement. It was surrounded by massive churches and magnificent mansions to fashion a dream-like appearance. There were tourists everywhere and the plaza was crawling with tour-operators, restaurants, cafés, bars, and souvenir stores.

I went to one of the cafés located at the corner of the plaza, where I could get a good view of the entire city with its back-drop of mountains robed in green with little houses on them. Soon, it was raining again with the sun hiding behind the clouds and my ears soothed by listening to the drizzle. I brought myself back into that moment where I was struggling to breathe a little from rambling around in the city's high-altitude.

I ordered a *mate de coca*, also known as "coca tea," which is made from dried coca leaves that are native to the Andes and naturally assist the body in dealing with the change of altitude. Sipping the herbal coca tea, which had a similar taste to that of green tea, I kept on observing the beautiful sight out of the café's tiny window with my laptop's screen reflecting on my eyes.

℘ ℭ

Suddenly, a strange feeling surfaced leaving me in a state of perplexity from all the events taking place during my travels. "Is all of this real or a mere creation of my imagination?"

Previously, I used to think that many of life's occurrences that we couldn't explain logically could be termed "random", "accident" or simply a "coincidence", but with time I realized that there are no coincidences in life, and my own journey had become a living proof for that. We hold a specific purpose in our lives, and every action we take to walk on the path for that purpose is what drives these so-called coincidences. They seem random and accidental at first, but slowly you notice a pattern. Every action you take, physical or even mental, has an effect of some sorts. It all starts from your mind, with every cause having an effect. So, when you learn to break out of the mental conditioning limiting the flow of your imagination, you can unleash your mind's full potential to create these so-called 'coincidences'.

It's crucial to start taking these so-called "coincidences" very seriously because nothing is of a random nature. Every little event while walking on a path true to ourselves has some sort of significance, but we tend to ignore it. We just have to look at our lives from a widened perspective, which leads to an awareness where it all makes sense. While traveling as a backpacker, occurrences of these "coincidences" are magnified and thus assist in understanding this quickly.

Although, there are different ways of traveling in today's world and for the sake of preserving the true essence of traveling, it's important to distinguish backpacking from other ways people travel. Tourism has become an extensively commercial industry; billions of dollars are spent every year by travelers around the world on their vacations. Many countries promote tourism to boost their revenue and there are always many travelers visiting any specific country.

Backpacking is an inexpensive and unique way of traveling, where you are not just visiting a country for the sake of it, but are there to experience the specific country's life at the bottom-most level. Backpacking can nurture your mind by adding layers of perspective on the different mindsets of people and provide you with a wholesome experience.

Backpacking is not intended for you to visit a country just so you can take selfies with its famous monuments to post on social media, nor is it to complete a bucket list, indulge in luxury or just party in bars or clubs. Not that there is anything wrong with those things, but they don't deliver you the learning experience that you gain from traveling as a backpacker, out in the world seeking more from life than its usual façade. Real change intervenes when an individual is traveling to explore themselves inside and out, past time and space, beyond the frivolities of life.

True backpacking amounts to a "school of life," which teaches you how to live and connect with other human beings regardless of where they come from. It reveals the internal power you have from constantly being vulnerable. It helps you discover real love in people and sync with them in a way that earlier you didn't even know was possible. It makes you a positive force aware of your feelings, and empathetic and kind toward others. It strengthens you emotionally, because of how many times you fall in love but learn to let go as you realize nothing in this world is permanent and change is inevitable. You don't fight impermanence or run away from it, but learn the art of surrendering yourself to it. You let life show you everything it's got for you. You learn to welcome the good and the bad with a smile, because the school of life doesn't just bless you with the good but also the darkness in this world, to provide you with experiences that can foster your overall growth. You understand the real value of life and the importance of living it for the common good of all people.

This "school of life" concept of traveling is not new. In earlier times, we used to call these people explorers, who spent their entire lives studying different cultures, or searching for land beyond their own or seeking the truth. Many civilizations have been built because these people were courageous enough to go explore and find the unimaginable. If not for them, the world wouldn't have become so connected and globalized.

During my Ayahuasca ceremonies in the Amazon, I was fully introduced to my evils. I burned with immense suffering in hell, where no person deserves to be, to gain innumerable teachings, and one thing I learnt was that it's easy to say I want to live my life for my passion and do what I love, but the real path to finding our purpose in life is a very challenging one. It requires sacrifice, bravery, courage, and constant reaffirmation from the inside of our core: what I am seeking is only moving me in the direction of what could be the truth that holds me together and keeps me breathing for what makes my heart beat.

೮ ೪

As I was leaving that café situated in the central plaza, I received a message on Facebook from a friend of mine Lisa, I'd met during Week 2 of my pre-Ayahuasca diet at Puriwasi, Lima. When I was leaving for Iquitos, Lisa was there to say goodbye to me in Lima and was departing for Cusco the following day. I'd told her just before heading for the airport that I might be going to Cusco in late April and if she was still there, I'd hopefully see her. She'd replied that she'd message me around then. So, she did, and it "coincidentally" came on the date I arrived in Cusco. It said, "I'm still in Cusco. When are you coming here?" She gave me the address of a house on *Calle Matara*, which was even less of a distance away from the central plaza than my hostel. So, after walking around a bit more in the main square of Cusco, where it was raining again I made my way toward the address Lisa had given me.

It was an enormous house built in Spanish style, which was being operated as a guesthouse by a lovely Peruvian family. I entered the house through its rustic Spanish-styled wooden front door to stand in the large open courtyard of a mansion-like house, which even had a well implanted in its middle. I thought I was standing in the central section of a *haveli* (traditional mansion built in India, which usually carry some sort of historical significance).

It was an ancient house offering a relaxing atmosphere and was not very busy. Lisa was standing in the verandah of the first floor when I entered. She sighted me right away and made her way down the floor to welcome me to Cusco with a kiss on both cheeks and a warm hug. It was incredible to see her again, a charming woman filled with positive energy and doting spirit. Her first language was French, and she was almost fluent in Spanish, but she could only speak in broken English. So, we communicated in a mixture of Spanish and English, or *Spanglish*, which made for hysterical dialogue that both of us dearly relished.

Lisa then introduced me to her best friend, Delphine, who'd joined Lisa in Peru recently. She was a beautiful woman with a burnished skin, lengthy smooth brown hair, large hazel green eyes, and an exquisite nose with a shiny gem drilled on its left side, which further glorified her striking smile. Delphine couldn't speak much English either but like Lisa, she was also a phenomenal human being.

The rest of that evening went by hanging out with Delphine and Lisa, sitting under the sky in the courtyard. Even with the language barrier, we were still able to communicate easily and appreciate one another's company. I really liked the guesthouse because of its serene, quiet and low-key environment. So instead of continuing to stay at Puriwasi Cusco, the next day I moved to the guesthouse, where the Peruvian family gave me a private room for an even cheaper rate of 20 soles per night. It was a no brainer.

My next couple of days went by hanging out with Lisa, Delphine and Samirah, whom I'd invited over when I was checking out from the hostel. She'd solemnly agreed and was as surprised as I was, when she first saw the huge open courtyard. After dwelling in Miraflores for so long and working at a bar, that place was perfect for me with its very peaceful atmosphere. Having my own room at such a low cost was a bonus.

A. Revolution Within

It was one of those instances that made me calculate the advantages of connecting with people while traveling and building genuine relationships with them as you go. Having already spent some sincere time with Lisa in Lima, where I'd let down all my superficial guards and wasn't afraid to show my real self, allowed her to feel comfortable and safe about letting her guards down so that we could candidly embrace our vulnerability together as humans, and it really just boosted our bond into something of real dignity.

Many variables can play a role when you connect with people, but some variables like being genuine, honest, kind, non-judgmental, caring, and empathetic with your actions and words help take your connection to the next level, making it truly profound. Neither party involved is in it for any selfish reason but to purely give just for the sake of giving.

There's no pressure to act a certain way so that the other person likes you, or to say things in a manner that the other person wishes to hear. It's a divine exchange of selfless love and willingness to give, without having any selfish intention of receiving something in return.

Today, all we care about is how we are perceived by others. We have lost ourselves so much in the process of creating a brand out of ourselves that we don't even know who we really are – and in this process, we miss out on experiencing the real beauty of life.

If you are thinking about a direction where your intuition fingers what could be the truth for you, you might just be moving in the right direction – where your mind is learning the art of questioning the countless notions that we have been twisted into blindly believing all our lives. Your mind could be rejecting delusions and labels that it has been mentally constrained to believe all your life, just for the sake of believing something, an unthinking belief that doesn't spin out of the vortex of what sustains the truth deep within yourself.

Take religion, for example. Around the world, billions of people affiliate themselves with various religions. They practice religion based on the values and beliefs that have been passed on to them from their parents who got it from their parents, thus establishing it as a heritage. It includes "knowledge" about how to act or behave for finding heaven, nirvana, enlightenment – call it anything you want based on your religious beliefs. But what is interesting, is that the majority of people who associate themselves with a religion and believe in its god do that because they have been told to do so.

This is not condemning religion or people's faith in a religion: it is a beautiful thing and provides hope to millions of people. But have you ever asked yourself, "What if I'd been born in a family that practiced a different religion from my family?" or "What if my family was not religious at all?" or "What if I was born in a tribe somewhere in the jungles of the Amazon, where they don't even know what religion means?"

These are the questions that every human to ask to understand the basis of the society's foundations.

Do we believe in religion or god just for the sake of it – or have we experienced a connection with god, spirits or anything that can't be explained to people who haven't had that same experience because it's something inexplicable? Do we disbelieve in religion or god because it can't be proved by science – or we are just not religious or spiritual? Are we unsure what to believe in, as it is too taxing for the brain to think about?

These are a few open-ended questions with no right or wrong answers, but they do raise an important point, "Why do we let any of these beliefs affect our societies as a whole?"

The purpose of any religion is for its followers to feel connected with the divine. Its purpose is not to provide various definitions or be made into a propaganda for the masses to just blindly follow. It's something of a personal treasure, which shouldn't be publicized or used to mislead others for selfish reasons.

The connection with the divine energy is with something beyond us and has the power to be our true guide on our solo journeys. It shouldn't be marketed so that practitioners end up spending hours in religious places pretending to pray or display their sanctity, without their knowing that they might have just been indoctrinated into doing that.

If that person is not even aware of himself or herself, how can they ever connect with god, or a universal energy? Its name doesn't even matter; the point is to have an actual belief in a divine energy that springs from deep within ourselves to truly connect us with what's real, not with some façade that has been fabricated over the period of many centuries.

In my home country, India, a land of many religions, there exists an old saying in Hindi, "*Bhagwan sabke andar baste hai,*" which literally translates to "god resides within all of us". It's a saying that can be heard flaunted around India by many but practiced by only a few. Instead of focusing within, we spend our entire lives focusing on externalities because of the pain and ego that breaking out of the brand we were born into would cause us.

We think we are powerful because we can fight to protect our beliefs and have been brainwashed to believe it's our responsibility to do so – even to the point of killing another person because of our beliefs, thinking it will bring us peace and closer to god. Our entire way of thinking is controlled by people in power so that they can stay in power. When we read about recent history, specifically Indian history, the British empire was always a part of it and its simple strategy for conquering the world was "divide and rule".

For the entire existence of humanity, that's exactly how we have been ruled by those in power, the people backstage who don't show their faces because they work behind the scenes to keep us in the dark. They use fear and anger to govern us. We will always be ruled by someone if we stay divided. Only when we unite as one in the name of truth, will we have real power because nothing will be able to break us, especially the faceless creatures working from behind the curtains. There's nothing stronger than the human spirit coming together and uniting as one body.

In this spirit of humanity, I pledged to myself in the Andes mountains: "I will live my life working for the day, when the heart of every living being on this planet can beat as one." If all of us make that pledge, the revolution in our hearts will certainly ignite and we will attain freedom.

೫೦ ೧೫

Lisa and Delphine left for Bolivia after two days in Cusco where we indulged in the memories of our backpacking journeys, and I continued to lodge in the same big house with the Peruvian family. Soon after their early morning departure, I decided to pamper myself for my remaining days in Cusco before possibly leaving for a trek on the Andes mountains, by exploring more of the city and determinedly using few hours of each day for writing.

Samirah, who was still staying at Puriwasi with her friend Svea, joined me later that morning to accompany me to visit the local *Mercado*, *Mercado San Pedro*, approximately ten minutes away from my guesthouse along *Calle San Pedro*. It was a lively and stimulating market, which offered a variety of cultural delicacies, beverages, coffee, clothes, accessories, knitted sweaters; basically, everything Peru had to offer, *San Pedro Mercado* had it.

Afterwards, I separated from Samirah and went on my own adventure of wandering around the streets of Cusco. I had the clear intention of getting lost and discovering a new café that would appeal to my senses so that they could shut off from the outside world and I could immerse myself inside the laptop screen to write.

Not until dawn, did I leave that café to head toward Puriwasi Cusco, where another friend of mine from California, Camille was to arrive. We'd met in Puriwasi Lima a couple of days before I'd departed for Cusco. She'd come to the hostel looking for a volunteer opportunity, to design a new artwork on one of the walls of the hostel in exchange for free accommodation. But because the walls of the Puriwasi Hostel in Lima were fully furnished, Sergio assigned her the project of recreating the walls of Puriwasi Cusco.

Camille was a gifted artist who was traveling around South America and whenever she arrived at a new destination, she'd find a hostel and show her previously-crafted designs to the owner and strike a deal with him or her: free accommodation in exchange for her designing one of her stunning works on their hostel's walls.

Earlier that day in a random café, I'd finalized the date for my trek in the Andes, which was scheduled after two days. So, the later hours of that night and the next day were mostly spent with the girls: Samirah, Camille and Sveah. I happened to have a really good time with them as they were just really entertaining to be around.

I welcomed Camille to Cusco that night. She'd arrived earlier that day after an exciting bus ride from Lima, but when I met her, she was still feeling the effects of the altitude because her bus ride had swirled around through many mountains for several hours to reach Cusco. Camille had already met Samirah and Sveah even before I had arrived at Puriwasi, Cusco, where all of us eventually saturated ourselves in company of some other travelers until the night wore out.

The next day, I unexpectedly ran into Camille again on *Calle Santa Clara*, a street across from the famous historical building of *Museo y Catacumbas del Convento de San Francisco de Asis de Cusco*. We visited some of the historical monuments and glanced through local stores, which offered various kinds of Peruvian artwork and clothing. Then we continued winding around the streets of Cusco toward *Calle Hatun Rumiyoc*, where the famous Twelve-Angled Stone in a wall displays the masonry genius of the Inca Empire. The streets offered many clothing stores, and one shopkeeper even got us to buy some Peruvian clothing. I don't know how she did it, but she totally pulled it off and lured me into buying a large poncho, that was white in color with brown and black stripes. It was made of Alpaca's skin (an animal found in South America like a small Llama, which belongs to the camel family). The poncho was beautifully warm and would turn out to be very beneficial during my trek in the mountains.

Our drifting through the streets of Cusco finally halted at the central plaza, where we sat on the steps outside *Catedral de Cusco* to soak in the warmth of the sun which perfectly counteracted the chill of the breeze on our faces. We were feasting our eyes on the mountains below the sun, when Camille said to me, "Tell me about your Ayahuasca experience." I turned around to look at her and started narrating the story. Her majestic face was glorified by the rays of the sun, her wavy golden hair was flowing in harmony with the breeze, while her ocean-embedded large eyes were shining like treasured pearls in the prismatic reflections produced by the natural light.

Camille was planning to do Ayahuasca in the near future so I felt compelled to tell her my story. When I'd finished reciting it, she silently said "Hmmmmm…" and then presented me with the most affectionate of smiles.

The sun was slowly hiding behind the mountains turning the sky into a spiral of red shades, when we began our walk back to Puriwasi, where we regrouped with Samirah and Sveah. I spent a couple of hours with the girls and a few other travelers before leaving for my guesthouse, for my last night as I was leaving for a trek the next morning.

The One

What makes us one,
Is our ability to see the one.
The one, that rests in all of us.

It's the only one that matters.
It's the only one that counts.
Because what makes us one,
Is what makes us breathe.
And what makes us breathe,
Is what makes us one.

So, be with the one.
The one that is in you.

IV. AMONG THE GODS

I LEFT MY GUESTHOUSE EARLY next morning before sunrise with a local guide named Freddy, I'd managed to find through a connection of mine. Freddy was an extremely knowledgeable guide with his roots dating back to the Inca empire. His facial attributes were a testimony of that, and plainly his historical grasp of the Peruvian culture was comprehensive. An experienced trekker, Freddy was to accompany me on Lares Trek, a four-day high-altitude trek that would take me through remote villages and communities high up in the Andes. The trek would end at Ollantaytambo, a town in Scared Valley also renowned for having an Inca fortress. From Ollantaytambo, I would board a train for Aguas Calientes, which is the village closest to the most recognizable attraction in Peru, Machu Picchu.

When traveling through a country as a backpacker, its major tourist attractions are not something that irrevocably grab your attention over the stimulation of building relationships with locals, meeting fellow travelers, gaining new experiences and learning through really immersing yourself in the culture of the country together with an intuitive zeal for grasping a deeper meaning in life.

The idea is to become a local as much as possible and learn about the intricacies of ordinary life through an experience that might at least slightly resonate with the everyday life of a local person. Visiting a tourist attraction is not equivalent to experiencing a country at the level that yields an impact down in the gut. There's so much more a country has to offer than the usual touristy stuff, and all you have to do is something on your own. Being a solo backpacker allows you to pursue your own path and listen to what your heart really wants to do.

At first, I wasn't very keen on visiting Machu Picchu as there was so much pressure to visit it if you were in Cusco. But that detracted from the importance of the powerful energy of Cusco's spiritual divinity: it had been built by the Incas as a holy place and pilgrimage site for the seekers of the sublime. Branding it as something less than that degraded its revered essence.

With my inner voice telling me to go there, I decided to visit Machu Picchu but made a choice to treat it as more than just a monument or a tourist site. What it would exactly turn out to be, I would find out for myself when I stepped into the mythical city that had been built by the Incas in the fifteenth century.

Lares Trek is one of the least commercial treks offered in the region, and it was to provide me with a great opportunity to trek past local villages and interact with various Andean communities living among the mountains. A descendant of the Inca civilization, Freddy began reciting his historical lessons about Peru in his macho but sweet voice early morning on a van-ride toward the village of Lares, where we'd begin the trek. There were two other travelers on the ride, Rik and Julia for our little trekking group.

Rik and Julia were a couple from Central London. Rik was a tall Dutch man originally from Netherlands, who now worked as a marketing manager for a Financial company based in London. His wife Julia was originally from Russia and worked as a marketing manager for an oil company.

They were both very ambitious but didn't let that affect their thoughtful and humble personalities because of their common love for traveling. Being married and working for big companies hadn't stopped them from coming to South America and going on trekking adventures. It was their way of staying inspired in life, and keeping their feet grounded rather than getting lost while working their way up on the corporate ladder.

Something that's phenomenal about traveling is how it links you with people you never imagined yourself being around in your home city. Coming from working in the renewable energy industry and mingling with people working in the oil industry was not something I could have foreseen, but having fostered the mentality of accepting all humans as one regardless of what they did for work helped me connect with humans without judgment and simply stand with them heart-to-heart.

Rik and Julia were extremely knowledgeable about the world, and great company. Julia was the quiet one of the two, and Rik always had a theory to state because of his background in Psychology. I loved hearing his various psychological theories about people, cognitive behaviors and how marketing influenced people.

The three of us and our guide Freddy spent four days trekking among the clouds of the Andean range with layers of mountains hiding behind frozen crystals, to bless us with views that couldn't be anticipated. I was completely disconnected from the civilized world once again and united with the Andean mountains and the divine energy that lodged within them. We occasionally came across villages, where we would eat with the villagers. The women and the children were dressed in their colorful attire and welcomed us with their open hearts. When not trekking, I meditated or simply gazed at the spectacular and fantastic scenery of the Andes.

Seclusion from the outer world, while constantly moving in a meditative state of mind on the quiet and peaceful mountains among the radiance of nature, blossoming flowers, abundance of green, endearing streams, hovering birds, docile Llamas, falling stars, melting nights, chirruping wind, and the dreamy lights opened a space for holding that joyful feeling in my heart that I could eventually transfer to others through my writing. It grew with every step on the plush blooming mountains of Peru, and would guide me in the future to recite the Peruvian journey with honesty and the pure intention of conveying the mammoth change that had been fostered in my being.

That space allowed me to focus on my breath whilst reflecting on my time in the jungle, so I wasn't merely thinking about the past but recreating its events to allow me to repeatedly re-live them and integrate their many Ayahuasca teachings. Breathing in that space required an immense amount of concentration, but it gave me an unparalleled strength to stick to my life-path and work toward my true purpose. It was a crucial lesson: all the answers are to be found within. Your heart is always right and the decisions that come from the truth in your core can never be wrong, regardless of what others say. If your true inner voice is telling you something, you'd better listen to it.

Our lives are meant to be lived for such moments when you feel content about who you are and clear about what you need to do. Death can greet us without invitation and can provide us with the motivation to actually experience the moments of purity that we all have the capacity to attain and provide our lives with the meaning it deserves. We need to reject the idea that we live to die, and live fearlessly so that we feel truly alive in every moment of our precious lives.

On the last day of our trek, when we were headed to the town of Ollantaytambo to board a train for Aguas Calientes, another person joined our little group for the day, a man named Joseph, a New Yorker who'd originally been going to join us for the entire trek but couldn't at the last-minute. He was friends with Freddy, so he'd decided to come for at least one day, which was enough for him and me to strike a sympathetic chord.

He was a slender-looking guy in his forties, which could be guessed by the small number of wrinkles on his oval-structured face and frisky greyish hair over his crown. He had a husky voice, which together with his brilliant sense of humor made him a charming individual to be around. He also had a little beard on his face, carried a big nose and a loud heartwarming deep manly laugh. We had our first conversation along a trail on a mountain, with a splendid view all around.

I asked him how long he'd been here for, and found out that he'd rented an apartment in Cusco almost a month ago, and had been staying there. "That's cool!" I said, "So, how come you are not coming to Machu Picchu with us?" He responded playfully, "Because I've just come from there, and that was my second visit." I laughed and asked him, "How come?" Then he told me his love-story about how he'd met a Peruvian girl in Cusco and she really wanted to visit Machu Picchu, so he'd ended up taking her, even though he'd already been to the site. His story definitely brought a smile to my face.

He was such an interesting man that our whole day to Ollantaytambo went by just talking to each other.

As our conversation further advanced, I discovered about Joseph's multiple accomplishments. He was a very talented individual: a published author, director, screenwriter, app designer, business consultant, entrepreneur, and even held an MBA degree from UC San Diego. On top of all that, the reason he knew our guide Freddy was because he was voluntarily helping him develop a phone app for his travel business!

I asked him at one point, "Joseph, you have done so much in life but is there any one thing that you really want to do in the future?" He replied, "Yes, my end goal is education. I want to make an impact in the world by providing quality education that focuses on liberal arts for underprivileged children across the globe, and maybe start an exchange program between the United States and some other countries." His answer had me totally sold on his idea. It was so refreshing to hear that.

Soon after our arrival in Ollantaytambo, a tiny town filled with tourists and restaurants, we had to get on the train for Aguas Calientes. Joseph departed for Cusco, but we exchanged contact details for when I returned to Cusco.

Our journey continued on a spectacular train-ride, Peru Rail built specifically for getting to Machu Picchu. It cut through the rupturing mountains, across flowing rivers and between festooned trees, enticing scenery like none other. I felt like I was in a fairytale movie where the train was taking us to some enthralling kingdom of dreams. Machu Picchu, being one of the most visited places on the planet, the train was packed and so was our destination, the town of Aguas Calientes. It was flooded with tourists from every corner of the world.

Aguas Calientes and its economy had been built solely for foreign tourists visiting Machu Picchu. It had had all been set up by the Peruvian government as a gold-digging operation among foreign tourists. Everything was so expensive and overvalued, that ordinary

Peruvians couldn't even think about visiting Machu Picchu. It was a rare sight and tragedy both at once. There was nothing much to do in Aguas Calientes itself other than shopping and eating at overpriced restaurants.

Freddy took us to a decent hotel near the train station around *Calle Tusuq*. The first thing I did was take a warm shower. Four days of trekking and camping in the mountains with no shower, had made me look like a caveman! Coming back to civilization after being on top of the mountains for several days really made me appreciate the little things in life like a warm shower. After the shower and checking my phone, I made my way to a nice little restaurant nearby, with tables placed out under the sky on the cobbled streets for dinner with the others.

Plenty of buses ran specifically for taking tourists back and forth between Aguas Calientes and Machu Picchu but Freddy cautioned us that even before sunrise the line for getting on a bus was going to be long. Next day, we woke before sunrise as planned to stand in one of the longest lines but with the promise of soon reaching the numinous city we had come to visit from lands faraway. The wait didn't seem that long as Rik was telling me about his final thesis for his Master in Psychology. I always enjoyed listening to Rik and his psychological theories about the functioning of our minds, and he explained everything very concisely, while his hands actively participated in the telling. It went on throughout the bus ride until our arrival at the entrance of Machu Picchu, where another long line awaited us.

Eventually, we walked past the big rocky gates at the front to enter the spellbinding ancient city, which was covered in mist. Freddy said, "I have been to Machu Picchu many times, but it looks different every single time." The sun was concealed behind the clouds, not yet blessing the city, which was erected upon dry-stone walls in the Inca's mortar-free limestone architecture. Huyanu Picchu, the towering mountain behind Machu Picchu that completes the view of Machu Picchu wasn't even visible. The mist enveloping the city presented me with a blissful, ethereal and enchanting moment of solitude when all the tourist bodies around me disappeared and left me awestruck beyond belief.

The Citadel was phenomenal, and the view changed with the passing of every second as the wind swirled the mist around the mountains mesmerizing the eyes of viewers. Soon, the sun sprung out of the mist into the vast sky above the mountains to glorify the holy city, which came to life as it received blessings from the sun god.

Every site in the city had been planned and built for a specific purpose, using the correct geometric alignment and having architectural significance for the Inca empire. It was a city with many temples and sacred plazas, that made it truly divine in nature and a remarkable human achievement. I couldn't comprehend that the Incas had built the city in the fifteenth century on top of a mountain at such a high altitude. Even though the city had a substantial number of tourists in it, the powerful energy within the city blinded me from the others around me leaving me in a lengthy state of admiration. I could feel the mighty vitality governing that sublime site all the way up to my head; there was a magnetic push from beneath my feet levitating my soul toward the sky.

After giving us a very informative tour of the city, Freddy left us to explore the site for ourselves and told us as he was leaving that he would meet us back at Aguas Calientes for lunch, giving us loads of time to just be in that enchanted place and take in everything we could.

Huayna Picchu, which was earlier covered in mist, revealed itself around that time to greet us with a smile, leaving Rick, Julia and me with no option but to climb it for a panoramic view of Machu Picchu. The climb was very steep, and I don't know what happened to Rik and me, but we decided to run up the stairs in a deadly manner. We didn't want to stop even for one breather and did the hour-long climb in just half an hour. We even pushed Julia into running along with us. There was such satisfaction in pushing the physical limits of my body in that powerfully energetic place.

Finally at the top of Huayna Picchu with our hearts pounding intensely, lungs heaving prodigiously and eyes looking down at the majestic city of Machu Picchu, there was a great feeling of being liberated. All my body was vibrating with the sweeping charge being transmitted all around that divine location. I stood among the gods detached from the world and hidden among the clouds on top of that mountain to worship their creation.

The energy electrified me and we soon began descending the mountain. Rik and Julia were just behind me when, a couple of minutes into the descent, I let my overflowing vitality flow through me and discharge into a dash down Huayna Picchu's stairs. Leaping over multiple steps on the way and flitting past many people, I bolted down. The people quickly moved to the sides of the path without my needing to warn them, as they could feel the stream of energy being radiated from me at a distance. The instinct to ride the current of energy down the mountain was so strong, there was no space for fear. It was ecstatically pleasing to do without a thought that I could possibly get injured. The path down the mountain was narrow, steep and slippery, making it far from ideal even for walking and somehow, I was running on it. I was in complete unanimity with the energy dominating my nervous system throughout the run and in less than fifteen minutes, I reached the bottom of the mountain thus ending the outflow of energy and attaining existential equilibrium.

At the end of the run, a noiseless inner voice surfaced to convince me that a nameless potent force had been guiding me throughout my Peruvian Journey. The run down the mountain was its cryptic message asserting, "I am here to guide you to overcome every hurdle that will arise on your path of freedom." All the decisions I had taken since listening to my inner voice in New York on that stormy night had been influenced by this same vigorous energy, which exists in all living beings even without us being aware of it.

It was this same energy that had unified me with Mother Ayahuasca, who'd granted me further belief and faith in my inner voice, which always resonates with the universal truth that can be found in all of us. It was so clear to me that the tough decisions I'd taken in New York, which required me to risk everything in life and embark on an unknown path challenging the norm, would not have been possible if that inner voice hadn't stemmed from virtue and true honesty, which lies concealed within all of us. It didn't matter how many people questioned me, challenged me or called me out for what I'd done, because I knew the voice that had emerged from deep within my core was something of true substance.

Every decision I've made in life listening to that voice has only led me to walk on the path of truth and feel profoundly at one with myself and the world. That wouldn't have been possible if that inner voice wasn't directly connected to a universal energy, existing beyond the realms of mind and matter.

I stood securely at the bottom of Huayna Picchu after concluding my redeeming run to leisurely gain control of my breath and for my heart to start beating at its regular pace. For a fleeting moment, I closed my eyes to receive the blessings from the sun god soaring above the mountains, and shining warm rays directly on my face. The energy from the sun regenerated every cell of my body and triggered the eternal flame within me into gently opening my eyes and staring at that marvelous star, with immense gratitude flowing out of my heart in reverence for the mighty force that had brought me to the sacred land of Machu Picchu.

Rik and Julia arrived at the bottom of Huayna Picchu shortly after I'd resurfaced from my momentary lapse from time. We approached the end of our visit to Machu Picchu quietly sitting on a rock taking in everything the spellbinding surroundings of the ancient city had to offer for one last time.

On our return to Aguas Calientes, we went straight to the restaurant where Freddy was to be waiting for us, for an enjoyable and celebratory feast to mark the end of our successful expedition. It was time then to pick up our bags from the hotel's storage and make our way to the train station for our train back to Ollantaytambo.

The passenger chairs on our magical train to Ollantaytambo were grouped with a shared table, and our little group was put with two other small trekking groups. They'd visited Machu Picchu after completing a different trekking route to ours, but organized by the same company Freddy worked for. We also returned to Cusco together from Ollantaytambo in a shared van. So, for the remainder of the voyage, our group had become larger with the addition of five more people.

One of the two groups comprised of three solo travelers: a young Japanese man, an older man and a young nurse from the US. The other group consisted of two women in their forties from the US as well, best friends who were traveling together. One of them had left the US at an early age to live in Costa Rica and the other resided in North Carolina. They'd taken time off for themselves to get a break from their busy full-time jobs and household responsibilities as mothers and wives.

Having visited Machu Picchu earlier that day, all of us were in elated states of mind, which only assisted us in having a good time on our way back to Cusco. There was a very swift transition from the train to our shared van-ride at Ollantaytambo station, and with the addition of five more lively people to our group the travel time to Cusco seemed minimal.

We reached Cusco around 8 pm. Freddy dropped everyone at their respective accommodation and, there were more goodbyes as the van stopped in front of my old mansion of a guesthouse. I hugged Rik and Julia inside the van, and outside the van told Freddy how awesome a guide he was, and thanked him for taking us on such a wonderful adventure.

None of them were aware that they'd become a part of an incredible transformative period in my life. It had been a crucial time for me, as I'd been very focused internally on the drastic changes occurring within my being throughout the trek. Having people around me who genuinely cared for me and were inspiring in many ways only aided the whole transformative process.

Realizations that arise in the mountains during an effort to connect with yourself and nature can lead to the creation of an untiring spirit true to its purpose and run on a harmonious channel springing from the oneness of this universe.

V. THE HUMAN SPIRIT

I WALKED INTO THE SAME Peruvian household I'd been lodging in before leaving for the Lares Trek. The young Peruvian girl at the reception remembered me and gave me the same room I'd occupied earlier. It was going to be my room for the remainder of my stay in Cusco.

After settling in my old room, I left the house to grab some food nearby on *Calle Matara*, and around that time I received a message from Joseph asking if I was back from Machu Picchu. I asked him if he wanted to come over to my guesthouse and join me for the evening. He arrived shortly after I'd finished eating my dinner, and as he was a writer and a traveler, our hours went by talking about the process of writing.

During our discussion, Joseph asked me what had inspired me to take on the project of writing a book, so I told him about my whole journey including the life-changing impact of the Ayahuasca ceremonies which had revealed my purpose to walk on the path of truth. My real inspiration for writing was to share this sense of truth with everyone.

"… That's great …" said Joseph, silently sitting back into his chair. His ears had popped up when he'd heard the word Ayahuasca, and he told me that he was planning to visit the jungle in a couple of weeks and was keen on doing Ayahuasca. I knew from the resolute look in his eyes, just how serious he was about it. So, I only suggested one thing to him, which is what I told everyone I crossed paths with who was determined about doing Ayahuasca: "Be sure of why you want to do it. It's not to be treated as an experiment because it's a concentrated healing process, which can demand you to go beyond your limits. Which is why it's essential to have a strong reason for doing it. You might have to face some intense moments during the ceremony and having a strong reason will provide you with the inner strength you'll need to overcome them." Looking straight into my eyes, Joseph said, "I agree and totally understand that."

The moon was dawning over us amidst the clouded sky. The hours of our conversation faded with the nocturnal longing to retire for the night.

Over the next couple of days, I adopted my usual routine of writing at the café during the day, and gathering with fellow travelers for a lovely evening after the sunset to include Joseph in the evening gatherings. He was on a similar work routine to me, which allowed both of us to be productive during the daytime and devote our evenings to meeting new people and gaining more insights for the creation of more stories.

My first morning back in Cusco after returning began with a solo wander all around the city. Firstly, I went to the *San Pedro Mercado* for a $2 meal from a local vendor, a lovely Peruvian woman who owned a tiny portable food-booth where she offered only one dish: delicious chicken noodle soup, which comforted my throat in Cusco's chilly weather conditions.

While exploring the food culture of a city, local markets are the best places to visit to try the food authentic to that city. Local markets do not aim to meet the fancy needs of tourists, but solely present the limited options of the specific local delicacies of the city. Contrary to the common belief, the chances of getting sick in a proper restaurant are higher than in a local market, because the market vendors are constantly preparing fresh food to meet the excessive demand and no food is preserved for days in a refrigerator.

After devouring the flavorsome chicken noodle soup, I left to savor the streets of Cusco and let my intuition guide me until I felt drawn to walk into a café. This practice let me become a soul-less entity disconnected from the madness of the world for a short period of time, so that I could generate a state of harmony in combination with clarity in my mind – until a café would captivate me.

It was my first day back in a proper city after completing the pilgrimage on the holy land of the Andes. It had made me want to live every moment of my life being grateful for the life I had, to immerse myself completely in joy, and further share it with others. It was also a reminder to constantly work toward making a positive impact on the lives of other beings.

The café that finally caught my attention was called *Museo del Café*, not a typical café but also a coffee museum, which offered a combination of things for customers to do. I simply sat down in its café section, which had an elegant and antique feel to it and provided a suitable environment where I felt comfortable and could express my thoughts and ideas.

There is something satisfying about working in a shared space that attracts individuals to it. It somehow functions as a stimulus for my mind by allowing me to simply observe people, and study them objectively as reflections of myself. Maybe that's what leads to an epiphany, which can be expressed in the form of my work. The interactive space also facilitates meeting like-minded people, I can share my thoughts with and learn about their ways of receiving information from the world.

The café had a sophisticated interior design, complimented by relaxed furniture and a fresh roasted-coffee-smell floating in the air, which made my nose feel alive. As I was working in my own little world dissolved inside my laptop screen, I could hear various languages floating around, which kept my awareness intact about the crowd around me. After writing for several hours, I took a short break to look around the space and observe distinct individuals who caught my attention. People-watching can be a delightful hobby for just appreciating the differences in human nature and studying people's reactions from a distance. It's a good way to take a break.

After that, I brought my focus back to my laptop screen and continued writing for several more hours until I looked outside the window on the wall to my left. The sky had changed its colors, and the greyish spreading on it indicated it was time to stop writing and get myself back to the guesthouse. I was getting together with Joseph later that night to go out in Cusco's main square and become a part of the lively atmosphere that Cusco was famous for.

৪০ ৫৩

Joseph and I met near *Catedral de Cusco* around 9 pm. He suggested we just walk around and see what caught our attention. I was totally on board with that idea. As we were walking and talking, he told me that he had finalized his decision to go to the jungle at the end of the month for Ayahuasca, and would begin the pre-Ayahuasca diet next week. I felt very happy for him because I knew he was going to have an unbelievable experience, and I was pleased to have played a promising role in his decision-making process.

We walked past the main square toward Cusco's lively streets, which were thriving with energy generated by the influx of hundreds of people, who'd come to Cusco from all over the world. It was a euphoric gathering with a blissful atmosphere. I ran into many travelers that night I'd met during my time in Peru, including Samirah and Sveah, who'd gotten back from visiting Machu Picchu that day itself. Their group of two had increased in number, as two other friends of theirs from Germany had joined them for the rest of their trip.

It was a night to be lived, be alive and be free to celebrate the gift of life. I had finally let go of everything to eternally merge with the flow of the universal energy and experience the truth of my actuality. All the sacrifices I'd made in the process of listening to my calling, the immense suffering I went through during the Ayahuasca ceremonies and the difficult decisions I'd taken to leave everything and walk further away from my old pointless superficial life blossomed in that moment of true divinity. The constant battle in my head had come to an end and I could appreciate the real harmony that had been awakened deep within my soul.

It was a celebration of the divine light that exists in every living being, which make us stronger as the days pass and life becomes more meaningful in its wonders.

℘ ◎

The day after that splendid night of celebrations was my final day in Cusco before leaving for Puno, a city in Southern Peru, to visit Lake Titicaca, South America's largest lake and world's highest navigable body of water. That last day in Cusco included an hour of pausing and reflecting upon the sublime days spent in the mountains of

Peru building new friendships, attaining more realizations and uncovering how I'd continue my on-going journey of "seeking truth". That journey had kept on blessing me with experiences unknown to the masses of the society – which only confirmed the importance to keep on writing about it.

This reflective pause occurred in company with my laptop, seated alone in a tiny eccentric café operated by a local artist somewhere amidst Cusco's craziness. It ceased when my eyes met the moon, flaring through the café's only significant window and dazzling my senses from the dusky sky above the mountains. It was time for me to return to the actuality of the day and enter the last phase of my stay in Cusco, with Joseph, Samirah and Camille, who was still working on her wall-painting at Puriwasi Cusco. It was Samirah's last night in Cusco as well, as she along with Sveah and the other German girls was leaving next day for a city called Arequipa, where I'd eventually reach after visiting Puno.

While we were brainstorming our travel ideas that night, Joseph decided to join me to Puno the next day, so I was excited to have a wonderful travel companion tag along with me. The only person I had to ultimately say goodbye to at the end of that night was Camille, who was going to stay in Cusco until she completed her wall-painting at the hostel. I was glad to have had met an individual like her during my travels, as she was just a breath of fresh air who always seeded her surroundings with offshoots of love.

I realized at the end of that night that a big part of a traveler's lifestyle is to constantly meet new people and build memorable relationships with them in the short span of time you have to spend together. This is an extraordinary thing as it links you with wonderful people all around the world, but there is also a cost attached to it.

A. Bondage from Love

For travelers, one of the most demanding tussles can be to maintain mental equilibrium in the face of often having to say goodbye to a dearly loved new person. For maintaining equanimity of mind, it's vital to perceive every moment for what it is: impermanent. Every moment with a new person is temporary – and this is true for the whole of our lives. As soon as we can accept the reality of impermanence, we'll cease depending on beautiful but temporary moments for our happiness. A balanced sustainable life focuses on staying true to the moment we are in.

One of the great learnings from traveling applicable to daily life is that it is imperative to keep moving forward no matter what has happened in your past, good or bad, or what you expect from your life in the future. Being completely present in the present is the most powerful tool, and also the most difficult to master, but it holds the key to a harmonious and self-contented mind.

As you grow and discover more about such powerful instant-connections with individuals from different parts of the world, you acquire an instinct to distinguish really special bonds, and recognize the strong impact an individual has had on you in a short span of time. It might sound cliché, but it's the quality not the quantity of time that really matters. Having no surety of when you'll see an individual you shared a beautiful time with again can generate feelings of sadness and lead you straight into being stuck in the past. So, it's important to foster emotional maturity so that you can transform the sentiment of grief into appreciation of the relationship.

If you do come across a unique individual you share a really special connection with, he or she will leave you with an explicit belief in your heart that your paths will cross again for sure. In reality, both parties make a determined effort to see each another again.

The uppermost desire of travelers is to overcome their fears during the process of truly listening to their hearts. They don't let fear get in the way of their being able to explore the world. They're not afraid to book a ticket to a far-away destination and leave with just a backpack without worrying much about logistics. They take that first challenging step toward the unknown past the comfortable zone – where life's miracles happen. It might sound a little dramatic, but an example from one of my previous journeys illustrates it.

In the summer of 2014, I got an opportunity to live in one of Rio De Janeiro's Favelas to volunteer at a local school helping a non-profit organization to grow and build their presence. I met Christopher, an Austrian and my co-volunteer at the school I was assigned to. We came from completely different backgrounds, cultures and upbringing but something far more powerful created an unbreakable bond between us.

It was not all a fairy-tale though, as Tio Lino, the owner of our school died unexpectedly. He was a great man who'd dedicated his entire life to fighting the corrupt to provide education for the Favela's underprivileged children. A deeper bond was created between Chris and me, and after Tio's death we did our best to keep a positive momentum going in the school, to make it easier for the children to get over Tio's sudden death. We wanted them to realize that what Tio had stood for all his life was not going to be wasted and his spirit would live on in all of us.

After our time in the Favela ended, Chris and I continued walking on our separate paths but we knew that what we had as friends was truly special and wasn't going to fade away with time or physical distance. We'd stayed in touch even though we both had very busy lifestyles and big changes were regularly taking place in them. That same year, we saw each other in Thailand but didn't get to meet again until Chris visited me in October 2016 in New York, when I was working for the solar company. At the time, he was going through a difficult time, as his long-term relationship with his partner had just ended. Being there for him through that arduous time, tested my character as a friend and made me appreciate the importance of friendship. I understood that true friendship was not about spreading your wings with someone during a good phase in their life. The real beauty of friendship is to be found when you have your friend's back when he or she most needs it.

Before Chris left New York for Austria after his short but uplifting visit, we decided to meet again during Christmas New Year, which was only a couple of months away and we finalized Miami as our travel destination. But a bombshell hit me in December, and just couple of days before leaving for Miami was when I quit my job in New York and began following my heart to walk on an unknown path.

That one week in Miami with Chris became one of the most strengthening periods of our friendship. It ended 2016 and ended our old lives. While I was gazing at the glowing sky on New Year's Eve from the Miami beach, Chris was standing next to me and together we welcomed 2017 with a few pacts.

Our first pact was to focus our energies on finding our true purposes in life and to keep motivating ourselves to not dwell in the past. We were to constantly take positive actions to live lives that provided us meaning and fulfillment beyond materialistic pleasures. We were to not let anyone, or anything, come in the way of our heartfelt decisions. We were to use our energies wisely and spend our time with people who'd push us forward rather than pull us back. The priority was to build lives we wouldn't have to escape from, but live every second doing what we were born to do.

Our second pact was a promise that no matter what happened, we'd take time-out to see each other at least once every year. With a handshake on those pacts, the fireworks dazzled to welcome 2017 as we embarked on our separate journeys. I left for Peru following my calling from the Amazon and Chris got an opportunity from his company to work in Malaysia for a couple of months. Somehow, the biggest changes of our lives began at the same time on our separate journeys in places far away from home and during times of immense mental suffering. The pacts made in Miami were a constant reminder for us to have courageous hearts to overcome our fears. We continued striving to surrender ourselves to the world without self-doubt flowing in our blood streams, and were eventually rewarded with moments that changed our lives forever and truly defined our new paths in life.

Every individual enters your life for a reason, and when I met Chris the first time in Brazil, I knew instantly that I was going to be friends with him till I inhaled my last breath. Our friendship has only flourished with time, and somehow, we ended up playing major roles in helping each other transform our true selves.

In a moment of meeting someone exceptional, your life can change, but you never know how much impact any individual will have on your life. It's important to recognize those individuals you feel so connected with, as it defies rational reasoning. Our hearts hold the true strength and power that keep humanity together safely. If you meet someone you connect with beyond words, it's vital to be diligent about keeping him or her in your heart regardless of what the world says.

You have to work hard to create a reality out of your true dreams, which is truly yours and not derived from some preconceived notion.

Imagination is a gift humans have been blessed with and if you work on it, it can help you create something of actual significance. Nothing happens out of luck. The events in your life can't be explained but that doesn't mean they are coincidental.

Everything that plays out in life happens because of the actions, physical and mental combined, you intend to take. Running away from different realities or debating what's real or not is only a distraction from understanding the significance of the truth that lies within. If you truly believe in your abilities and don't let anyone thwart your journey to transcend your mental capacity, you will evolve into your true self.

And when you are lost or stuck or walking on the wrong path but with the right intention, extraordinary individuals will rise out of the darkness to guide you onto the right path and help you stay true to your purpose. They can act as major players in your journey of self-transformation. I realized that because of Chris, an extraordinary individual who came into my life just at the time when I needed someone to provide me with affirmative encouragement before beginning my transformational journey.

A traveler's lifestyle does contain many goodbyes, but they can help you achieve immense mental growth if you don't fall into the trap of living in the past. The goodbyes with Camille and the many other travelers I met during my time in Peru taught me that and how important it is to just be in the moment.

My friendship with Chris shows how some goodbyes are nothing but a "see you later," because your heart knows when it comes across a special individual, you are predestined to see again. These "see you later" individuals bring out the best in you and help you discover things about yourself that you didn't even know were in you. When you come across these "see you later" individuals, who won't be too many in number, you won't be able to keep them out of your life. They will always be with you, if not physically, but surely in spirit. They will believe in you when nobody else does, including yourself, and will walk with you till the end on this incredible journey that we call life.

The "see you later" individuals are easily distinguishable from the "goodbye" individuals, who come in your life for a specific period and provide you with memorable moments for a particular phase. To sustain mental equilibrium, it's very important not to crave blissful memories with those "goodbye" individuals. Your relationship with the "see you later" individuals is so selfless and pure in nature that it blesses you with the marvelous experience of sharing an unbreakable bond with another person – which you didn't know was even possible.

These "see you later" individuals are one of the many reasons you risk everything to go on a life-changing journey: they help you uncover the mysteries of love beyond self.

$$\wp \, \wp$$

After those ecstatic exultant last few days in Cusco, I was ready to move forward and explore a new destination. I slept like a bear that night and woke up the next morning as if I was coming out of hibernation. It was around 8.30 am when I woke up and looked at my bus ticket, and after two seconds of staring at it my eyes grew wider and wider. I jumped out of my bed only to realize: I'd missed the bus!

The bus, which I'd thought was to leave Cusco at 2.40 pm, was supposed to arrive in Puno at 2.40 pm. There was no point in even going to the bus station because the bus had already departed half an hour before. Instead of mourning it, I started to figure out my next step.

Till then, I'd never missed any flight, bus or a train ride during any of my travels. This was a first time! Maybe my subconscious mind had chosen to miss-perceive the departure time to keep me in Cusco longer. I used Facebook Messenger to contact Joseph and tell him that I'd mistakenly given him the wrong booking details, but he'd already sent me a message saying that he couldn't find any bus leaving Cusco at 2.40 pm. That definitely brought a laugh to my face. I called him immediately and told him why I'd missed my bus which made him laugh as well.

We found out that there were a few other buses leaving for Puno at night and soon after the end of our call, we met at my guesthouse and took a taxi to the bus station barely a fifteen-minute ride away. We bought two tickets for a bus departing Cusco at 10 pm that night for Puno.

After buying our bus tickets for Puno, we went to the *Plaza Mayor de Cusco* to make use of our unanticipated day in the magnetic city of Cusco, to do what any other reasonable traveler would have done on a sunny thriving day like that one. It was our final showdown with the streets of Cusco, which we conquered by visiting various bars, eccentric cafés, restaurants, and heritage stores, all run by locals that we'd developed friendships with over the course of our stay there.

It was a wonderful last day in Cusco with Joseph, which I hadn't asked for but nevertheless received as a gift from the universe. We were so immersed in the activities that presented themselves, that we completely lost track of time and only just managed to make it to the bus station before our bus left for Puno – after running the last stretch at the bus station so it didn't leave without us. With a hands-down salute to Cusco, we continued our journeys to the next destination.

VI. FLOATING THROUGH PUNO

THE BUS RIDE TO Puno was an overnight journey on restful reclining seats, which following our frivolity-filled day made it easy to doze off during the smooth drive. My eyes were exposed to the air early next morning before sunrise in Puno. As Joseph and I had not booked any accommodation in Puno, we just grabbed a taxi from the bus station and asked the driver to take us to a nearby hotel. He took us to a random 2-star hotel, where we got ourselves an affordable shared room at 25 soles per person. It was still quite early when we arrived, so as soon as we got a room there, we each slept for few more hours before getting acquainted with Puno.

We woke up to the first glimpse of light reflecting through the cracked window of our room, and after quick showers, we left the hotel to find food for ourselves. Puno was a typical industrial town and the major attraction there was Lake Titicaca, the largest lake in South America containing many known islands that were home to diverse indigenous communities. It geographically separated Peru and Bolivia, and thus acted as the link between the two countries, offering travelers an opportunity to cross the Peru-Bolivia border via water. Puno's raison d'être was as a junction for travelers, who'd explore the lake's islands or cross the border.

The coast of Lake Titicaca was only a fifteen-minute walk away from our hotel, and our plan was to go find a boat to take us to one of the islands on the lake. It seemed like a straightforward plan when we left the hotel, but it didn't work out as we'd intended! That is one of the aspects of traveling that you have to accept – or you'll always be frustrated. You have to learn to find beauty in the unexpected and be open to whatever happens on the journey. Traveling teaches you acceptance because events take place regularly that you can't anticipate.

Puno's restaurants didn't have much to offer other than the standard Peruvian food options, which didn't fit with Joseph's diet. It took us a while to find a spot, where Joseph could get something suitable to eat, and I had to settle for a Peruvian breakfast that consisted of chicken and spaghetti at a tiny local restaurant not too far away from our hotel.

While traveling, sometimes you have no option but to be flexible with food and eat for survival, based on whatever food choices a destination has to offer. Before coming with me to Puno, Joseph had been staying in a rented apartment in Cusco with a kitchen, which made it possible for him to cook according to his dietary needs. Having your own kitchen where you are temporarily living can be very helpful, but when you're on the move in a small city with limited options and no kitchen at your convenience, you can encounter problems.

Seeing Joseph struggle to find even one item of food that met his dietary restrictions, had me recognize the poor eating habits we have in our societies. When I'd returned to civilization after my week in the jungle, my whole focus had been to live a balanced and healthy lifestyle, where I could be a little more malleable about my food choices, but it was crucial to continue the practice of healthy and minimal eating, which I'd adopted during the Ayahuasca process.

That whole cleansing process had made me aware that we eat way more than what our bodies need and that, on a daily basis, consume packaged or fast food, which is no less than poison for our bodies. When Joseph and I were meandering around the streets of Puno looking for food suitable for his vegan diet, it was easier to find packaged food and drinks instead of a piece of fruit or any healthy item.

It's the same in even the most remote villages today. Locals might not even have access to their own native fruits or vegetables as they're exported by big companies and sold to large food corporations, who then sell them at ridiculous prices in expensive supermarkets in developed countries. The locals are then forced to eat or drink poisonous packaged food, which is the only thing they can afford to buy to sustain their livelihood. Food is a necessity for all living beings, but some humans are controlled by greed and use it for their own selfish ends.

The entire Ayahuasca diet process, when I felt clean and physically healed because of what I was consuming, made me realize how so many diseases that exist in our world today, which weren't even around hundreds of years ago could be totally eradicated, if we just changed our eating habits.

During my stay in the Amazon Jungle, the elder shaman grew fresh and organic food in his own permaculture farm for the entire village, feeding many people and making them completely independent of any packaged food. It resulted in a lifestyle that cherished eating locally-grown food, rejected the practices of the food corporations around the globe and led to sustainable and healthy living in harmony with nature. That was when I realized the importance of taking back control of our lives from the hands of big food corporations, who manipulate food prices, destroy local habitats, ruin natural eco-systems, brainwash the masses, hurt local economies, reject empowerment of people, carry malicious intentions, unbalance the world, and are purely driven by greed.

It's not feasible or practical for everyone to create their own farms to evade the practices of the big corporations, but we can reject the systems and leaders who support these big corporations. The power doesn't lie in their hands, but in ours and it's time we took it back to build a society that functions for the betterment of all living beings on our planet.

It's critical to call out these big multinational companies who control the provision of basic human necessities like food, water and electricity to everyone. They should be strictly regulated for the harm they are causing to nature and millions of uninformed people around the globe. Their endless desire for power and control over others have blinded the individuals running them so much that they can't see what they are doing to the world.

We should not let our societies be governed by individuals in power, who divert our attention away from the real problems threatening our planet toward futile issues that don't matter, but which exacerbate division and confusion in the world. If we don't take action against these evil practices now, a planet might not exist where future generations can co-exist in a harmonious manner with similar comforts to what we have today.

Instead of worrying about who is to blame or where to point the finger, we need to recognize that we are not any better or worse than the controlling individuals living in the shadows. We are equally as guilty. The same evil within us is what drives their actions, and when we look deep within our souls to fathom the darkness governing our actions, only then can we comprehend the existence of the individuals who pull the strings from the shadows.

They are nothing but reflections of us, and unless we can suppress our own egos, we cannot expect the individuals in power to act on our command. We as a generation have a responsibility to create a better world for future generations, and we can't do that with pure honesty if we can't transform ourselves beyond ego and selfish desires. There will be a time when we will have to hand over our planet to the next generation, and they will want us to bestow on them a world that can be built upon continuously for the betterment of all, including all the living beings that co-exist on it with us.

The best way to take a stand against these malpractices by big companies doesn't require regular individuals like you and me to go out of our way to take extreme measures. Instead, we need to pursue our own self-transformation, by building self-awareness and educating ourselves about these important issues. That process slowly leads to us crafting a lifestyle that is in accord with Mother Earth and her natural eco-systems.

Every action in the right direction matters and has a positive effect on your life. You can start by adapting habits that help you build a healthy sustainable lifestyle: reject packaged/fast food, develop healthy eating habits, buy locally-grown foods, minimize unnecessary plastic waste, don't consume more food than what your body needs, focus on water sanitation, create better waste management systems in-house, educate your peers and children about climate change and the malpractices of the food industry, choose to walk/bike instead of driving for small distances, be physically active, reject consumerism culture, use your energy wisely, practice minimalist living, raise awareness among the uneducated, discard superficial ways of life, and constantly work toward self-transformation, and so on.

These are some of the many habits you can adopt to progressively bring about a revolution in the world. As you continuously grow and educate yourself and others on this journey, you will only become more pro-active over time and will automatically have a constructive influence on the people in your surroundings. It all starts with you and the actions you take to bring your communities together and be as empowered as you can be. Acting independently of the malpractices of large corporations and the corrupt intentions of your leaders, you will automatically start walking on the path of making a real positive change.

୫୦ ଓଃ

When our food quest in Puno ended, we finally began walking toward the edge of Lake Titicaca to figure out how we could make use of our only day there effectively, as I had reserved a bus ride for Arequipa the next day. The lakeside was situated at the far end of the city from our hotel on Titicaca Street. It was a quick walk and it had many souvenir shops and some travel agencies around it for tourists, but wasn't busy at all.

Instead of going through a travel agency, Joseph and I spoke with a local guy at the lakeside who recommended we get on a boat, which would take us to one of the floating islands on the lake. We negotiated a price of approximately $6 per person for a round trip journey to the islands of Uros, one of the most prominent island groups on the Lake, which has been inhabited by local indigenous communities for many years.

The boat we got on was a modest one for local Peruvians, making us the only foreigners on board. Even though Puno itself was not a fascinating city, Lake Titicaca was truly astonishing. Its large water body was serene, which, combined with the slow boat ride, made for a peaceful expedition to the island. We passed between several floating islands, home to many indigenous communities on our way.

The islands had been created by the indigenous communities using the totora reeds that grew in the shallows of the lake. The base of an island wasn't more than two meters wide and the island was approximately fifteen meters square. One island was strong enough to hold several huts, a single one lodging one indigenous family. The huts were crafted out of the same totora reeds used to build the foundations of the floating islands and their beautiful canoes.

It was captivating to witness their natural and simplistic living. The creative use of natural resources without harming the eco-system they lived in was commendable. To support all their basic electrical requirements, they even used solar panels, installed on top of their huts using a thin pole grounded into the base of the island, for keeping the panels intact throughout the island's subtle movement.

On our arrival at one of the Uros islands, we were greeted by its community leader. He was dressed in typical colorful Andean clothing and wore an intriguing round hat. He spoke Spanish and used some broken English words at times to communicate with us. He was thrilled to have two foreigners on his island. He gave us a short informational talk about the islands and the culture of the communities living on them.

It was astonishing to be standing on the spongy surface of that floating island, which weighed so little that it was possible to make the entire island quiver with a single jump.

Seeing the solar panels on top of the huts took me back in time, to when I was door-knocking in Brooklyn with the pure intention in my heart of motivating homeowners from various backgrounds to go solar. I was door-knocking in an affluent neighborhood of Brooklyn during the Presidential Elections between Donald Trump and Hilary Clinton. The homeowners primarily identified themselves as Republicans and diehard Donald Trump supporters. Like him, they were strong deniers of climate change and wanted nothing to do with solar. What made sense financially and morally didn't matter as their minds were completely compromised by the voice of their beloved leader.

ഇ ൠ

Coming back from that flashback, the first thought in my mind was that these communities were doing way more for the world and future generations than most of the inhabitants of the civilized societies. Maybe instead of rejecting the lives of indigenous communities, we should try to learn from them, as they live sustainable, healthy and simple lives in accordance with nature.

They are not selfish or overpowered by greed, but welcoming and empowered by kindness. Their hearts are much bigger than all ours combined, and no amount of money or gigantic houses can provide us with the contentment they already have in their lives. They don't reject strangers coming to their islands, but enrich them with loving kindness and hospitality. When I was in Brooklyn, plenty of homeowners screamed at me, swore at me and smashed doors in my face. At times, they treated me as if I wasn't even a human being, but it never affected me because deep-down I always knew that their reactions derived from the fear, pain, anger, and suffering that had overpowered them.

These two demographics fall on the opposite ends of the spectrum, which is a great way for us to understand the fundamental differences in the mental conditionings of individuals based on the environments they live in. We live in a society where we are conditioned to be envious of people who have a fortune and can access all kinds of materialistic pleasures. We think they've made it in life and have achieved everything there is to life. But that definition of success is flawed. It is based upon tangible and invaluable assets, that are mere fabrications of our institutionalized money-driven systems, with no significance beyond the physical. It is detached from the truth that is concealed somewhere deep in our subconscious, where the answer lies about who we really are. Our conditioning suppresses the truth further, making us suffer even more. Only when we can rid ourselves of these societal conditionings, can we explore the real truth that endures in the depths of our minds.

We have been conditioned to look down upon individuals who belong to such indigenous communities, assuming that what we have is a better life, but really it's the complete opposite. We are the ones relentlessly raging in fury, not able to stay satisfied and joyful deep inside our core. We lack the ability to generate deep feelings of compassion and empathy for our fellow living beings. We do exponentially more harm to the planet than indigenous communities, who live a life in harmony with nature and not against it.

We are the ones who struggle to appreciate the little things in life and can't focus our attention on things that really matter. We have lost our ability to selflessly love others and instead, submerge ourselves in a bottomless pit of ego and ceaseless desires. We think these indigenous communities have nothing to offer but actually they have already achieved everything worth real value that humans can attain, and we are the ignorant ones interminably fighting with one another for no real reason.

೫ ೬

The time on Uros went by in cultural exchange with its indigenous community and absorbing more of their simplistic ways of living. It reminded me why I'd left New York and a feeling of thankfulness arose toward the universal energy that had led me to leave and helped me break free of the conditionings that used to subjugate my mind.

They later served us a delicious meal using trout, the most popular eating fish on Lake Titicaca. By the time we reached our hotel again, our tiredness collected over last two days of traveling by the bus, exploring Cusco and visiting the Uros Islands demanded a siesta.

Joseph was still asleep when I woke up, so I quietly moved out of my bed, grabbed my laptop and disappeared to wander around the streets of Puno. While I was roaming around its narrow streets, I noticed many Pizzerias, which was intriguing. Puno had no history with Italy and no Italians lived there, but there was Italian food everywhere. It's extremely interesting as a traveler to see certain trends in a city with no context or reason for them. I kept walking around the streets to get a feel for the city, until I came across a small bar located on Lima Street which seemed like a suitable place, where I'd feel relaxed enough to write. It had limited seating in a comfy setting. The tables glittering from the dim lights reflecting upon their shiny glass-surfaces created an irresistible atmosphere.

I set up my computer on a table next to another one where two female travelers were seated, and across from a large table where a group of elderly tourists were seated, their thick Australian accent easily giving away their nationality. I ordered a warm drink, which was served in an old-fashioned tumbler. It consisted of coca leaves infused with locally fermented alcohol for warming the body and fighting Puno's freezing conditions. The warm drink in a cozy environment in the chilliness of Puno was a great stimulant for words to flow from my mind onto the laptop.

Before beginning the writing, I had a pleasant interaction with the two women sitting next to me. They'd been traveling and working around South America for several months. They'd met in Cusco and decided to travel together for a little while, similar to what Joseph and I were doing. One of them was from Germany and the other from Austria, which obviously reminded me of my best friend Chris. She was the first Austrian I'd come across in Peru and after a lovely conversation with the two of them I began writing.

Going to a random café or bar and conversing with strangers to share a delightful moment before starting writing was very helpful for me to get into the flow for creative thinking. A couple of hours went by until Joseph showed up, which was my signal to stop work and leave the bar with him so that we could find ourselves a restaurant nearby to get some dinner.

It was a simple but elegant restaurant, where we indulged in a feast for the night. During dinner, we discussed many topics as usual; there was not a single time when Joseph didn't have something interesting to talk about. One of the topics was creative work, and he made an exquisite remark about creativity that was to stay in my mind for all times: "The ultimate form of human experience is to create something from nothing." It was clear to me that our existence as human beings is truly a blessing because of the ability we have to constantly create. It really is sensational that we can use that ability to do what no other animal is capable of: transcend our minds and build upon the awe-inspiring works of our ancestors.

Our ancestors made huge sacrifices in their lifetimes for us to access their discoveries and knowledge through various media. We cannot put a price tag on the sacred knowledge that has been passed on to us from past generations. It's inestimable and it demands that we take on the responsibility of building upon that knowledge and passing it on to the coming generations. That systematic transfer of knowledge has created a new platform for the young to learn from the wisdom and experience of their ancestors. Teachings from past ages can be used effectively by aspiring talented minds for building on past knowledge and producing new original artworks, that come out of their sheer transcended minds.

With the end of our dinner, Joseph and I began walking outside the restaurant while brainstorming about what our next destination would be. I told him that I'd already booked a bus from Puno that was to leave for Arequipa the next afternoon – so that became our next destination. It had a great reputation as a city with a rich culture and astonishing architecture. It was also very famous for the Colca Canyon, the deepest canyon in the world and home to Andean Condors, which are gigantic South American birds from the vulture family.

Arequipa was to be my penultimate destination in Peru before returning to Lima for one last bash – and to conclude my Peruvian journey, as my flight out of Peru was to depart from Lima in a week's time. I had to make my way toward Arequipa and then book a flight to Lima from there. I also wanted to spend my journey's last night working with Franco at Puriwasi Lima, because the best way for me to end my Peruvian story was to be at the place where it had all begun.

The bus I'd booked was leaving the next afternoon, and fortunately for us, as we were brainstorming our travel plans, we came across the bus company's office: it was "coincidentally" right outside the restaurant we'd had dinner in! Joseph looked at it and said, "Why don't we ask them if they have a bus leaving for Arequipa tonight? That way, we won't have to stay in Puno tonight and can be in Arequipa by tomorrow morning. It will save us a day."

It couldn't have been a more ideal scenario. It was as if someone had been listening to our conversation and magically presented us with what we needed at that exact moment. We went inside the tiny office run by an elderly Peruvian woman. I asked her in my broken Spanish, "*Tenes ... un bus que parta hacia Arequipa esta noche?*" She said, "*Si.*" I showed her my ticket on my phone, and asked her if it was possible to alter my bus reservation – and it was! So, I quickly got my ticket amended. Joseph decided to buy his ticket at the bus station, as it would be cheaper there and many seats were available.

The rapid decision-making and instantaneous follow-up invigorated us so we made to our bus on time. In just a few hours, we were sitting on its reclining seats for our ride to Arequipa to conclude yet another chapter. The last chapter of my journey was to start with my eyes being greeted by the sun, mounting itself over Peru's canyon city.

VII. THE AREQUIPA CANYON: RATATOUILLE

I WAS LOOKING BEHIND MY eye lids into the blackness of my mind when our bus arrived in Arequipa thirty minutes prior to the estimated arrival time of 5 am. With a sense of relief, I got off the bus to witness the changing colors in the sky. The rosy layers of assorted shades summoned by the rising sun were taking over the murky horizon, heartening me with confidence that this was exactly the place I needed to be before closing my Peruvian chapter in Lima. Coming earlier from Puno to Arequipa had been a wise decision, which was confirmed by later events in Arequipa.

Joseph and I took a taxi from the bus station toward the *Plaza de Armas* in Arequipa, only a fifteen-minute ride away. The backpackers hostel I was to check into later that night was situated nearby, and Joseph had booked a private room in a hotel, that was also near the Plaza. I'd arrived at my hostel way earlier than was originally planned and was hoping that a staff member would be awake to let me enter the building and do an early check-in.

We both knew it was time for Joseph and me to go on our separate paths and continue our solo journeys again. There'd been no hard feelings between us, as we were both on the same page. Our time together had been a stirring exchange of ideas, values, theories, beliefs, imaginations, and emotions that arose out of the feelings that made us human. Our time together was to be retained and treasured by us as individuals who'd traversed paths on their numinous journeys in an illusory outer world.

Joseph and I had gratifying see-you-later hugs as we reached the backpacker hostel on *Calle Mercaderes*, and then turned in opposite directions on our independent ways.

Embracing the emotion that arose in my belly every time I had to let someone go was a prevailing practice of mine. I used it to overcome any remaining anonymous emotional blockages, the ones that usually stop us from having the feeling of appreciation flow through our veins into our heart. It's pivotal to let this emotion of appreciation flow and allow the heart to burst into tears of joy, so that it can release deep-rooted emotional blockages, which will otherwise contain us throughout our lives. In this manner, we alleviate ourselves from many years' worth of emotional burdens, that we only discover in the process of discovering our true selves.

Standing on the brick street in front of the hostel's slender door staring at the door bell, I wondered if someone would wake up to open the locked wooden door for me at such an early hour. Fortunately, after pressing the doorbell a couple of times, a traveler staying in the hostel woke up and unlocked the door for me to get inside the building. I climbed up the narrow stairwell that stretched up to the reception, where an old Peruvian gentleman, the owner of the hostel, was sleeping. I gently woke him up and instead of being grumpy, he welcomed me with a big smile on his chubby face that brightened up my morning. He was a short but very cute man with a flabby physique, who looked like a teddy bear.

As I'd arrived earlier than the check-in time, he informed me in his drowsy voice that the hostel would not have any beds available till mid-day but he was kind enough to let me stay in the living room until check-in time. So I lay down on one of the couches to rest for a couple of hours. The owner provided me with a warm blanket and as soon as he covered me with it, my eyes shut themselves and put me into the dead-asleep stage for a couple of hours.

My first morning in Arequipa began with the sunlight filling the living room. I still had to wait for several hours before a bed was available, so I decided to walk out into the brightness of the city. I went to the reception to ask for a recommendation for a good café located near the hostel. The owner was not to be seen anymore but a nice Peruvian woman was sitting at the reception and she recommended an old Peruvian café a couple of blocks away. She described it as the place that brewed the best coffee in Arequipa. She got me excited about the coffee, and curious about what made it the best!

It was a timeworn family-run café operated by a beautiful elderly woman, and the secret behind the delicious coffee was that she used an old brewing machine, that is she had to brew the coffee herself! It took all the time in the world to be prepared and was ultimately enriched with an immeasurable sum of love.

I placed myself on a chair inside the café periodically sipping the warm flavorsome Peruvian coffee, served to me shortly after its tender brewing. With each sip of the coffee, my mind screened images of my impactful times in Peru. In five days, I was to fly out to end my journey in Peru and begin a new chapter of my life in the Himalayas, totally inspired by the events that had taken place in Peru, especially in the jungle.

My stories about my unification with Ayahuasca and other rousing travel memoirs along with realizations and teachings I gained from many unpredictable encounters originated in hopes of inspiring the young to walk on the path of self-discovery, while living for something beyond themselves, to make the world a more harmonious and peaceful place.

Reconciling with Mother Ayahuasca was only the beginning of my transformational journey. My next steps of rambling along the path of truth were to occur in the coming months when I'd actually be writing the story whilst living among the Himalayan peaks in the region of Ladakh, and uncovering more of myself through deep meditation practices, leading up for me to adopt Buddhism as my sole frontier in life.

Walking on the path of liberation is not a one-off activity: it's a continuous process. It requires strenuous mental, physical and emotional effort from you every day of your life. You have to remain determined and shore-up your will-power so that you keep advancing on the path that you've chosen for yourself. You need patience for absorbing every second of the journey, and unceasing persistence to not let external voices affect your decisions. At times, you'll have to make sacrifices and say "no" to things you know are detrimental toward your real growth, even though it might seem unreasonable at the time, but over time you'll understand that it really was a distraction that would have stopped you from reaping long-term benefit – which is only availed if you stay true to your purpose at all times.

Your purpose will move your heart and strengthen your mind so that you can face the challenges that will arise constantly, without letting fear overpower you. The divine energy that drives you toward your purpose, needs to be protected and used wisely and not drained in unnecessary action. The deific energy will push you to give your best at every step of the journey to make your life worth living and truly satisfying. You'll be content deep within yourself and accept life for what it is, without needing any sort of external entertainment to provide pleasure for you.

My visual re-screening of the last three months in Peru terminated as I swallowed the final sip of my coffee and took myself back to the hostel. The bed was still not available but the receptionist suggested I wait at the hostel rooftop until check-in time. It was an enormous roof, which offered a 360-degree view of the entire city of Arequipa, and I knew right then that it was the spot where I'd spend the majority of my time in the coming days. It was time to pause after all the running around from Cusco to Puno to Arequipa. I didn't want to spend my last days in Peru thinking about what I needed to do or see in a new city. I wanted to solely devote my every second to just being present in that majestic setting.

The rooftop view encompassed the entire city of Arequipa, including snow-capped El Misti Volcano, a stratovolcano, and the fantastic Chachani Mountains, which encircled the city of Arequipa and hallowed it with their presence. *Plaza de Armas*, barely two-hundred meters away, provided a clear sight of the city's colonial buildings and an unobstructed view of the titanic granite cathedral gate of *Basilica Catedral de Arequipa*. The city's striking architecture was designed to contrast with the snowcapped volcano in the backdrop and present an opportunity to appreciate the seamless coherence between the scenic beauty and humanity's architectural genius.

I placed myself at a spot at one of the tables where I could immerse myself in the picturesque view of Arequipa and simultaneously work on my writing.

It so happened that Samirah and the German girls were all staying in that hostel in Arequipa at the same time as me. Our travel plans coincided to re-unite us once again. Many of the new faces staying at the hostel smoothly integrated with us to create another of those coherent groups packed with outliers from different parts of the world.

The next couple of days in Arequipa imitated my routine in Cusco. I left the hostel in the mornings to wander around the streets of Arequipa, until I discovered a local café where words poured out through my finger-tips while I sipped a cup of coffee and then after numerous hours of writing, I'd drift toward *Ratoutille*, a restaurant that became my holy spot in Arequipa.

I'd noticed *Ratoutille* on my first day walking around in Arequipa, after leaving the hostel post-check-in with the innocent intention of getting lost in Arequipa for couple of hours. The "losing myself in a city" drill began whilst observing other sculptures in *Plaza de Armas* only to find myself drifting through one of the stony streets out of the plaza in the opposite direction from my hostel. I continued my rootless meandering passing many local food vendors, smelling the flavors and spices of Arequipan cuisine and fully relishing the aromas in the air in that particular street, eventually coming upon a white castle-like edifice titled *Ratatouille*.

The little castle had a blackboard outside its entrance, with the statement "10 soles lunch options" on it. I entered the extravagant building only to be teleported somewhere in Europe. A young cheerful couple saluted me with their affection and served me delectable food cooked out of pure love. I couldn't believe that the restaurant offered such a delicious meal and profound service, all for 10 soles: it was preposterous.

I returned to that restaurant every day for the rest of my time in Arequipa and brought along all the other fellow travelers from the hostel. The waitress, Lie, was originally from France and became very fond of me in the coming days. She was a slim-figured, tanned woman, with green eyes, enticing lips and smooth bronzed hair that fell over her curvaceous shoulders. Her coquettish smile, liveliness and a magical talent for making customers feel enchanted by her presence, produced the most hospitable ambiance I had ever felt in a restaurant. It was an impeccable eatery, where I spent all my Arequipa afternoons in creating fond memories of my last week in Peru with fellow travelers and Lie. Arequipa was a delightful finale to the whole Peruvian journey.

The night before my last day in Arequipa, Samirah and her friends left Arequipa for another Peruvian city. Of course, I recommended Puriwasi Lima to every backpacker I met during my travels, so Samirah and her friends were to check in there on the morning of the day I was to fly out of Peru. We'd see each other for one last bit! A few other travelers I'd met in Arequipa were also going to stay at Puriwasi on my recommendation and would be there on my last night in Peru too. All these incidents were entirely unplanned and just fell into place somehow. It was pretty amazing!

I'd previously decided to fly back to Lima and spend my last night working at the bar of Puriwasi with Franco, because I'd promised Franco that I'd return even if it was for one night. My flight for Lima from Arequipa was to arrive the night before my last one and the thought of ending my Peruvian journey at Puriwasi brought a sense of completion to the story.

My Lima flight was to leave Arequipa in the evening and I left my backpack in the storage room of the hostel, after checking out in the morning. The hours were spent at Ratatouille absorbing every little second of that day. I sat at a large wooden table in company with other travelers from my hostel. The sun was glowing at its peak and Lie was working her magic amongst the crowd as she'd done every other day. It was a pleasing and entertaining afternoon, which became even more pleasant as another very distinctive individual joined our little clan.

She was seated in an elegantly casual manner right across from our table when my eyes caught her attention. She was encompassed by a mystifying air. Her biscuit-shaded wavy hair wrapped around her sleek neck, and the pale skin of her face contrasted with the dark glasses she was wearing. Her exquisite bodily figure, covered in a blue denim jacket was poised on the chair, while she looked upwards into the sky holding a cigarette in her left hand and a cup of coffee in the right. Her presence was entrancing and in the flicker of an eye, I stood up to walk in her direction. In a matter of seconds, I was staring through her dark glasses right into her luminous cerulean eyes.

Even though I didn't smoke, I asked "Do you mind, if I ask you for a cigarette?" She responded with a demure "Yes," her strong French accent an undeniable indicator of where she was from. Whilst she was handing me the cigarette, I asked her, "Would you like to join us at our table?" She retorted with a bewitching "Yes." As she elegantly stood up to follow me, she kissed my cheeks and said, "I'm Valentine." I playfully smiled and replied, "*Mucho gusto* Valentine... I'm Kart."

With her "yes", our little group got larger and the afternoon became livelier. Valentine brought an alluring energy to our table. The hours went by in no time and after saying goodbye to Lie, who wasn't happy that I was leaving, we all returned to the hostel's rooftop to witness the sun set behind Arequipa's snowcapped volcano. Valentine joined us as well, and though we'd talked for just a few hours, it seemed like we'd known one another for a long time: our connection felt so profound. There was some serious back-story behind our coming together, as such happenings while traveling are more than just fleeting coincidences. It's truly magnificent how a couple of hours of staring into someone's dreamy eyes can leave you more captivated and more dazzled by their presence than anyone else you've ever met.

It was unfortunate that I had to leave for the airport with the downing of the sun, as it did not leave an opening for Valentine and me to spend more time together. I said, "Goodbye" and hugged the entire group and made my way down from the rooftop to the hostel's reception to call a taxi. Valentine accompanied me as well, as she was to leave for her lodging when I departed for the airport.

I thanked the receptionist for their hospitality and grabbed my backpack from the storage to make my way down the staircase, which permitted only one person to walk at a time and led outside to the streets of Arequipa. Valentine and I were standing on top of that slender staircase, facing one another with our bodies touching and eyes in sync. Her smooth fingers were stroking through the rough stubble on my face and my hands were caressing her delicate neck. Our hearts had overtaken our bodies to merge our energies into one, and in that moment our lips met. Time came to a halt, and the world around us paused. The eternal meeting of our lips was relinquished as she put her hands in mine to stare deep into the fresh soul that had just been resurrected.

"Wow! I can't believe we met just few hours ago."

She smiled with adoration in her sparkling cerulean eyes and replied, "I wish you weren't leaving."

"We are going to meet again. I can't tell you when, but it will happen," I told her.

With that statement, I embraced her one last time and said, "Ciao amor."

The drive for the airport was pleasant and introspective in nature, parallel to every other taxi drive during my transitioning stages. It was always wonderful to have bright visions of the preceding period flash in front of my eyes one last time before beginning a new chapter. On reaching the airport, I went straight to the check-in counter, where I was told by the airline staff that the flight to Lima had been slightly delayed. It wasn't the most ideal scenario as I could have easily spent some more time with Valentine, but instead of lamenting the delay I happily accepted it and decided to just relax at the airport while waiting for an announcement about my flight.

At the airport convenience store buying some snacks, I ran into the American women I'd met on the magical train ride back from Aguas Calientes to Ollantaytambo. Bari and Kelly were to board the same flight as mine. Our flight ended up being delayed for approximately three hours, which resulted in our getting more familiar with one another. They told me about their children, husbands and how this was the end of their much-awaited "girls' trip." Arequipa was also their last destination, and they were to fly out of Lima the coming day too. They were wonderful company at the airport, and Kelly even offered me a ride back to Miraflores in her hotel taxi. "I'll be more than happy to give you a ride with me," she said. That was perfect, because the delayed flight limited my options for shared van-rides from the airport. Bari was to stay at a hotel next to the airport, as her flight out of Peru was early in the morning.

Such are the wonderful perks of meeting people and building genuine connections with them while traveling: something always works out, and you get to experience the kindness of strangers. It also works as a constant reminder that the world functions on the kindness and compassion we generate toward one another: it is the core of what keeps our world running. What goes around, comes around and even if you don't get it back, it doesn't matter. Your conscience will be clear before retiring to bed, as your actions will have peacefully resonated with the idea of working toward the greater good even in the littlest of gestures.

There is immense beauty in humankind and generating sincere empathy toward fellow beings is the pure essence of that beauty. It's one of our biggest strengths and the primary element binding us together as a species. The day when all of us can learn to empathize and think about others before ourselves will be the day when world will automatically change for the better.

"Avianca Flight 816 to Lima will now start boarding," announced the flight attendant, and minutes later I flew in the air amongst the invisible clouds on a course of reshaping the world so that we could reach for our freedom blazing amidst the heavens.

Wings of life

Flying... flying it was ...
To the end.
The end of what was now.
Now, had to end....
To end an anomaly.
An abstract creation...
That had become a reality.
A reality, that had to end...
To give birth.
Birth to a new life...
Life that was alive.
Alive was the breath...
Breath, that lived.
Lived to persist in a moment...
A moment, that had to end.
To begin a new life.

A. Beyond Time

I arrived in Lima at a dark hour for the final steps on my Peruvian journey. I re-linked with Bari and Kelly at the baggage claim at Lima airport and I joined Kelly on the ride to Miraflores. The taxi driver was glad to accommodate me for an extra 10 soles, and soon we were on our way. As it was about 2 am when we had landed in Lima, there was no traffic to avoid.

We were both sleepy during the ride and conversed slowly, matching the sea breeze flowing in beautifully through the car windows to please our senses. It was a welcoming gesture from the ocean, who was delighted and jubilant to have me back in Lima. Soon, we were at Kelly's hotel and after saying goodbye and thanking her, I directed the driver in my Spanish toward Puriwasi, "*Ahorra Avenida Ricardo Palma, por favor,*" and she drove in the direction of the triangular region in Miraflores. When we reached the intersection of *Avenida La Paz*, where Puriwasi was, I handed the driver her 10 soles and said, "*Gracias*." She smiled at me and then I turned in the direction of Puriwasi for the final get-together. I walked up the hostel's familiar stairs to the reception, where to my surprise Sergio was working the night-shift.

I said to him, "*Hola amigo, como estas?*" with a grin on my face. To which he replied with, "*Muy bien* Kart. Good to see you, amigo! How are you?" I told him I was great, and that it was good to see him as well. I then asked him if he had a bed available for the night by any chance. Discouragingly he informed me, "No beds are available tonight; you will have to sleep on the couch in the living room."

I didn't mind sleeping on the couch, as I'd gotten used to crashing anywhere. I told him I was going to leave my backpack in the storage and sleep upstairs in the living room until the morning. "*No problemo*," he replied, "and I will give you a bed tomorrow morning by check-in time." He also told me that I'd be working at the bar the next night with Franco. I responded with, "*Perfecto amigo*. That's why I'm here," and then made my way up the stairs to slumber on a large bean bag.

I thought it was funny how Sergio didn't even ask me if I wanted to work at the bar, but just told me that I'd be working at the bar, as if he already knew that was going to happen. Even for my last couple of nights, I'd be staying at a hostel without spending any money and cherishing the wonderful community-based environment.

Next day was my last whole day in Lima, as my flight was scheduled for 7 pm the following day. I told myself, "This is it. Tonight, will be my last night in Peru."

I didn't do much for my last day. I simply spent its day light hours at a coffee shop doing some writing, followed by a casual walk around the streets of Miraflores to commemorate all the extraordinary memories from my time in Peru. The walk concluded at the triangular region, where I sat down for hours in the middle of *Parque Kennedy* thoroughly immersed in a time-lapse and feeling grateful for everything that had happened over the course of the previous three months.

Around then, I received a message on Facebook from Valentine. She'd sent me a photo of a flight ticket. I looked at it: it had her name as the passenger on it and the flight was for that night from Arequipa to Lima. I was surprised for a second, but then felt ecstatic. "Is she coming to Lima for my last night?" and I answered myself out loud, "Yes, she is!" I eagerly messaged her, asking "You're really coming to Lima?" She replied, "Yes, why not?" Her decision to book a flight to come see me was an affirmation of what we'd both felt in that moment, when our bodies had fused to electrify our hearts and blend us into a single entity.

Not wanting to let that memory of touching her lips take me away from Lima in the current moment, I brought myself back to Miraflores to be in what the present was offering. At the brink of dusk, I navigated back to Puriwasi, to reconvene with Franco and then indulge in the activities of the bar as my farewell.

The rooftop was still the same with its cozy setting. Standing behind the bar was my brother, Franco. Straight away, I said, "*Hermano... que tal?*" He quickly came outside the bar and welcomed me with a tight squeeze, yelling in my ears, "*Hermano*!! It's great to see you!" It was like I'd never left the rooftop and felt joyous to be standing in front of Franco again. I told him it was my last night in Peru, and I was really glad to be spending it with him there at the rooftop. He smiled with a pinch of sadness in his eyes and said, "It's been great having you here my brother. Let's have a good last night before you leave for your next adventure."

It wasn't a busy night and the people at the bar were travelers I'd met in Arequipa. My beloved friend Jack, the eccentric writer, also came by for a couple of hours to say goodbye and wish me his best. It was equivalent to hosting a gathering for friends at my house, and I couldn't have asked for something as real and nice for my final hours in Peru. After closing the bar, Franco and I and some of the other travelers planned to go out for a bit to celebrate my last night.

While we were about to close the bar, in walked the mighty Valentine. My eyes were wide open, and my mind was not able to comprehend that she'd actually come. I'd told Franco about her earlier, and even he was enraptured by her sudden entrance. Her timing was flawless. I welcomed her to Lima with a wistful kiss on her cheeks and told her, "You are something else." She smiled exquisitely and raised herself on her toes to kiss me back while confidently muttering, "I know."

The stage was set, the actors were in motion and so the last act took off in Lima with my ultimate group. Franco took us to a dance spot where the night advanced impulsively with our feet tapping on the dance floor in rhythm with beats reverberating throughout our bodies. Hours flashed by in seconds to the moment when I heard a whisper in my ear from Franco, "I have to leave," which was also an indicator for me to leave.

I said to him, "I think all the rest of us are going to leave with you." We left the dance place and were standing when Franco told me, "It's time for me to go home brother!", which was the moment I'd hoped wouldn't come, but balancing my spirit we firmly hugged each other. I told him that he'd have to come visit me in India, which he promised he'd do. He left after our hug, and I was brimming with a heartwarming emotion because of having met such a startling friend in a foreign land. I was sure that Franco and I had known each another from lives before this one.

The other travelers decided to go back to the hostel, but both Valentine and I looked into each other's eyes, and wordlessly agreed to go on a carefree walk through the quietness of Lima's night. It was a few more hours until the dawn of the next day, which would mark the end of my last night in Lima. I was fully prepared to make the most of the remaining few hours of my journey. There was something alluring about walking in the solitude of a city, just before sunrise. Everyone was deep asleep dreaming in another reality. The sun hadn't risen to commence the next day, and the city was simply peaceful at those hours. It was utterly silent and no one, but us, could be seen on the streets of Miraflores.

I asked Valentine if she wanted to go to Miraflores's boardwalk overlooking Lima's coastline. She agreed gaily so we went. That was one of the best parts of Lima: you could see the entire coastline and immerse yourself in the movement of the waves, crashing upon the city in thunderous procession.

I couldn't have asked for a better way to spend my last few hours in Lima until the sunrise. We sat on top of the hill facing the vast ocean. The moon reflected upon the sea and then flickered on Valentine's eyes. The sea presented a musical performance that could have mesmerized any audience with its spell-binding wondrous elements. The night rolled up its sleeves to dance through the wonderful performance, and was suffused with the sun's emissions as it drew closer to the end. It was an act of nature that will stay with me through my lifetime. Having Valentine as a genial companion for those priceless hours made everything even more memorable and magical, and by the end of the performance we had merged with the ocean to be ignited as one soul to laud the perennial beauty of Mother Nature.

℘ ☙

I made it back to Puriwasi around 9 am and realized I had to check out in a few hours. Not sleeping through the night hadn't made me feel tired. I felt absolved from the meaningless burdens that hold us back from transcending ourselves.

At my check-out time, I saw Samirah, Sveah and the other German girls standing next to the reception desk. I was pleasantly surprised to see them, and wordless when Samirah said, "Hey!" with a big smile on her exquisite face. Other travelers from the previous night were there as well, and then Valentine walked in to check-in at Puriwasi, as her prior hostel was fully booked for the day.

It was breathtakingly overwhelming to have so many of the travelers I'd met during my time in Peru, standing in that limited space at that precise moment. I froze for a second, as I couldn't believe that it was happening and asked myself, "Is this for real?" It was like being in a dramatic movie scene.

I interacted with everyone and checked out at the same time cheerfully, but then I realized that I had to depart for the airport in several hours, which also meant that I had to say goodbye to all of them. It was undeniably sad but not disheartening. I was vastly satisfied that I'd lived the last three months tearing apart the scraps of distortion in my intellect that had degraded my heart and imprisoned it from me.

The coming hours passed in company with some travelers and Valentine at an old Peruvian café, situated beside the tip of the triangular region in the heart of Miraflores. Devouring my last cup of coffee in a country that had given me so much more than I could have ever envisioned, I felt more grateful than I'd ever felt before.

I asked myself when I would visit Peru again – but I didn't have the answer for that question, and I wasn't saddened about it either. I felt quite satisfied with not knowing the answer.

My time in Peru had shaken me apart to foster the growth of a new-born in the image of our heavenly body, which is locked away by the corrupt who steer people away from their true path. But as we learn to break free from the vicious cycles that govern our societies, we also learn to walk on the path of truth. When we unchain ourselves from our conditionings to see things as they really are, not as we would like them to be, we can hear the voice of the heart, which can only be heard then.

A new quest was to begin as I boarded my flight out of Peru, but I was ready for it as my heart was at peace with my mind. It was going to be a continuous process of fully taming my mind and emancipating my heart, but at least the path was clear, and the obstacles would be welcomed as part of the spectacle called "life", which blesses us not only with joy, happiness and love, but every single emotion that a human being is wired to feel.

I knew who I was and what I needed to do. Yes, evolution, growth, knowledge, and learning are pillars of enrichment for our species, but there is more to life than just logical thinking and intelligence. Three months in Peru really had helped me understand that at an experiential level, so I could get beyond such complexities and keep it simple by focusing on strengthening my core values of love, compassion and kindness, while walking on the path that was true to myself.

The Truth

Love others more than you can love yourself.
Give without wanting to receive.
Be compassionate beyond reach.
Empathize with every soul.
Learn to live, not to die.
Die without fear.
Fear is the enemy...
Enemy is to be defeated.

Surrender to the world.
World is beyond measure.
Measure is what makes us relative.
Relative is our time.
Time is all we have.
All we have is nothing...

Nothing... you say?
What is it, that you want?
Are you willing, to risk it all?
Risk it all, for what?
For you, to discover the truth.
Truth? Truth of what?
What is the truth?

Truth is what you are.
Discover, who you are.
You are the ultimate truth.
Truth will lead you to the path.
Path that is truly yours.
Yours, to be found.
Found, only by you....
You? Who are you?

It was the end of a chapter, which had once been an implausible dream. The dream had encompassed reality and grown into an even larger dream.

The endless circles of these dreams had me walking away from that café to the hostel, saying "Goodbye" and "See you later" to everyone who'd stamped their presence upon my heart.

As I rode in the van to the airport, no illustrations appeared in front of my eyes. My breath was in sync with my mind, and my mind only conceived a single notion: it was the end of what had been the most life-changing journey, and I flew out of Peru leaving a part of my heart with it forever.

ABOUT THE AUTHOR

BORN IN GWALIOR, A historic town in India, Kartikeya Ladha grew up immersed in the richness of India's vibrant customs and family life, and educated in a rigid educational system at The Scindia School, a relic from the days of the British Raj.

After completing high school, Kartikeya left India to attend Northeastern University in Boston, USA, where he concentrated on Management and Entrepreneurship. Soon after graduation he moved to Brooklyn in New York and worked for a start-up solar company as a door-to-door salesman and soon became a team leader.

It was one of the most successful community solarization programs in the U.S. Kartikeya fearlessly knocked doors in Brownsville, tagged by TIME magazine in 2012 as "Brooklyn's Most Dangerous Neighborhood". He educated hundreds of households about climate change and motivated them to take positive action for the environment by embracing renewable energy.

Kartikeya quickly became the company's highest earner and enjoyed all the delights of fast city-living – until an inner voice surfaced out of the darkness compelling him to renounce his long-held plans of building a life in America and go seek the truth of human existence.

His quest for the absolute truth led him onto an unknown path and inspired travels around the world to faraway lands, while he went beyond life's usual norms to unearth his calling in our magical world. In the process, he initiated an endless stream of rediscovering himself as a human being, while trying to serve his life's heart felt mission.

His first book, "Dream Beyond Shadows" captures tales about many insightful stories, based on the experiences he gained from a trailblazing expedition to Peru, South America.

Made in the USA
San Bernardino, CA
26 May 2020